THE CRAZY
YEARS

WILLIAM WISER

THE CRAZY
YEARS

Paris in the Twenties

with 74 illustrations

G.K.HALL&CO.

Published by G. K. Hall & Co.
A publishing subsidiary of ITT

This G. K. Hall paperback is reprinted by arrangement with Atheneum.

First G. K. Hall printing 1985.

Library of Congress Cataloging in Publication Data

Wiser, William.
  The crazy years.

  Reprint. Originally published: New York : Atheneum. 1st ed. c1983.
  Bibliography: p.
  Includes index.
    1. Paris (France)—Intellectual life—20th century. 2. Arts—France—
Paris—History—20th century. 3. Artists, Expatriate—France—Paris. I.
Title.
DC737.W57 1985   944'.36   84-23489
ISBN 0-8398-2859-4 (pbk.)

Table of Contents

CHAPTER ONE

Last Rites, First Folly

He was Modi, she was Noix-de-Coco – or he called her Haricot Rouge that winter of the Great War when the lovers ate nothing but red beans. Modigliani had plucked a fresh and tender blossom from among the young students at the Colarossi art academy: Jeanne Hébuterne, 19, the painter's last great love. He painted her in the languid, sensual, elongated pose of the Modigliani woman; she left home to share his wretched life on the rue de la Grande-Chaumière, she bore his child. For a time there was a monthly allowance from the art dealer Zborowski – as much as 3,000 francs – but the money went for wine and absinthe, hashish or cocaine. Once in a drunken frenzy or a drug-induced hallucination, Modi dragged Jeanne into the street by her braids and might have beaten her insensible but for the intervention of a concierge. To Zbo he said, 'Jeanne and I, we're agreed on an eternal joy,' – whatever that meant, in Montparnasse, 1919.

Truly theirs was a winter's tale from Henri Murger's *Scènes de la Vie de Bohème*. When Amedeo Modigliani died of tubercular meningitis at l'Hôpital de la Charité, his brother Emmanuele wired Kisling from Rome: 'Bury him like a prince.' Kisling's clumsy death mask had torn away bits of Modigliani's face: Jeanne Hébuterne, in the last months of a second pregnancy, saw the corpse only for a brief last look; she did not allow herself to weep, nor did she kiss the ravaged face adieu. Her parents took her away, back to the Hébuterne flat on rue Amyot: Jeanne's unnerving calm aroused their concern, she could not be left alone at Modigliani's atelier. Despite a brother standing watch, Jeanne leapt to her death from a fifth-floor balcony. From the position of the body it seemed she must have plunged backwards so as not to look down at the paving stones far below.

Modigliani's portraits of Jeanne Hébuterne
(above) and himself, 1919–20.

Like a prince, Modigliani was borne to Père Lachaise cemetery in the plumed black carriage of the *pompes funèbres*. A retinue including Zborowski, Derain, Brancusi, Lipchitz, Survage, Léger, Soutine, Valadon, Foujita and Picasso followed the prince to his tomb. There were those among them who believed the Belle Epoque had truly ended that January of 1920 when Amedeo Modigliani was buried. Later the Hébuterne family relented and allowed Jeanne to be placed beside Modi at Père Lachaise.

*

Four months later, that same year, the Twenties might well have begun on a section of railroad track outside Montargis.

In the early morning hours of 24 May a platelayer named André Radeau was walking the crossties through the Bois de Leveau along the Paris-Lyon-Marseille line, 113 kilometers from Paris, when he was accosted by a barefoot individual, clad only in pyjamas, moving towards him in the dim light.

'You won't believe this!' called out the apparition. 'I know it must sound incredible, but I am the President of France!'

The gentleman in pyjamas was scratched and bruised. He claimed to have fallen from the presidential train en route to Roanne. André Radeau escorted the distraught fellow to the gatekeeper's lodge at the next crossing. There, in a one-room cottage, the gatekeeper Dariot and his wife were as perplexed to receive this unexpected guest as Radeau had been to encounter him on the PLM tracks.

The stranger introduced himself as Paul Deschanel, the President of France. He then asked Dariot to notify the *sous-préfet* at Montargis of his accident. The gatekeeper assured the gentleman he would do as he wished, but made no move. Instead, he joined his wife and the platelayer who were whispering together in a corner.

'Madame,' intoned the visitor. 'I can see that your husband does not believe I am President of the Republic. Have you ever seen a photograph of Paul Deschanel?'

The gatekeeper's wife had taken shrewd notice of the gentleman's attire. The pyjamas were of impeccable quality; his feet – except for a trace of cinders from the roadbed – were pink and clean, with well-trimmed toenails. If he was a lunatic, he was a distinguished one.

'Yes,' replied the good woman, 'I have a photograph of him on the mantelpiece.' This was a picture of President Deschanel clipped from *Le Petit Journal* and set in a cheap frame, flanked by blurred likenesses of Joffre and Clemenceau. The man did have the same white mustache and haunted look about the eyes as Paul Deschanel, but in all honesty she was obliged to reply, 'I'm afraid you are not much like him.'

'True, I am in pyjamas. But that does not prevent me from being President of France.'

His protests continued even as she sat him down upon the bed; then – while he insisted her husband call the *sous-préfecture* – she washed his skinned knees and elbows. As if dealing with a recalcitrant child, she put him in her own as-yet-unmade bed still warm from the bodies of her husband and herself. Meanwhile the platelayer went in search of the nearest doctor.

When Dr Guillaumont arrived he was accompanied by a gendarme. From the doctor's examination it was apparent that the stranger had, as he insisted, fallen from a train. Dr Guillaumont applied antiseptic to the superficial injuries and administered an anti-tetanus injection. By now it seemed reasonable that the gendarme inform the *sous-préfet* of the gentleman in pyjamas at the gatekeeper's lodge who claimed to be the President of France.

It was Monday of Pentecost, an official holiday. Monsieur Leseur, the *sous-préfet*, decided to investigate this curious incident in person – but there were no taxis. Also (not unusual) the phone was out of order.

From the station in Montargis, Monsieur Leseur sent a telegram to Roanne inquiring about the presidential train. Was or was not the President aboard? The first reply was that the train had arrived in Roanne but that President Deschanel had left word with his valet not to disturb him before 8 a.m. Meanwhile the *sous-préfet* had engaged a local pharmacist, Monsieur Damas, to drive him to the humble cottage in the Bois de Leveau. Upon hearing that the object of their efforts was a man clad only in pyjamas, Monsieur Damas, accustomed to emergencies, had the foresight to bring along a spare suit of clothes. A second reply from Roanne made their errand all the more urgent: President Deschanel was indeed missing from his compartment on the train.

By now a great many observers were assembled in the single room of the gatekeeper's lodge, gathered around the bed where the gentleman in pyjamas – who may or may not have been the President of the Republic – sat propped against a collection of pillows, holding court, trying to remember how he had got onto the railroad tracks at Montargis.

Members of the presidential staff arrived that afternoon to confirm that the disoriented stranger installed in the gatekeeper's bed at Bois de

Leveau was Paul Deschanel, the French President. From Paris came the President's wife, along with Alexandre Millerand, leader of the National Assembly and next in line for the Presidency. These two delegations arranged to collect the President like some parcel gone astray. They dressed him in the pharmacist's spare suit, put a pair of white socks on his feet; he wore slippers borrowed from Dariot the gatekeeper. The President complained of *un trou dans le mémoire*, but in spite of a hole in his memory he was aware of the odd misadventure and would in no case return to Paris by train. He was driven back to the Palais de l'Elysée in a convoy of several motor cars.

The story given out to the press by Millerand was that President Deschanel had retired early in preparation for a day of speechmaking in Roanne; the presidential train was traveling at no more than twenty-five miles per hour to insure the President a good night's sleep – thus, when he fell from the train, he was not more seriously injured. It seemed he had opened the window to his compartment and leaned out seeking a breath of air. The window was of faulty design, the President leaned too far. Newspapers duly printed the dispatch, but conjecture crept into the editorials: somehow the official explanation lacked substance and detail. *Chansonniers* lost no time putting the adventure to verse.

> Il n'a pas oublié son pyjama
> C'est épatant mais c'est comme ça.

> (He didn't forget his pyjamas,
> Astonishing, but that's how it is.)

Elected in January of 1920 (when Modigliani was dying at l'Hôpital de la Charité), the new President was already showing signs of an erratic and unstable mind. A cabal of ministers and senators promoted Paul Deschanel over Clemenceau in a political maneuver to keep The Tiger from being elected to the highest office in the land. The obscure Deschanel was duly elected President but could never quite recover from his unexpected triumph over the formidable French hero, Clemenceau. Deschanel's remarks and behavior at public receptions became increasingly bizarre. At the British Embassy, Deschanel set forth such extravagant proposals the diplomats thought he might be drunk. After a speech, a group of schoolgirls presented him with a bouquet; he then tossed the flowers, one by one, back at them. On one disturbing occasion he wandered away from an official delegation to embrace a tree beside the path.

Following the episode of the presidential train, Deschanel went to the Chateau de Rambouillet to escape the capital and the pressures of office at the Elysée. One morning he walked away from the dreary order of business at a state meeting – a natural enough impulse – in the direction of the tempting lakeside, and from there continued his stroll into the lake, fully clothed. His valet saw him striding through the water, and plunged in after him.

By autumn, Deschanel's brief term of office came to an end at Malmaison, an institution on the outskirts of Paris for the treatment of nervous disorders. On 23 September, Millerand became the new President of the Republic.

During Deschanel's manic-depressive term of office, two playful but serious revolutionaries of art – Francis Picabia and Tristan Tzara – came to Paris from Zurich where they had founded a new movement destined to sow anarchy in the established patterns of French culture. The movement was called Dada, the first word the founders had come across in *Le Petit Larousse*, a nursery term for rocking-horse. According to the tenets of the new faith, visiting Montargis in one's pyjamas, wandering into a lake in a business suit, falling in love with a tree, was evidence of the essential Dadaist in us all (even the most hidebound politician) and precisely the example the President of France should set.

Surely Deschanel was the harbinger of the age. In those early months of 1920 may have come the first suggestion of the Twenties as *les années folles*, the crazy years.

CHAPTER TWO

Parade's End

The first time a flimsy, crate-like Gotha aircraft flew over the rue St-Honoré, an antique dealer wearing a spiked helmet from the Franco-Prussian War fired his hunting rifle at the interloper. Impossible that Paris could ever become a military outpost and enemy target. Those who were curious enough went to the Bois de Boulogne to hear the cannonade. During the 1918 bombardment, one million Parisians fled to the relative safety of the countryside: as the ghostly zeppelins drifted above the Seine bearing a deadly cargo of explosives, those who had not fled the city took shelter in wine cellars or along the underground quays of the Métro. Gertrude Stein and Alice Toklas went into the concierge's lodge so as to have six stories above their heads: it was true, said Alice, that one's knees really did knock together as described in poetry and prose.

German gun emplacements ranged within ninety miles of the capital, close enough for Big Bertha to blast at the very heart of Paris. After the klaxons sounded All Clear the city became a vacuum, eerily silent. The streets were empty after dark except for roving patrols of *hirondelles*, the police who bicycled along the boulevards, the pointed ends of their capes swept backwards like the wings of swallows. At dusk the city took on the pale color of absinthe – nine out of ten street lamps were extinguished under wartime restriction. Night life had all but ceased except for the *caf'-conc'* on the rue de la Gaité, kept open for soldiers on leave. The remaining street prostitutes around the gare Saint-Lazare ducked into shadow when the *hirondelles* cycled by.

Children and the aged were evacuated as much to escape the penury of wartime winters as from danger of zeppelin raids. (The Mexican painter Diego Rivera lost his infant son to cold and hunger.) Coal was rare, shipped from England or brought in from the Cévennes mountains south of Lyon now that the rich coal-mining region of the

north-east was occupied or under fire. Parisians waited in everlasting queues for a ration of *boulets* made of coal dust, peat and straw. The intervention of a cabinet minister was necessary to obtain a cartload of coal for the sculptor Rodin, dying of pulmonary congestion. The Japanese painter Foujita was so impressed when a girl named Fernande broke up a Louis XV chair to make a fire for his visit that he proposed marriage to her. Between the stately lines of chestnut trees in the Luxembourg Gardens were patches of beans and carrots; even the fashionable Parc de la Muette in Passy had been sown with potatoes.

There were, as ever, Americans in Paris – but few. The unconventional daughter of a clergyman, Sylvia Beach, traveled between Paris and Belgrade (where she distributed pyjamas to Serbian troops) during the war, and in Paris witnessed a direct hit from *Grosse Berthe* on the church of Saint-Gervais when the cathedral was filled with worshipers: ninety-one were killed outright, another eighty-six gravely injured. Ernest Hemingway was standing near the Madeleine when the façade of that church was blasted, his first wartime experience. Another volunteer for ambulance duty, John Dos Passos, saw one shell explode harmlessly in the Seine: immediately fishermen went out in boats or used nets at the quayside to scoop in the stunned fish.

Paris, said Malcolm Cowley, was all the lovelier under the threat of death. For many Americans the rite of passage to the European conflict was a tour of duty in the overseas ambulance corps; several of these 'gentleman volunteers' were writers, or would-be writers. They were a handful of friendly visitors – Malcolm Cowley, E. E. Cummings, John Dos Passos, Dashiell Hammett, Ernest Hemingway – with no personal share in the larger event taking place, but whose senses, Cowley noted, were sharpened by the thought of dying the next day. A passion for Paris often developed during this indoctrination tour in the besieged city, an ambulance driver's love at first sight would persist as a lifetime affair of the heart. The Great War was the largest adventure on the horizon, and Paris, its reconnaissance post, was the most beautiful city in the world.

The banker J. P. Morgan's erratic nephew Harry Crosby enlisted in the Norton-Harjes Ambulance Corps, his first flirtation with the danger and risk of death he craved, and an episode in his life that would wed him forever to Paris. Ernest Hemingway caught only a glimpse of Paris before he went on to serve with the Red Cross in Italy. E. E. Cummings and John Dos Passos went to the north-eastern front in separate units of the Norton-Harjes Ambulance Corps in France. The

The nave of St-Gervais after a direct hit from *Grosse Berthe*.

Paris of World War I was a brief but central experience in their young lives, a wartime interlude that would affect the sensibility of their formative years and color the literary work to come.

*

E. E. Cummings arrived in Paris a virgin at 22. 'They carried us to a foreign country,' explained Malcolm Cowley, 'the first that most of us had seen; they taught us to make love, stammer love, in a foreign language.' 'La Ville Immense', Cummings called the city – 'la femme superbe et subtile'. The association of Paris to Woman was inevitable for the Boston-bred young man whose father was a Unitarian minister and an official of the Watch and Ward Society. Paris, empty of men, but everywhere provided with 'the finest girls God ever allowed to pasture in the air of this fresh earth', made it hard for a young poet to resist the 'Tu viens?' whispered from all sides. Deliberately or by chance he did not locate his unit headquarters for five truant weeks during which he wandered Paris at will. Women were everywhere, openly available, hovering in his path. 'Tu viens?' This extended idyll all but obliterated thoughts of Boston; the young man's puritan upbringing was no defense against falling in love with a prostitute.

He met Marie-Louise at Sultana Cherque's restaurant, the Oasis, on the rue du Faubourg-Montmartre. When Marie-Louise completed her classic tour of the territory between République and the Madeleine, she and Cummings would sit among the pimps and street girls of the Oasis until dawn. In college French the poet stammered his love to this foreign delight. The affair was no wartime transaction between Montmartre tart and doughboy on the loose: Cummings was genuinely enamored of her and she, to all appearances, was attracted to him.

Contrary to every tradition of the professional *fille de joie*, Marie-Louise invited the young man home with her to a tiny flat on the rue Dupetit-Thouars, and into her bed – although they did not consummate their love in the way that would seem most natural to Marie-Louise. Nevertheless, the two slept together through the late mornings in the most innocent of intimacies. Five weeks were hardly enough for Boston's blue-eyed boy to wriggle free of Watch and Ward. Impossible to imagine the French girl's reaction to this persistent chastity – but Marie-Louise continued the relationship with her American naif right up until Cummings, a virgin still, reported for duty.

At the front, ambulance driver Cummings became involved in a Kafkaesque affair that colored his remaining time in France and

Some *filles de joie* at ease in the Sphinx.

provided the material for his first book. In defense of a friend who had written an indiscreet letter about the low morale of French troops (the letter, naturally, was intercepted by the censor), Cummings, along with his friend, was accused of sympathy with the enemy. The two American volunteers were interned at the detention center of La Ferté Macé, a concentration camp for military misfits.

It took all the political pressure the Reverend Cummings could summon, via a series of letters to President Wilson, to secure his son's release. When Cummings was finally allowed to leave La Ferté Macé, he was to report directly to the US Embassy where he would be notified of transport home. He had three days in Paris before his ship sailed.

At the Hôtel des Saints-Pères in the heart of the Latin Quarter he washed away the dirt and vermin of prison life. Ambulance duty, and the grim reality of La Ferté Macé, had altered certain New England concepts of morality. The young poet stepped out into the rue des Saints-Pères alive to every sensation, excited by every possibility. As he went in search of his particular love along the streets she was known to frequent, Cummings fell in love with Paris all over again.

It was time to dispense with a virginity he could no longer tolerate, in the city where such a loss or gain so conveniently transpires. But prostitutes are the night's most impermanent creatures. For all the substance he could find of his evanescent butterfly, Cummings might have imagined the girl. She had left the flat on rue Dupetit-Thouars. He retraced the erratic path of her working nights from République to the Madeleine – a vast territory encompassing three arrondissements; he lingered at curbsides and *coins de rues* where her solicitations would most likely take place. Again and again he returned to the Oasis where they had so often met and talked away the small hours before dawn. But the poet was never to recapture his first love except in verse. This was the last year of the Great War. So many had passed through Paris, had fled, had died, had disappeared.

The final night in Paris Cummings was overcome with the desire to end his troublesome innocence: he had become a man in every way but one. Late, at the Oasis, the pretty waitress Berthe shared a table with him, and a bottle of champagne. Before the city stirred to life again at dawn, and he was due to take the boat train to Le Havre, Cummings accompanied the sweet and compliant waitress to her *chambre de bonne*. Berthe became the last-minute substitute for Marie-Louise, love partner by proxy, a bittersweet farewell to Paris.

For Dos Passos the wartime adventure had taken place 'on the fringes of the great butchery'. He shared the meager salary of a French private, the *poilu*'s few centimes and a liter-ration of wine daily, but ambulance duty was almost as rearguard and tame as it was for Jean Cocteau. (Cocteau served as an 'officer' in Misia Sert's private ambulance corps, costumed in a stage-military uniform designed by Coco Chanel.) Whatever guilt, disappointment and frustration Dos Passos felt about his passive involvement removed from the battlefront, he sublimated in Paris after the Armistice. There he wrote his first successful novel, *Three Soldiers*, a fictional version of the war. His own oasis in Paris was Madame LeCompte's hotel-restaurant Le Rendezvous des Mariniers, on the quai d'Anjou.

From this sanctuary on the medieval Ile St-Louis, Dos Passos circled outward along the stone quaysides and through the incredible tangle of streets on both sides of the pont Marie to explore the city he found more intense and satisfying than military life had turned out to be. On at least one extended promenade, Dos Passos was accompanied by Fernand Léger, who had just been mustered out of the French army where he had served as stretcher-bearer at Verdun and been gassed at the Aisne. (Of his military experience, Léger said: 'Three years without touching a brush, but contact with reality at its most violent, its most crude ... the war made me mature, I'm not afraid to say so.') Dos Passos had no wartime adventure to match the painter's 'contact with reality', but a walk with the older man was a revelation: a way of looking at smokestacks seen from the Montmartre funiculaire; the flat planes of a river barge as mass, a sill of geraniums as detail. Léger was in the process of adapting his Cubist techniques to a particular vision of the machine age. In Paris, where the several branches of art meet so familiarly, Dos Passos was invited to share the painter's perceptions.

While Dos Passos was involved in the excitement and stimulus of postwar Paris, E. E. Cummings wrote him of his boredom and unhappiness at home. His outraged father was planning to sue the French government for the false incarceration of his son. As an affidavit for the case, he encouraged Cummings to record his prison experiences – although the young man nourished no special grudge against the French. On the contrary, Cummings was as rabid a Francophile as ever: his hapless arrest and military detention only reinforced a growing resentment of all bureaucracy and authority. But the poet began to put down his impressions of La Ferté Macé episode to satisfy his father's scheme: the affidavit, however, grew beyond any such legal intent to become that classic document of World War I, *The Enormous Room*.

*

The little ladies of Paris had fascinated Cummings and Dos Passos from the first. Dos Passos referred to his excursions in search of architecture and *les petites femmes* ('alas, the remorseful prophylaxis after') while Cummings would recall Frenchwomen of his own in the lines:

> little ladies more
> than dead exactly dance
> in my head, precisely
> dance where danced la guerre

Demobilization brought home an army of women as well as men. The little ladies were streaming back from the front, where professionals had operated clandestinely as canteen girls, or openly in the 'red lanterns' for enlisted men and 'blue lanterns' for officers.

A new recruiting drive was on, for prostitutes to serve in the brothels of the capital. Known as *maisons de passe, maisons closes, maisons de tolérance*, the houses of prostitution had not altogether languished during the war – with the troops of three allied nations passing through Paris – but air raids, police restrictions, and the military patrols in search of deserters disturbed the tranquil flow of business. As an influx of foreign visitors joined the returning *poilus* seeking the classic pleasures associated with Paris, new and exigent tastes required the famous houses like the One-Two-Two (de la rue de Provence, behind the Galeries Lafayette) and the historic Chabanais (beside the Bibliothèque Nationale) to seek fresh recruits from the chorus lines of the Folies-Bergère and the Casino de Paris. Girls from the provinces took the familiar road to the bordels of the big city, pimps awaited them at the gare de Lyon and the gare Saint-Lazare.

The flourishing upturn in the flesh trade during the Twenties encouraged Marthe Lemestre to establish a three-star house of rendezvous, Le Sphinx, the first important *maison close* on the Left Bank. 'Martoune' obtained the backing of four respected investors (one of them a bank) for her palace of unrivaled opulence. Set in the somber neighborhood of the Montparnasse Cemetery, the house was easily distinguished by its stucco Sphinx added to the façade of 31 boulevard Edgar Quinet.

Martoune inaugurated the establishment modestly enough with a staff of fifteen *filles de joie* – but girls of reputedly superior gifts. Eventually as many as sixty charming hostesses entertained hundreds of clients nightly, not only as bed partners but often simply as salon companions, graceful tablemates with whom one discussed art and the issues of the day over a bottle of Taittinger. With complete confidence fathers brought their adolescent sons to Le Sphinx for a traditional initiation into the carnal mysteries.

The wine list at Le Sphinx was as extensive as the choice from the cellar at Maxim's, an understandable investment for the house since a considerable part of Maxim's clientele were familiars at Le Sphinx. Of the three important houses (Le Sphinx, the Chabanais, the One-Two-Two), Martoune's Le Sphinx was the most avant-garde, with Art Déco interiors in Egyptian motif instead of the gold leaf and drapery, candelabra and canopied beds traditional to the older houses. Le Sphinx was the first building in all of France to install air-conditioning.

*

Sexual tolerance is a given of Parisian attitudes, including the freedom to be homosexual. Inevitably a colony of the third sex, uninhibited by legal or social pressures, became an accepted component of the mixed milieu. One's choice of partner, and the form of lovemaking that choice took, was a private matter between lovers (and possibly one's concierge). Homosexual exile in Paris was a tradition that might extend from Oscar Wilde at the turn of the century to his granddaughter Dolly Wilde in the 1920s.

France was a convenient channel crossing from England, Paris the destination of social outlaws of whatever sexual inclination, even for a single permissive weekend. At the end of World War I, Vita Sackville-West – author, intimate of the Bloomsbury circle – embarked on a passionate escapade in Paris with Violet Trefusis. Violet had only just married Denys Trefusis, an officer recently returned from the front, but her liaison with Vita predated the nuptial ceremony, and was a more compelling commitment, Paris a more tempting idyll, than a tame honeymoon in London. Vita darkened her face with dye and wore a stained bandage around her head – bandages, in postwar Paris, being a common enough sight – to dress as a sailor. Violet called her 'Julian'.

In her diary Vita wrote of the heady sense of freedom she felt as she strolled the boulevards and back streets of Paris with Violet beside her: 'I never appreciated anything so much as living like that with my tongue perpetually in my cheek, and in defiance of every policeman I passed.' It is doubtful whether a French policeman cared if she dressed as a boy or not. Even as the two husbands converged on their errant wives, Vita went on: 'There was no abatement ... in my passion for the freedom of that life.'

This was 1920: freedom was in the air, in Paris, at the beginning of the decade.

CHAPTER THREE

News of Paris

During Vita Sackville-West's fling with Violet Trefusis, Vita's husband, the diplomat Harold Nicolson, was attending the 1920 Peace Conference at Versailles. The end of The War to End All Wars had brought the Big Four to the Hôtel Crillon, with its vista of renewed horse-cab and motor traffic around the obelisk at the place de la Concorde, to squabble over questionable promises and secret treaties while Europe was being carved into a new design. Under the elegant chandeliers of the Crillon, presidents and prime ministers dismantled two empires, deposed four kings, and brought forth three new republics. The press corps gathered under the arcades on the north side of the *place*: Paris had become the focus of international news.

Censorship had ended with the Armistice. French newspapers extended their daily editions beyond the single page imposed as a wartime measure to save paper. The journals could flaunt their political affiliation once more with editorials on German reparations and annexation of the Saar. Wire services and foreign-language dailies opened agencies as close to the Champs Elysées or l'Opéra as possible. For those who were already Over There and wanted to stay on in the favorite city of the postwar world there was a scramble for appointments to Hoover's American Relief Administration, but legions of young hopefuls jostled for posts as stringer-journalists covering the Peace Conference.

Rookie newsmen moved from the US Army publication *Stars and Stripes* into the Paris agencies of Reuters, the United Press and the Associated Press. John Dos Passos and Vincent Sheean became roving foreign correspondents, with Paris as a frequent stopover or convenient headquarters. Dorothy Thompson covered the Peace Conference from the *Philadelphia Ledger*'s Paris office. Captain Walter Lippmann had served as propaganda officer with General Pershing, then became press attaché to President Wilson, with the prospect of elucidating Wilson's Fourteen Points to Anglo-American readers.

A young Irishman with an interest in art, Arthur Power, began seeking out painters in their studios (he looked for them first in Montmartre, but discovered that most had migrated to Montparnasse), and from these peripatetic interviews talked his way into writing a column 'Around the Studios' for the Paris *Herald*. In much the same way Elliot Paul took a job at the Paris *Herald* writing 'From a Litterateur's Notebook'. Harold Stearns arrived in Paris on 14 July 1921, the French Day of Independence, a celebration – with dancing in the streets and *feu d'artifice* beside the Seine – he considered appropriate to his own declaration of independence from America. On his very first outing to a racetrack, Stearns picked the winner of the Grand Prix de Paris, a circumstance he also considered significant: he became the racetrack reporter 'Peter Pickem' for the Paris edition of the *Chicago Tribune*.

Still, it was a time of hustle and luck: jobs were not easy to find – Matthew Josephson became desperate and pawned his wife's wedding ring at the municipal pawnshop Le Mont-de-Piété just before he got a job with an English-language racing sheet, *The Paris Telegram*.

A midwestern journalist, James Thurber, had been inducted into the Army in the final months of the war. He was trained as a code clerk, received sailing orders, and arrived in France two days after the Armistice was signed. When Thurber reported for duty at the Hôtel Crillon, his commanding officer informed him with undisguised sarcasm, 'I requisitioned a code *book*, not a code clerk.' Thurber was the tenth such mistake in as many weeks. Nevertheless, in the confused laissez-faire operations of those postwar months, Thurber was allowed to linger, or malinger, with nine other redundant code clerks at the chancellory of the US Embassy, 5 rue de Chaillot. The wide-eyed Ohioan had stumbled into the ideal sinecure.

'Finie la Guerre' was the street song of the moment. 'Girls snatched overseas caps and tunic buttons from American soldiers, paying for them in hugs and kisses, and even warmer coin.' Eventually Thurber was to collect warmer coin of his own when he took what he called 'the first step aside'. The girl was a dancer, Ninette, from the Folies-Bergère. After a long separation, Thurber, like Cummings, attempted to search out his first love – but Ninette had married another doughboy, been to the American midwest and back to Paris; meanwhile, Thurber too had married, the meeting with Ninette had been inspired by guilt and curiosity: *finie l'affaire*, but not the affair with Paris.

Colonel McCormick of the *Chicago Tribune* could not resist the challenge of launching a Paris edition of the *Tribune* to compete with his arch-rival James Gordon Bennett who had long cornered the English-language news market with his Paris *Herald*. McCormick appointed David Darrah to run the *Chicago Tribune*'s Paris edition, and Darrah sought out such journalists as George Seldes and Vincent Sheean to work for the new daily. The third US journal to open a bureau in Paris was the *Brooklyn Eagle*, edited by Guy Hickok, on the boulevard de la Madeleine.

The news desk of the Paris *Herald* was known for its staff of literary hopefuls with unfinished novels in their suitcases: on his second trip to Paris, a civilian now, Thurber also carried with him the inevitable first draft of a novel. He was unable to get a job in the Paris *Herald* newsroom – there was a long waiting list of apprentice newsmen hoping for jobs on the English-language dailies – and it looked as if Thurber and his new bride would have to return to the US when finally Thurber convinced David Darrah that he was not a poet. Darrah had been besieged by what he considered literary types looking for a job on the *Tribune*, and what he needed was somebody who had experience writing headlines. Thurber had been a reporter for the *Columbus Dispatch*: he was hired, to begin work the next night – the pay was $12 per week.

Thurber found himself working alongside another aspiring novelist, William Shirer. Later Shirer confessed that once he had met the expatriate writers Hemingway, Fitzgerald and James Joyce, he had abandoned all hope of writing fiction. Thurber also came to the conclusion that he was no novelist: he threw away his half-completed manuscript to concentrate on the short humorous pieces for which he became known.

The newspaper mogul James Gordon Bennett boasted, even to his employees, 'I can buy all the brains I need for $25 a week.' To take revenge for the meager salary – a marginally living wage only because of the favorable exchange rate – reporters treated the news as something of a joke, extending the most trivial items into extravagant features or inventing unverifiable dispatches out of whole cloth. Paris was the newsman's playground, work and pleasure were meant to overlap. After the paper was put to bed, journalists from the foreign dailies met at Le

Chien Qui Fume in Les Halles, still alive and bustling with fruit and vegetable vendors under the arc-lamps of the market sheds. In this hectic atmosphere of camion horns and *les forts* hauling crates for the wholesalers, the reporters swapped notes and anecdotes, ate onion soup and drank with the prostitutes and market loaders while the rest of Paris slept.

The publishers who were quick to seize on the growing American presence in France and to extend the hometown news to editions in Paris unintentionally provided a conduit of literary talent by way of their overseas operations. Correspondents James Thurber and Janet Flanner served their apprenticeship as journalists in Paris, then scaled their work to the higher demands of the fledgling *New Yorker* (Janet Flanner as the magazine's Paris correspondent 'Genêt'); the working style of newspaper prose helped sharpen the novelistic technique of John Dos Passos and Ernest Hemingway; Elliot Paul and Eugene Jolas would use newspaper work as a starting point for their later careers as editors and publishers. When William Bird first came to Paris he directed the Consolidated Press office on rue d'Antin, but left the agency to become an expatriate publisher of the Three Mountains Press in a cellar-printshop on the quai d'Anjou. In this way, many of the reporters and editors of Paris-based journals would move on from the newsroom to produce what Ezra Pound defined as literature: news that stays news.

*

When Sherwood Anderson brought the news of Paris to a group of young writers in Chicago, Ernest Hemingway had just turned 21. Hemingway was editing a house organ, *The Cooperative Commonwealth*, to earn money so that he might marry his fiancée, Hadley Richardson. The young journalist had worked briefly on the *Kansas City Star* and had contributed features and articles to the *Toronto Star* at a penny a word. Hemingway nurtured an outsized ambition to write prose fiction: newspaper work was his first tentative approach towards a literary career. Editing *The Cooperative Commonwealth* was a dullish stopgap job until he could take Hadley to Europe on their honeymoon: he was already changing his salary into Italian lire in anticipation of the trip.

The great adventure in Hemingway's life until that time was, like so many of his contemporaries, ambulance duty during the recent war. He had narrowly escaped being blown apart on the Italian front during the Austrian offensive at the Piave in 1918. For the remainder of his life he would bear the psychic as well as physical scars of that wartime episode.

Ernest Hemingway, on the mend in Italy, and his nurse,
Agnes von Kurowsky.

He likened the trauma to the sensation of having for an instant met death – the soul slipped from his body like a silken handkerchief drawn from a pocket – and in the next instant he was restored to life. His wounds were treated at the Ospedale Rossa in Milan where he fell in love with his nurse, Agnes von Kurowsky. Theirs was the supremely romantic affair Hemingway would celebrate in his second novel, *A Farewell to Arms*. In that story the heroine dies in childbirth, but the unhappy truth was that Hemingway's first love threw him over to marry an Italian officer.

Despite whatever intrusions reality made in the Hemingway remembrance of things past, he remained a romantic where his own past was concerned. The original excitement of that adolescent love affair overcame any bitter aftertaste of the ending to romance. Ernest convinced Hadley that they should spend their honeymoon in Italy, where the young soldier had been wounded in two important ways. He managed to suppress whatever brooding under-thoughts still haunted him from that brush with death. He dwelt, in his enthusiasm and imagination, on the glory of his great adventure.

Meanwhile Sherwood Anderson was delivering his rapturous report on Paris as a literary paradise, the ideal place for a young writer to launch his career. Hadley became as excited about the prospect of Paris as Ernest: the Italian plan was abandoned. (Later Hemingway did revisit the Piave, and observed: 'Chasing yesterdays is a bum show – if you have to prove it, go back to your old front.')

Anderson provided the couple with letters of introduction to Gertrude Stein, Ezra Pound and Sylvia Beach – Americans all, three important sources of influence and advancement in a writer's apprenticeship. The last night in Chicago Hemingway showed the attractive side of his character: Anderson heard a knock at his door, and opened to the shy, grinning, giant-of-a-man. Attempting to repay a debt in his own way, Hemingway presented the older writer with a rucksack of canned goods, making a gift of the last food stores he had hoarded for the stint in Chicago.

Ernest Hemingway and his new bride took the converted troopship *Leopoldina* on its rough winter crossing to France. He carried with him the letters from Sherwood Anderson: 'I am writing this note to make you acquainted with my friend Ernest Hemingway, who with Mrs Hemingway is going to Paris to live, and will ask him to drop it into the mails when he arrives there ...'

CHAPTER FOUR
Introductions

Newcomers to Paris were unaware that prices had quadrupled since the beginning of the war. Some items had increased ten times over: tobacco was 100 per cent higher, soap 500 per cent. Unemployment was naturally severe after demobilization of the largest army France had ever assembled; pensions for the aged were on the way to becoming worthless. But the incoming horde took little notice of the price of bread officially raised from fifty to ninety centimes. The critical downward spiral of the French franc was only another inducement that lured the first wave of Americans to Paris. The same day newspapers announced the bread increase, 1 January 1920, the dollar stood at 26.76 francs – a single American greenback could purchase a month's supply of bread.

The former zones of industrialization in north-eastern France were devastated and depopulated – not only the French, but most European economies were ruined by the war – while the United States had flourished during 1914–18, and at the beginning of the Twenties was the world's leading industrial power.

But the outward aspect of Paris was unchanged: the city smiled beguilingly at its visitors although a poverty of means and spirit lay just behind the façade. Those with money – gold, or currency redeemable in gold – were the new pilgrims. Following the 1924–26 financial crisis in France, the dollar would rise to a record high of fifty francs. A lopsided economic balance opened the way for a dollar-rich invasion of expatriates to France. As little as $80 purchased tourist-class passage across the Atlantic; the truly adventurous could work their way to Le Havre 'shoveling out' in the fetid holds of cattle boats. A modest allowance from home would subsidize an American in Paris for what appeared to be forever, a windfall made that first tentative Grand Tour possible.

In 1919 F. Scott Fitzgerald earned a mere $800 from his writing; in 1920 his income soared to $18,000. He had just married the southern belle Zelda Sayre (who had turned him down as a poor prospect in his $800 year) and by Valentine's Day Zelda was pregnant. The newlyweds were anxious to make lavish use of the first profits from Fitzgerald's best-selling *This Side of Paradise*: Paris seemed the very paradise in which to spend the big money. The glamorous Fitzgeralds were a symbol of carefree high-living, ambassadors of the jazz age, and – since a pregnant flapper would have little status in Manhattan – Scott and Zelda decided to bring the jazz age to France.

That same summer, Fitzgerald's Princeton friend 'Bunny', the literary critic Edmund Wilson, was in Paris for his own urgent and certainly Parisian reason. Wilson was in amorous pursuit of the violet-eyed Edna St. Vincent Millay. (Who could resist a poet not only beautiful but with the wit to reply to a keep-off-the-grass sign – *Pelouse défendue* – in the Luxembourg Gardens: 'Mais nous ne pelousons pas!'?)

The Fitzgeralds sailed on the *Aquitania* snobbishly delighted to read their names inscribed on the first class passenger list. Maxwell Perkins, Fitzgerald's editor at Scribner's, had supplied letters of introduction to French and English authors: at this stage of his career Fitzgerald was in adolescent awe of established literary figures abroad, and had every intention of using the Perkins-Scribner's connections as a passe-partout from the New World into the Old. In Paris, Scott and Zelda camped on the doorstep of Anatole France but did not meet the illustrious Frenchman. They did meet the Irishman, James Joyce. On that occasion Fitzgerald declared his everlasting obeisance to Joyce's genius, and threatened to jump from a window to demonstrate his sincerity. Joyce persuaded him not to. ('That young man must be mad.')

Scott and Zelda went to the Folies-Bergère where the presence of so many American doughboys – returned from the trench warfare Scott missed – may have dulled the flesh-and-feathered spectacle. They trekked with numb indifference through the galleries of the Louvre, and, with a hangover each, toured the halls of the Palais de Versailles. (A visit to Napoleon's chateau at Malmaison had ironic significance: in that suburban village was the Malmaison clinic where Deschanel underwent treatment for nervous disorder, the same clinic the Fitz-geralds would revisit at the end of the decade when Zelda began to show signs of mental breakdown.) Against the current belief of Americans that 'they do things better in France', Fitzgerald concluded that Europe was of antiquarian interest only.

Frenchmen demonstrate a great love for Americans – immediately after a war – but Scott and Zelda were from that other America France cannot tolerate. Their hotel manager did not see the humor when Zelda fastened the elevator cage with a length of rope, to be sure of having the elevator at their constant disposal. Scott was not gifted for languages and made no attempt to come to know his French hosts. Like so many touring Americans, the Fitzgeralds were only happy in the company of fellow Americans. The French either ignored the golden couple of the jazz age or deplored them. Champagne lacked the kick of bathtub gin, Paris was a bore. It was as if Scott and Zelda had come to the wrong party, too early, and could only recall with overwhelming regret the wild party they had just left.

Although Edmund Wilson realized that Fitzgerald's 'access of conscious charm' was unlikely to charm the French, he urged the Fitzgeralds to stay on – but Scott informed him that Paris as a center of culture was washed up. 'Culture follows money', he declared, therefore New York was destined to be the next metropolis of all that mattered.

So the Fitzgeralds sailed home to Manhattan where Scott was the Prince Charming of all the sad young men and Zelda (once delivered of her firstborn) could be the belle of the ball forever. When the real party got under way they would be back. Paris in the mid-Twenties – crowded, excessive, frenetic – was exactly the fete they were seeking all along.

It was Edmund Wilson who abandoned Paris for all time. Edna St. Vincent Millay made known her preference for a handsome British journalist. Wilson briefly consoled himself with one of the little ladies of Montmartre: he even attempted to convince Loulou that prostitutes should organize. (On the metal sides of the foul-smelling *pissoirs* was painted the slogan, inspired by the recent Russian Revolution: L'UNION DES TRAVAILLEURS FERA LA PAIX DU MONDE.) Loulou was amused by the naiveté of the idea. She wondered if Wilson was in any way related to President Wilson, whom she considered *très chic*. A prostitute can be a charming café love and loving armful, but Loulou's company did not make up for the affair with Miss Millay. A rejection from the lovely poet who burned her candles at both ends was, in effect, to be spurned by the muse, to receive the cold shoulder of the city of art.

'Is it not extraordinary,' wrote James Joyce, 'the way I enter a city barefoot and end up in a luxurious flat?'

The first flat to house the Joyce family was a rent-free 'matchbox' lent by Madame Savitsky, Joyce's translator in Paris, on the rue de l'Assomption – a street-name the word-conscious Joyce may have considered apt. At the urging of Ezra Pound, James Joyce came to Paris early in 1920 for a two-week visit: he would stay twenty years. After a journey of 'silence, exile, and cunning' by way of Trieste and Zurich, Paris seemed the next logical stopping place. Joyce had got the message in Zurich from Ezra Pound – who had it from Jean Cocteau and Francis Picabia – that Paris, eternally susceptible to the miracle of rejuvenation, was entering a new golden age. In Zurich Joyce had exhausted funds and friends: a quixotic lawsuit launched against an employee of the British Embassy further reduced his resources and welcome. After the wartime ordeal of living on English lessons and poet's wages, Paris was indeed a return to Eden for Joyce.

Ezra Pound had already quit the London scene where he and Wyndham Lewis were at the vortex of the Vorticist movement. He diagnosed London as moribund, afraid he might 'wake up one morning with web feet' after having fled the United States for the same reason.

Pound introduced Joyce to his own patron, the American lawyer John Quinn, who became interested in Joyce's nearly-completed novel *Ulysses* and offered to contribute $1600 toward its eventual publication. The indefatigable Pound was assembling a coterie of Joyceans – admirers, and possible supporters – in Paris. Pound's tagline after each discussion of the Irishman's dilemma was, 'You must help Joyce'. Ezra Pound could be endlessly resourceful and completely selfless in his efforts to help another artist or musician or writer in whom he believed.

The two writers, James Joyce and Ezra Pound, were remarkably different in appearance and manner. Joyce, with his neat haircut and rimless glasses, dressed as conservatively (even in hand-me-downs) as his means allowed. Next to him, Pound cast an almost satanic image: he affected poet's garb of loose collar and careless *cravate*, often a cape, worn with a sinister wide-brimmed Spanish hat. Gentlemanly James Joyce was the most retiring of men, with a ritual of elaborate courtesy meant to keep society at bay. Joyce was stiff and uneasy with new-found acquaintances, while Pound was at his voluble best, opinionated and direct, meeting and knowing everyone, astir in every intellectual stew.

James Joyce – Paris 1920.

Despite his reticence, Joyce allowed himself to be fed to the lion-hunters by Pound. In his poverty, Joyce naturally gravitated toward the solvent. Through Pound, he was invited to the Natalie Barney salon where he first met Madame Savitsky, who not only agreed to translate *A Portrait of the Artist as a Young Man* into French, but generously provided the destitute author with her rue de l'Assomption apartment.

Pound suggested to Jenny Serruys, the literary agent, that she might be able to help Joyce. James Joyce then fell into the habit of appearing at Miss Serruys's office to announce he needed a bed for his borrowed flat, or to ask where he might obtain a table to write on. Miss Serruys was good enough to look after the writer's day-to-day needs, lent him money, and even introduced her fiancé into the league of friends who helped Joyce: Joyce was very happy to accept a discarded army overcoat from the young man – the best coat, Joyce emphatically declared, he had ever worn.

Three days after his arrival in Paris Joyce was presented to the proprietor of Shakespeare and Company, Sylvia Beach.

'Is this the great James Joyce?' asked Miss Beach.

'James Joyce,' replied Joyce, shifting his ashplant walking-stick to shake the hand of the diminutive figure.

Sylvia Beach, with her gentle sensitivity to literary genius and superhuman patience with literary temperament, was to be an even larger force than Ezra Pound in the advancement of Joyce's career. Very soon Joyce asked her if she would send any stray students of English his way; he had made a bare livelihood teaching English in Trieste, and he was prepared to do the same in Paris.

Not all Joyce's new acquaintances paid unreserved homage to him, and several were put off by the cool social manner or his obviously superior opinion of himself. When the American wife of a Japanese painter, Mrs Yashushi Tanaka, expressed admiration for Yeats, Joyce offered the snide opinion that Yeats had achieved eminence only because he had been the lover of Lady Gregory, and she had paid his way into the limelight. To a French author, Edmond Jaloux, who had spoken of Flaubert, Joyce began a denunciation of Flaubert's style by lecturing on his mistakes in French. While Pound was briefly out of Paris, Joyce wrote to him: 'I heard and saw no more of the many lucky mortals who made my acquaintance here. I suspect that the pleasure my exhilarating company gave them will last for the rest of their natural existences. Except Vanderpyl.'

Ezra Pound browsing at Shakespeare and Company.

Fritz Vanderpyl was the art critic for *Le Petit Parisien*, and was good-natured enough to accept Joyce's opinion that art was of no interest, except portrait-painting. Vanderpyl thought Joyce looked very professorial in his neat dark suit and felt hat, except for the startling pair of dirty tennis shoes Joyce habitually wore that first year in Paris. (His remark about entering a city barefoot was close to the truth.) Ever needy, Joyce could drop his façade of formality in an instant to express a blunt request. Vanderpyl and Joyce had barely shaken hands when Joyce asked him, 'Can you lend me a hundred francs?' Vanderpyl borrowed the sum from a friend and passed the banknotes to Joyce, who was obliged to bring bills close to his failing eyes to make out the denomination.

Ezra Pound could not resist the opportunity to bring together the two great men of modern letters, T. S. Eliot and James Joyce. While Pound was briefly in London he learned that Eliot would be visiting the continent and contrived for Eliot to deliver a parcel to Joyce when he passed through Paris. The two men had very little to say to one another, perhaps because Joyce performed – as he invariably did in such circumstances – an off-putting show of courtly protocol. Wyndham Lewis accompanied Eliot throughout the visit, for which Joyce (flush for a change, in borrowed funds) played generous host. Joyce paid for every round of drinks, then invited Eliot and Lewis to an expensive meal at his favorite restaurant, Les Trianons. It was impossible for either visitor to pay for as much as a coffee. Eliot privately complained to Lewis of Joyce's excessive politesse and insistent largesse. Eventually the parcel from Ezra Pound was opened and found to contain second-hand clothing and a worn pair of brown shoes – the shoes, no doubt, meant to replace Joyce's lamentable tennis shoes.

Since the loan of Madame Savitsky's flat, Joyce had moved his family of four twice – but thoughtfully returned the items he had borrowed from Jenny Serruys when one of the flats turned out to be fully furnished. By the end of the year Joyce discovered the apartment of his dreams at 5 boulevard Raspail. Boulevard Raspail is a long somber residential avenue running from the Latin Quarter into the heart of Montparnasse: its rows of respectable but indifferent façades probably suited Joyce's idea of sanctuary – or he may have been pleased to live on a boulevard that honored Balzac at the junction of place Vavin. The apartment rental was far more than the writer could ever hope to acquire, but once again his Paris friends decided they 'must help Joyce' and agreed to subsidize the cost of housing the Joyce family. As to furnishings, Joyce was indifferent – except that he demanded a table with square edges to write upon, while Nora Barnacle (who would not become Joyce's legal wife until the end of the Twenties) converted each of their temporary living quarters into a passable replica of a flat in Dublin. It was on the boulevard Raspail, and soon after in an apartment lent by Valery Larbaud at 71 rue Cardinal Lemoine, that Joyce completed his masterwork *Ulysses* ending with the most resonant affirmative in literary history, Molly Bloom's classic 'yes.'

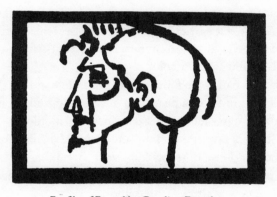

Profile of Pound by Gaudier-Brzeska.

CHAPTER FIVE

The Knots in Picasso's Tail

'Picabia is the man who ties knots in Picasso's tail.'
EZRA POUND

'Yes,' lamented Gertrude Stein, 'the old crowd has disappeared.' But even as she said it, an active contingent of the old crowd, her crowd, was moving back to its prewar premises. Paris came to life again, progressively, like a canvas by Vallotton. (When Vallotton did a portrait of Gertrude Stein, she remarked on the painter's obsessive method of painting from left to right, beginning at the top of the canvas, then down to the next section, until the surface was covered with paint and the portrait completed.) Slowly, arrondissement by arrondissement – but particularly Montparnasse, which had taken over from Montmartre as the latest outpost of the avant-garde – the portrait began to fill in and take on color.

The Germans had twice failed to break through at the Marne for an invasion of Paris, but now a peacetime invasion was taking place. Great colonies of the uprooted – Russian émigrés, in force – joined the returning soldiers swarming into the capital. From America 'the younger and footloose intellectuals went streaming up the longest gangplank in the world', as Malcolm Cowley visualized the 'great migration into new prairies of the mind'.

At war's end the artillery post on the roof of the Hôtel de Ville had been dismantled and the Cocteau-inspired cabaret, Le Boeuf sur le Toit (The Ox on the Roof), established. Kiosks were plastered over with ads for the new comedy *Phi-Phi* or Paul Colin posters of Mistinguett (singing 'Mon Homme') at the Casino de Paris. Except for a token force on occupation duty, the French army had demobilized. The survivors of Ypres and Verdun formed queues at their local city halls to marry wartime sweethearts and crowded around the Havas ads looking for employment. Zeppelin damage and Big Bertha scars were still visible; signs in the Métro requested patrons to relinquish their seats to *mutilés de la guerre*. The same taxis and couturier vans that had relayed troops to the Battle of the Marne were back on the boulevards in a familiar traffic tangle and cacophony of horns.

Of the old crowd Gertrude Stein knew best, Matisse had abandoned Paris for the Riviera, but Braque was back from the trenches where he had suffered a head wound that required trepanning. Wearing a turban of bandages he experimented with sand and plaster applied to canvas, working at his old studio on the rue Caulaincourt beside the Montmartre cemetery. But few of the Cubists went back to Montmartre: studios had become expensive in the burgeoning night-life district – a rural outpost before the war, with its antique windmills and sloping *terrains vagues*, its vineyards and terraced garden plots had by now been filled in by apartment blocks. Montparnasse was uglier, and lacked the rustic folklore of la Butte, but studio space was easier to find.

The Polish dealer Zborowski who had discovered and nourished Modigliani still haunted the *cités des artistes* of La Ruche and La Falguière as if another Modi might turn up among the destitute – but D. H. Kahnweiler, because of his German origins, had been obliged to sit out the war in Switzerland. Kahnweiler was back, and with undiminished optimism attempted to recover his confiscated stock of paintings and reassemble his coterie of Cubists. Only Juan Gris, ill and discouraged, appeared to need or want to settle again under Kahnweiler's wing. Picasso had become successful enough to move into bourgeois splendour at 23 rue La Boétie, next door to Paul Rosenberg's gallery at number 21. The Rosenbergs, Paul and Léonce, had replaced the devoted Kahnweiler as Picasso's dealers. Rue La Boétie was in fact the new street of modern art, with Paul Guillaume at number 108, and La Licorne, a gallery run by the dentist-connoisseur Dr Girardin, at 110 next door.

Despite death and defection, altered circumstances and changed attitudes, Paris was astir again. The Bateau Lavoir – so named by the poet Max Jacob because the ramshackle wooden structure resembled the laundry-boats tied up along the Seine – where the Cubists had lived and worked in picturesque misery (Picasso's tea froze in the pot overnight and was reheated for *le petit déjeuner* next winter's morn) was by now an abandoned ship. One of the first to evacuate the Bateau Lavoir was Max Jacob himself. During the war he had converted from Jew to Catholic, taken the baptismal name Cyprien, and now shuttled between Paris and the contemplative life at a monastery in the village of St-Benoit-sur-Loire. Picasso took pains to avoid meeting Max Jacob

(Cyprien) and André Derain: they only reminded him of the days of frozen tea in the leaky Bateau Lavoir. In a period of new attachments and shifting allegiances, the painters of the prewar Ecole de Paris had scattered to other arrondissements, principally to Montparnasse, according to their levels of success. Georges Braque and the poet André Breton remained loyal to Montmartre. The war had only interrupted Braque's interest in the Cubist concepts he had discovered alongside Picasso; Breton was brooding over the beginning dreams of Surrealism: the poet pinned a notice to a wall in his room on the rue Fontaine: 'Ne vas jamais à Montparnasse!'

*

The Parisian world of art could not long support a postwar vacuum of ideas: even a statement of anti-art or a season of comic anarchy would serve until a substantial movement should coalesce. Marcel Duchamp had managed for a time to shock bourgeois sensibilities by a reverse-art of 'ready-mades', exhibiting a shovel, a wine rack, a toilet seat as gallery pieces. This spirit animated the background to the first *dernier cri* of the decade. Dada was born in Zurich during the war (8 February 1916) when Tristan Tzara delivered the first Dadaist manifesto at the Café Terrasse, accompanied by Hans Arp with a brioche dangling from his left nostril.

The advent of peace negotiations in the Paris of 1920 brought two uninvited delegates to the capital – Tristan Tzara and Francis Picabia – determined to declare a new war in the art world. Revolution, not reconciliation, was the principal item on their agenda.

Early in the campaign, Picabia escorted his friend Tzara to 27 rue de Fleurus to announce to Gertrude Stein that Dada had arrived in Paris. Miss Stein was fond of Picabia, but she was neither interested nor amused by his proclamation. In her original and inventive way, Gertrude Stein might be thought of as a Dadaist unaware, but she was not likely to become part of a movement she had not discovered for herself. (Her own work had been ridiculed too often for her to offer her name to a group devoted to ridicule.) The Steins, Gertrude and her brother Leo, had purchased and pronounced upon the works produced under the various labels of Impressionism, Post-impressionism, Fauvism, Futurism (an Italian movement which caused more stir in Paris than in Rome), and above all Cubism – but Dada was not to receive the Stein imprimatur. Never mind; 'The true Dadaists,' declared Tzara, 'are against Dada.'

The first public Dada manifestation took place at the Palais des Fêtes on 23 January 1920. A stunned audience sat through a preliminary literary discussion passively enough but with visible discomfort; however, when Tristan Tzara read as a poem an insignificant newspaper item chosen at random, accompanied by castanets, cowbells, and rattles, the first major battle was joined. The whistling, hissing, outburst of insult was exactly the reaction the Dadaists had hoped for.

At the Salon des Indépendants the very next month, the Dadaists gave out the false report that Charlot (Charlie Chaplin) was the latest convert to Dada and would be present on stage. This announcement naturally attracted an overflow audience – Chaplin, of course, did not appear. As the Dadaists read aloud their poems and manifestos, the outraged crowd hurled vegetables (also a veal cutlet, in an instance of pure Dada) at the rostrum. The lights had to be switched off in order to evacuate the auditorium. By the time Tzara's *Vaseline Symphony* was presented at the Salle Gaveau that May, a contingent of gendarmes patrolled the aisles to deal with the riot that had become traditional.

*

Cubism had been equally revolutionary before the war, but by 1920 the movement had plunged beyond its breakthrough years. Although Braque was still experimenting in the Cubist manner and Léger had adapted Cubist techniques to an interpretation of the industrial age, only Juan Gris would continue to paint Cubist pictures until his death in 1927. The tightknit prewar group had splintered, Cubism was no longer avant-garde enough for a new age. Amédée Ozenfant pronounced the trend decadent (at any rate, the paintings were selling too well for modernist comfort) and in need of purification. Also from Switzerland, but no part of the Dada circle, Charles Jeanneret (Le Corbusier) joined with Ozenfant in the theory of Cubist purism, as expressed in the journal founded in 1920, *L'Esprit Nouveau*. Despite this attempt at spiritual renewal, Cubism was losing impetus. 'The Cubist bloc is breaking up,' wrote Blaise Cendrars. 'There is new beauty.'

Even though Picasso was one of its originators, Cubism was no longer part of his quicksilver interests. When the Salon des Indépendants held its 1920 exhibit reuniting all the Cubists of the prewar years, Picasso alone refused to show. He had quarreled, then broken with Derain and Braque in his denunciation of Cubism. 'I took Braque and Derain to the station,' said Picasso of his friends who went off to war. 'I never found them again.'

In Rome Picasso had fallen in love with auburn-haired Olga Khoklova, a dancer with the Ballets Russes. She was the daughter of an officer in the czar's army, and appeared to be of an upper-class background that made her all the more desirable in Picasso's eyes. She was not one of his easy conquests: a member of the Diaghilev troupe overheard Picasso at Olga's bedroom door asking to be allowed to see her, and her reply, 'No, no, Monsieur Picasso. I'm not going to let you in'. No intrigue in his company escaped Sergei Diaghilev, and he warned Picasso, 'With Russian girls, you have to marry them.'

They were married at the Russian Orthodox Church on rue Daru, the honeymoon took place at the Hôtel Lutétia whose wedding-cake façade dominates boulevard Raspail at the Sèvres-Babylone intersection. Marriage to Olga brought a complete change in Picasso's outlook and style of life. Olga created a household of upper-middle-class respectability in the heart of the Right Bank bourgeoisie. Since the name Picasso could now open doors to the wealthy and to the highest circles of Parisian society, Olga intended to leave her precarious dance career far behind and enter the ranks of the Tout-Paris. The Picassos received and were received. The high point for Olga in the social ascent was an invitation to the rue Masseran town house of Count Etienne de Beaumont.

The painter who had worn the stained corduroys of Montmartre, simple fisherman's garb, or the 'monkey-suit' of overalls when he worked, now purchased his first dinner-jacket. With it he wore the Spanish *faixa*, a cummerbund of red or black with fringed edges (an item he had formerly worn beneath his overalls to protect his kidneys against the damp cold of the Bateau Lavoir). The bohemian chaos Picasso brought with him from la Butte was confined to the painter's studio one flight above the smart flat on rue La Boétie.

With Olga as the model for a series of serene Greco-Roman figures of heroic proportions – airily dancing on Mediterranean beaches, or seated, solid as statuary – Picasso entered his period of Neo-classicism. Olga became pregnant; life was ordered, almost predictable. Picasso sought his way out of Cubism and beyond by studiously contemplating the antique past.

This was a fluid time, the future indistinct. What next? was a question that also vexed the impresario Sergei Diaghilev, who culled for his ballet productions only the most advanced ideas of the avant-garde. At this threshold of new beginnings – the Ballets Russes had

Picasso in his studio on the rue la Boétie; (inset) his portrait of Olga Khoklova.

been badly disrupted by the fortunes of war, the company in desperate need of a renaissance – Diaghilev had the happy inspiration to bring Picasso together with the composer Igor Stravinsky for a ballet project based on a theme by Pergolesi. Stravinsky and Picasso were alike in several ways: short of stature, with intense and animated expressions heightened by the fierce eyes of buccaneers. ('When Picasso looked at a drawing or a print,' said Leo Stein, 'I was surprised that anything was left on the paper – so absorbing was his gaze.') Both men were inordinately proud of their small feet and hands, both were health-conscious to the point of hypochondria. They shared with Diaghilev a superstitious dread of death. In 1920 these three temperamental moderns set to work on the ballet *Pulcinella*.

The first set designs Picasso conceived – in the style of the *commedia dell'arte* (the painter had always been fascinated by Harlequin) but updating the period to nineteenth-century Offenbach – were altogether inappropriate to Diaghilev's conception of the project. In an argument over side-whiskers instead of masks, Diaghilev suddenly tore the sketches to pieces, then ground the torn bits underfoot. Ordinarily this outburst would have led to an irrevocable break between the two men. Picasso's Spanish pride and Diaghilev's stubborn will could not accommodate opposition, yet Picasso – perhaps conditioned to Slavic turbulence by Olga's temper tantrums – managed to dominate his rage. As suddenly as he had exploded, Diaghilev became, as he could, all charm and persuasion. In a miracle of reconciliation Picasso designed new costumes, then altered the set. *Pulcinella* was the success Diaghilev needed to bring the Ballets Russes into the Twenties, a reassessment of the classic past filtered through the perceptions of a painter and a composer of genius.

*

At the time of the Armistice, Gertrude Stein remarked that Apollinaire's death had changed Paris. Guillaume Apollinaire had been the leading exponent of the avant-garde during the Belle Epoque: poet, critic, impresario of Cubism. He died not of his wartime injuries – a head wound that required trepanning like Braque's – but of Spanish influenza, the second great scourge of the infant century (influenza slaughtered a number equal to all the deaths attributed to World War I, an estimated ten millions). The story Gertrude Stein embellished and passed on was this: as Apollinaire lay dying he heard cries from the street, 'A bas Guillaume!', which in his delirium he thought were meant for himself instead of Kaiser Wilhelm. But Guillaume Apollinaire died three days before the Armistice, so he would not have heard the victory cry from his deathbed. Gertrude Stein loved a story that was a story.

Although she did mourn the passing of Apollinaire and the finale to the era he represented, Miss Stein was not one to languish long or regret forever a vanished time. (In a sense, the disappearance of Apollinaire as the ambassador of Art left that post vacant for Gertrude Stein.)

For Miss Stein, a way of marking the end of the war and the beginning of the Twenties was to replace the unwieldy Ford ambulance she had driven all through the war (her 'second-class hearse') with a pert two-seater she named Godiva because the new motor car arrived from Detroit in its natural state, stripped of accessories and trim. (A chain-smoker, she installed her own ashtray.) She was writing again, often from the lofty driver's seat of Godiva as she waited out a garage repair or sat parked at a Parisian curbside.

At one of the garages where Godiva was being serviced, Miss Stein heard a French mechanic – a cross-eyed, sweet-tempered, and conscientious older man – refer to his hopeless apprentice as one of *une génération perdue*. Men, he explained, become civilized between the ages of 18 and 30, but the war generation missed the civilizing period. Miss Stein later applied the term to those twenty-year-olds like Ernest Hemingway whose characters were altered and whose outlook was shadowed when the natural order of their lives was interrupted by war. The writer Matthew Josephson was present when Miss Stein labeled his generation 'lost', but he remembered the French phrase as *une génération fichue*, which means 'ruined' – thus the famous label may have been largely romanticized in the translation.

*

A grapevine of news and gossip, a network of introductions or the casual accident of a chance meeting began to link one outpost of the new age to the other.

Sylvia Beach had started Shakespeare and Company, her lending library of books in English, and mail-drop service – a kind of Left Bank American Express – first on the rue Dupuytren, then at 8 (later 12) rue de l'Odéon, across the street from Adrienne Monnier's La Maison des Amis des Livres. Sylvia Beach and Adrienne Monnier met when Sylvia's wide-brimmed hat blew off and Adrienne in her long thick peasant skirt went chasing the hat down the rue de l'Odéon. Les Amis des Livres performed the same literary services for French intellectuals as Shakespeare and Company did for the English-speaking community. Miss Monnier and Miss Beach remained friends and were never rivals – a rare and delicate accomplishment in the competitive atmosphere of The Quarter – thus the French and Anglo-American circles that frequented the rue de l'Odéon were sometimes concentric.

The two bookstores were, in their own ways, salons as well as *librairies*. At Shakespeare and Company, Gertrude Stein made contact with a number of new writers passing through or newly installed in Paris since the war. She could find reading matter in English, and was delighted that her own privately-printed *Tender Buttons* was among the books in the lending library. For Gertrude, bookstore browsing and gallery openings were social occasions as well as intellectual stimulation – the new writers and painters she met were invited to her studio-salon at 27 rue de Fleurus. At a Left Bank gallery Picasso, with whom Gertrude Stein had quarreled, came up to her and said. 'Hell, let's be friends' – so they shook hands and she invited him to her studio. The studio on rue de Fleurus became a crossroads meeting-place in the heart of Montparnasse for everybody who was anybody (or soon to become somebody) along with the idly curious or the curiously idle, any passing eccentric or new face in Paris willing to reply to the question Miss Stein's companion Alice Toklas asked at the door: 'De la part de qui venez-vous?'

Guests might turn up by no one's explicit instruction, or they might have been invited by the forgetful Miss Stein herself. Not that the *de-la-part* mattered as much as Gertrude Stein's keenness for new people, her swift instinctive summary of character, or her early discernment of originality in the most unlikely visitor. Her prejudices were legion, but they worked as often in the guest's favor as not.

Gertrude Stein and Sherwood Anderson – whom she immediately liked for his large Italianate eyes – met at Shakespeare and Company. Again through Sylvia Beach, Miss Stein met Ezra Pound, whom she was not sure about. Pound had known Yeats in Ireland and Eliot in England and now Joyce in Paris. Since James Joyce also frequented Shakespeare and Company, Miss Stein almost met him there but, in her words, not quite. Pound was a generous friend to writers and painters and musicians, as well as an influential force in the arts. (It was the influence that made Miss Stein unsure of Pound.) Through his editorship or association with 'little' magazines, he managed to help his gifted contemporaries publish their work, and he genuinely wanted to

Sylvia Beach at the entrance of her first bookshop on 8 rue de l'Odéon; later she moved down the street to number 12 (see page 129).

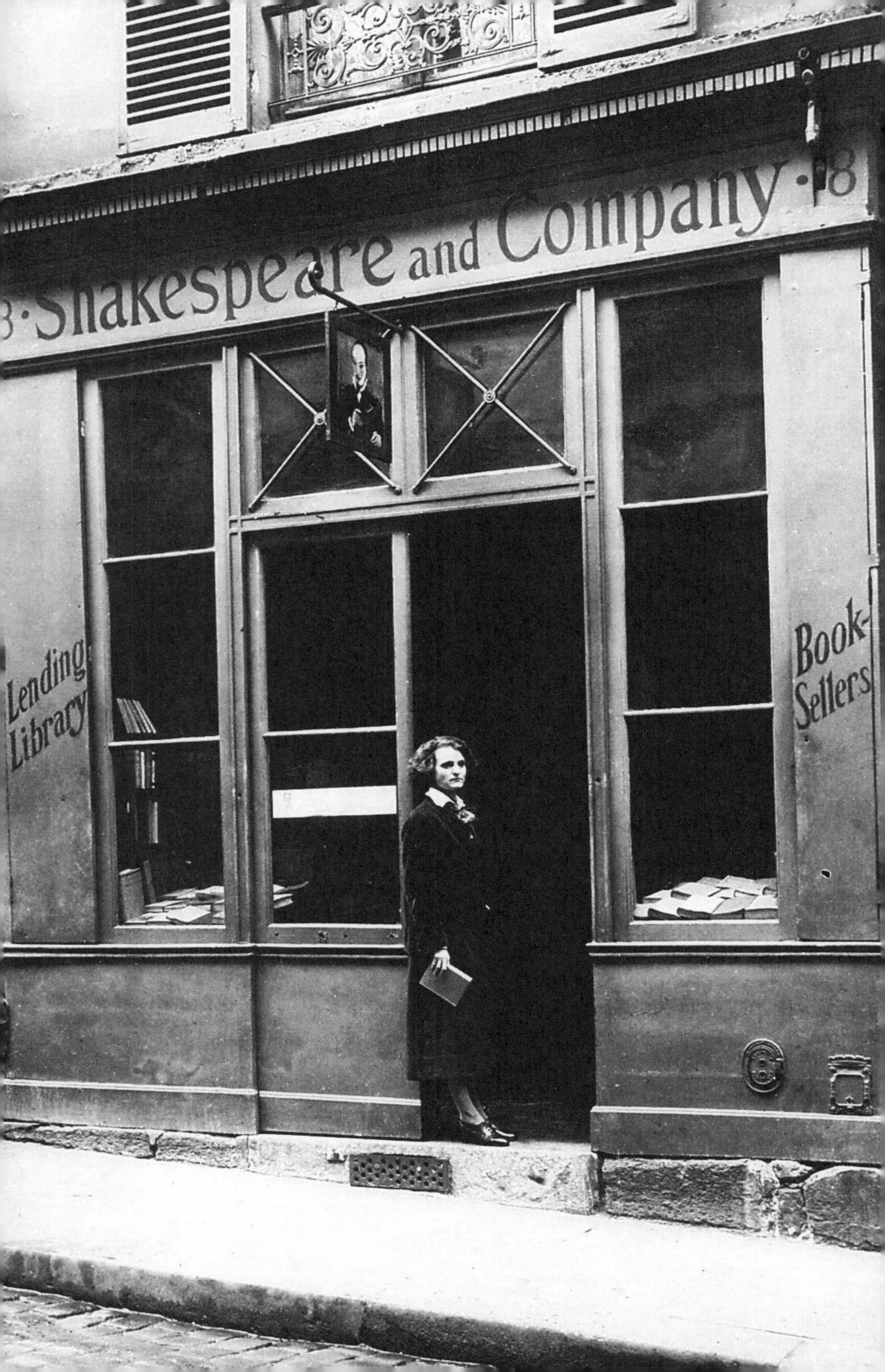

8 · Shakespeare and Company · 18
Lending Library
Book-Sellers

help Miss Stein. Gertrude Stein was practically unpublished at this time except for self-publication at her own expense, even though she was recognized throughout the literary underground of the day as an important new voice and guiding spirit to other writers. As anxious as she was to publish (her dream was to appear in the *Atlantic Monthly*), she was wary of Pound as a counter-influence with the young, and as a

formidable rival. Nevertheless, the two important arbiters of art met at Shakespeare and Company.

Pound was invited to visit the famous studio on rue de Fleurus where the water-stained walls were hung with paintings by Matisse, Derain, Gris, Braque, and most of the Fauves and Cubists who were unknown before Gertrude and Leo Stein began buying (and explaining, if only to themselves) their work. Miss Stein sat slumped heavily beneath the portrait Picasso had painted of her and she complained did not resemble her. ('It will,' said Picasso – and it did.)

During Pound's debut at the Stein salon he spoke at great length and with his customary enthusiasm. Gertrude Stein was not in the habit of being out-talked. In Pound's enthusiasm he fell out of Miss Stein's favorite chair, or broke it, according to a revised version of the incident. Gertrude Stein found Ezra Pound impossible to know, so she said, after he fell out of her chair. 'He was a village explainer,' she explained. 'Excellent if you were a village, if you were not, not.' After the first visit there were no others. Gertrude put Pound off by saying she and Alice were picking wildflowers that day, or that Alice had a toothache.

After the Ezra Pound fiasco, Sylvia Beach – the quiet diplomat of The Quarter and self-effacing go-between – was wary of introducing Gertrude Stein to a writer as reputable as James Joyce. Joyce and Stein were the two commanding presences of Montparnasse who neither met nor acknowledged one another's existence. Like Sylvia Beach, Ernest Hemingway came to know both: he discovered that one did not mention the name of one great 'general' to the other. At Gertrude Stein's salon, 'If you brought up Joyce twice, you would not be invited back.'

Yet the lines of communication were open: new cliques came into being as the older circles enlarged or faded from the scene. The Parisian network was extensive: vital connections were made by those asking what next? at the same moment.

CHAPTER SIX

Newcomers

'This Paris has shaken me from head to foot,' Joan Miró wrote home, and added, '– in the good sense.' Shaken he was, startled by the new and bombarded by sensation, but unable at first to translate the experience into paint upon canvas. The shy and introverted Catalan walked the streets of the great city in silence, and stared.

Both Miró and Picasso were from Barcelona, but Catalans of opposite character and talent. While Picasso may have turned his back on old friends of the Cubist years, he was expansively welcoming to the newcomer Joan Miró. Picasso took on the role of older brother and mentor to his fellow Spaniard: he settled Miró into a hotel room on rue Notre-Dame-des-Victoires where many of their compatriots lived – Picasso remembered his own painful transition to the bustling capital of the arts, and the need for Spanish companionship. To help launch Miró into the Parisian art world, Picasso introduced him to his dealer, Paul Rosenberg. He also bought two paintings from Miró, an even more effective way of expressing genuine interest in the younger man's talent.

For the first months Miró roamed the foreign city as a displaced person, overwhelmed by a turbulence of images and impressions. Back in the stark hotel room behind the Bourse, he was unable to lift a brush or make a sketch. 'I am pierced to the marrow of my bones by all the sweetness here,' he wrote, but he was obliged to return briefly to Spain, to get his bearings and set his course afresh.

In Barcelona Miró divested himself of all the work he had accomplished until then, a backlog of paintings he turned over to a dealer for a lump sum with the promise of an eventual show in Paris. At least he earned enough to live on for a year. He could never be the painter he needed to be without the stimulus of that hustling gray city in the north. When he returned in 1921 for a second assault on the capital he found a studio of his own, lent to him by the Spanish sculptor Gargallo.

The new address, 45 rue Blomet, was significant. Miró's neighbor in the same building was André Masson, living in the typically squalid style of the Montparnos, practicing a 'systematic derangement of all senses' partly accomplished by the drinking of absinthe. Miró's sense of order was exactly the reverse of Masson's chaotic bohemianism. When the two painters became friends, Masson was amazed at the whitewashed walls of Miró's studio, the neat and fussy arrangement of paint tubes and canvases, a fastidiousness that was fundamental to Miró's character.

Miró had already met Picabia in Barcelona and had been impressed by his energy, black humor, and 'wipe the slate clean' defiance. Picabia brought his companion Tzara to 45 rue Blomet, where, in the mixed company of Michel Leiris, Robert Desnos, Jacques Prévert, and Antonin Artaud, was born the Rue Blomet Group. They met in Masson's grubby studio, or in warm weather sat in the grassy courtyard under a lilac tree.

Miró, so poor he could afford but one lunch a week, fed himself on the animated discussions of the Dadaists. Too timid to express ideas of his own, Miró's head swirled with the passionate declarations-of-independence by this wild group of painters and poets. Philippe Soupault would insist: 'Cleanliness is the luxury of the poor – be dirty!' while Tzara intoned the obituary of the Cubists: 'Cubism, my friends, is a cathedral of *merde*.'

From 29 April to 14 May 1921, Miró showed his latest work at the Gallery Licorne on the rue La Boétie. Not one painting sold. Yet the critic Maurice Raynal spoke of Miró's 'temerity' in his catalogue notes – temerity, for the shy Catalan who had arrived in Paris with the mud of Montroig on his boots. Still a peasant at heart, Miró completed in 1922 the last of a cycle of Montroig-Barcelona scenes, *The Farm*. From that point he embarked on the revolutionary experiments meant 'to express the golden sparks given off by the soul'. The Rue Blomet Group merged with the Surrealists led by André Breton. With peasant caution, Miró joined the ranks of those who sought 'a kind of absolute reality, a super-reality'.

Cubism had dominated the galleries and studios until then with the cool and dispassionate studies of guitars, pipe shanks, and carafes. 'Je briserai leur guitar' ('I will smash their guitar'), Miró was to utter with his first surge of confidence and beginning command of French. The introverted youth from Catalonia had thrown in with the metropolitan set. 'Never again Barcelona, that's flat. Paris – to the day I die!'

*

The Hemingways arrived in Paris on the boat train from Le Havre in a jostling compartment full of boy soldiers. They checked into the inexpensive Hôtel Jacob and discovered a restaurant, the Pré aux Clercs – dinner for two from twelve to fourteen francs, Pinard wine at sixty centimes – at the corner of rue Jacob and rue Bonaparte. Rue Bonaparte reminded Hemingway of François Villon's Paris, when wolves would slink into the city under the public gallows at Montfaucon. In letters home he wrote of the priceless time they were having 'walking the streets day and night, arm through arm, peering into courts and stopping in front of little shop windows'. Their hotel room resembled a grog shop, he boasted to cronies in Prohibition Chicago. Rhum St James was fourteen francs a bottle. 'It is the genuwind 7 year old rum as smooth as a kitten's chin.' The franc, in 1921, was 'fourteen to a paper one'.

Hemingway had an instinct for finding cheap lodgings in unlikely neighborhoods. Their first home was a small flat in a marginal quarter off the rue Mouffetard. The place de la Contrescarpe attracted a floating colony of hard-drinking *clochards* who bought liters of raw wine or, for a few centimes more, drank rum at the Café des Amateurs on the square. The Hemingways lived around the corner at 74 rue Cardinal Lemoine (across the street from one of James Joyce's borrowed residences, at 71). Their acceptance of Paris on the sordid level, as well as the sublime, made it possible for the newlyweds to adjust to the rude surroundings and settle into the neighborhood as would any French couple in the same circumstances.

When Janet Flanner visited the Hemingway flat she climbed the fetid spiral staircase with water spigot and crude *pissoir* on every landing. The few rooms of the apartment were of indeterminate shape, all angles and unexpected corners, the furnishings heavy and ugly. The bathroom was no more than a recessed closet with water pitcher and bowl, no plumbing, only a slop jar. The slop jars were emptied out at the landings, garbage carried four flights down to the courtyard.

'You can live on less and less,' was Hemingway's motto at the time. Ernest and Hadley offered Miss Flanner an egg for lunch the day she visited. There were boiled potatoes and *vin ordinaire* – the Bois-

Charbon-Vin shop was just across the street. From the Mouffetard open market Hadley bought the cheapest legumes; a favorite was *poireaux* (leeks) which she prepared French fashion: boiled, then served cold with oil and vinegar. A goat-herd brought his *troupeau* along the place Contrescarpe in the early morning, playing a shrill tune on his pipes to alert customers. At night the *vidangeurs* passed with their horse-drawn pump, to drain the foul septic tanks in the quarter.

In order to write undisturbed, the young author rented a room at 39 rue Descartes where Verlaine was said to have died, thus paying indirect homage to the French literary past. True homage was paid to Flaubert, whose dedication to *le mot juste* was a driving inspiration to the beginning writer struggling to find exact words of his own.

With the chill rain of late autumn the walls stained with damp. Hemingway would look out across a gray panorama of rooftops from his attic window, the same view Verlaine had brooded over: an incredible complication of chimneypots, *bombé* sheet-metal roofing, church towers and twisted drainpipes from the Sorbonne to the vast esplanade of les Invalides. If the smoke from neighboring chimneys blew in an unobstructed line, he knew his own chimney would draw: it might be worth the investment of a bundle of firewood and a packet of twigs from the Bois-Charbon-Vin merchant.

By midwinter Hemingway was forced to seek the warmth of 'a good café on the place St Michel' to set down in blue French lycée notebooks the beginnings of those first stories of a remembered Michigan. When the sky lowered in winter and the city was a study in slate, the principal escape from gelid hotel rooms and unheated ateliers were the terraces of the big cafés, glass enclosed, warmed by charcoal braziers. 'The hot rum punch and checker season has come in,' Hemingway wrote home. 'It looks like a good winter. Cafés much fuller in the day time now with people that have no heat in hotel rooms.' That first winter was so cold 'all the fountains froze'. To warm the heart there was a selection of drinks including calvados, kirsch, and rhum St James. A single glass of wine or a *café filtre* entitled a client to sit for as long as he cared to contemplate the rows of exotic bottles: Amer-picon, Noilly Prat, Dubonnet, Byrrh – and, to a writer, the just as exotic customers – inside a lighted bistro whose walls and tables and zinc *comptoir* fused into a collage by Braque. The tales Hemingway wrote by hand in the blue lycée notebooks he later typed on a Corona portable typewriter Hadley had given him for his birthday.

For Sylvia Beach
Ernest Hemingway
M R Paris Aug. 1923

Hemingway photographed by Man Ray. The inscription is to
Sylvia Beach, August 1923.

Overleaf A Montparnasse café in the late 1920s.

At first he hesitated to use Sherwood Anderson's generous letters of introduction to Ezra Pound, Gertrude Stein and Sylvia Beach. Miss Beach received her letter much later, after Hemingway had discovered Shakespeare and Company on his own, and introduced himself. The bookshop was warm and well-stocked with books Hemingway was too poor to buy but happy to learn he could borrow. He called Sylvia Beach 'Madame Shakespeare', and wrote to her at 12 rue de l'Odéon in that name. Sherwood Anderson's photograph was among those in Miss Beach's private gallery of literary friends, but Hemingway did not inform Sylvia Beach of his friendship with Anderson nor produce the letter Anderson had written until, shyly, he presented his introduction to her long after he had become Shakespeare and Company's 'best customer'.

He then began to call on Gertrude Stein, and wrote to Anderson: 'Gertrude Stein and me are just like brothers.' He was both impressed and amused by his discovery of Ezra Pound, who at that time was learning to play the bassoon and made his own crude but serviceable furniture out of cratewood. 'Pound took six of my poems ... he thinks I'm a swell poet.' He boxed and played tennis with Pound, and sat at the feet of Miss Stein – then absorbed in the way of a perfect student the lessons he could best apply to his own lonely pursuit. As a student he accepted advice and criticism from both these original sources – at least during the initial literary kinships 'when the flowers of friendship bloomed', uncomplicated by the blood feuds of the late Twenties – but wisely the young writer kept his two instructors in the arts well apart, in neutral corners.

To relieve the hard discipline of sustained literary endeavor, the young Hemingway boxed or attended the spectator sports at Auteuil and the Vélodrome de Paris. Another escape from creative pressures was walking, in the city made for walking. Hemingway discovered parts of Paris that the devotees of the Dôme, the Coupole and the Rotonde would never quit their wicker chairs to visit: the outdoor boxing rings of Ménilmontant and the riverside restaurant Chez Robinson with tables set in perches in the trees along the upper reaches of the Seine. During his probing expeditions through the city, the writer collected those moments, public and private, he could draw from: an inventory of telling detail to give dimension to his fiction. He made casual friends of seven-day bicycle racers and grizzled fishermen on the quays of the Ile de la Cité dependent on the tiny *goujons* they caught to supplement pensions reduced drastically by the falling franc. He was a sparring partner to professional boxers, friend to café waiters, confidant of prostitutes. Along the open boulevards and down strange culs-de-sac the young heavyweight prowled the city he loved best, his personal domain.

Madame Shakespeare
℅ W. Shakespeare et Co
12 rue de l'Odéon

Envelope addressed by Hemingway to Sylvia Beach.

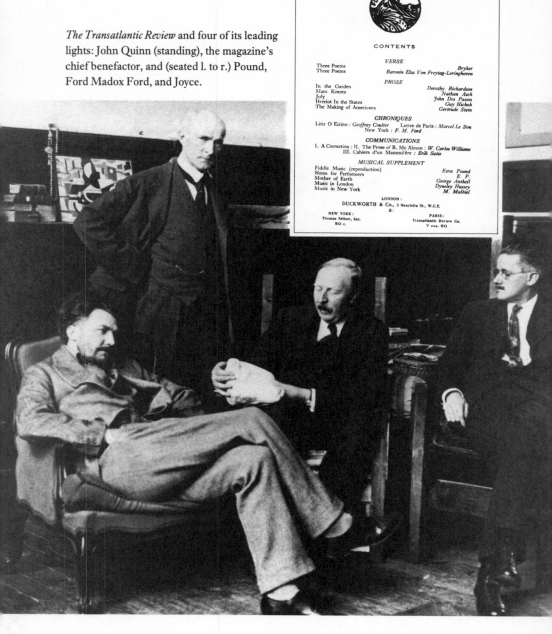

The Transatlantic Review and four of its leading lights: John Quinn (standing), the magazine's chief benefactor, and (seated l. to r.) Pound, Ford Madox Ford, and Joyce.

the

transatlantic

Edited in Paris
by F. M. FORD

review

VOL. II. No. 2
August 1924

CONTENTS

VERSE

Three Poems   *Bryher*
Three Poems   *Baronin Elsa Von Freytag-Loringhoven*

PROSE

In the Garden   *Dorothy Richardson*
Marc Krantz   *Nathan Asch*
July   *John Dos Passos*
Herriot In the States   *Guy Hickok*
The Making of Americans   *Gertrude Stein*

CHRONIQUES

Litir O Eirinn : *Geoffrey Coulter*   Lettre de Paris : *Marcel Le Son*
New York : *F. M. Ford*

COMMUNICATIONS

I. A Correction : II. The Prose of R. Mc Almon : *W. Carlos Williams*
III. Cahiers d'un Mammifère : *Erik Satie*

MUSICAL SUPPLEMENT

Fiddle Music (reproduction)   *Ezra Pound*
Notes for Performers   *E. P.*
Mother of Earth   *George Antheil*
Music in London   *Dyneley Hussey*
Music in New York   *M. Maltiel*

LONDON :
DUCKWORTH & Co., 3 Henrietta St., W.C.2.
2/

NEW YORK :   PARIS :
Thomas Seltzer, Inc.   Transatlantic Review Co.
50 c.   7 res. 50

CHAPTER SEVEN
Big Money and Little Magazines

I f Hemingway truly intended to be a writer, Gertrude Stein told him, he would have to give up journalism. 'If you keep on doing newspaper work you will never see things, you will only see words and that will not do...'

Although Hemingway was at first dependent on overseas assignments from the *Toronto Star* for a bare livelihood, he saw the truth in Miss Stein's warning. Journalism had contributed considerably to the stripped-down Hemingway style – bits of newspaper dispatches, experiences and observations he had picked up as a correspondent would emerge as the hard-edged concentrated literary vignettes of his first effort, *In Our Time* – but his newspaper prose would have had a trivializing and finally destructive effect on his fiction. Hemingway trusted Gertrude Stein's judgment in literary matters; he submitted his manuscripts to both Gertrude Stein and Ezra Pound, separately. 'Ezra was right half the time and when he was wrong he was so wrong you were never in doubt about it. Gertrude was always right.'

But Pound, the tireless broker of the arts, could be relied upon for practical help as well as counsel. When Ford Madox Ford came over from London to edit the newest of the so-called 'little' magazines, *The Transatlantic Review*, Ezra Pound convinced Ford to take on the experienced Ernest Hemingway as editorial assistant. The two men were mismatched in most every way, yet managed to collaborate in some makeshift fashion to produce the most important literary publication of the day.

The older Ford enjoyed the company of young aspiring writers, but he expected them to be respectful, if not awed, by his rank and accomplishments. As Ford Madox Heuffer (he changed the Germanic name Heuffer to Ford during World War I) he was an established novelist, and had shared a by-line with Joseph Conrad for one book.

Ford was mistaken in thinking his ambitious and increasingly self-assured young assistant would join a retinue of admirers who attended his teas and *bal musette* parties. Hemingway was glad of the job, but his relationship to the walrus-mustached editor was strained from the beginning.

Ford administered the magazine from a mezzanine cage-like office at the vaulted top of an ancient wine cellar on the quai d'Anjou. The sole occupant of the cage could sit, but was unable to stand erect. Since there was barely enough space for Ford's own bulky form, the cramped arrangement kept the two editors out of sparring distance. Hemingway, restless and full of youthful energy, read and edited manuscripts outside on the lower ramp of the quay where the gray waters of the Seine washed against the stone. He was happy not to have to share a birdcage with the asthmatic Ford, whose breath, Hemingway reported, stank of the grave. In wet weather Hemingway retired to Madame LeCompte's Rendezvous des Mariniers beside the pont Marie, where Dos Passos had written *Three Soldiers* after the war.

The wine cellar on the quai d'Anjou also sheltered Robert McAlmon's Contact Editions and Bill Bird's Three Mountains Press (the Three Mountains' logo, one wag remarked, showing Mons Veneris foremost). The centerpiece of the cellar was the seventeenth-century hand-press Bird had purchased from a French printer. Everyone took a hand at pulling the immense spoked-wheel handle of the press: at night Hemingway sometimes strolled down to the quai d'Anjou alone to set his latest work in type, then took proofs of the pages on Bill Bird's antique press to see how the story looked in print.

To Gertrude Stein's everlasting delight, Hemingway saw *The Transatlantic Review* as a showcase for her *The Making of Americans*; subsequently he talked Ford into publishing the unpublishable opus as a serial, beginning in the April 1924 issue. As a further favor, Hemingway volunteered to correct the thousand pages of copy – an incredible task the author herself was happy to avoid. Even as the friendship between Gertrude Stein and Ernest Hemingway began to deteriorate, Miss Stein remained grateful that Hemingway, after all, arranged to have *The Making of Americans* published in *Transatlantic*.

The Transatlantic Review was originally funded by John Quinn, the patrician lawyer from Chicago who sporadically supported Ezra Pound, James Joyce, and a number of painters of l'Ecole de Paris. (Georges Rouault had received sustenance from Quinn for years, and when finally the two men met, Rouault lowered his head and wept on his patron's sleeve.) In the early Twenties, John Quinn was the only discerning and eager client the Rosenberg brothers could find for works of modern art. However, Quinn was far less effective as a lawyer for the avant-garde causes he so readily supported as patron: he was defense counsel in the 1921 *Ulysses* trial, the United States *v The Little Review*, when the serialized portions of James Joyce's novel were considered obscene. Quinn lost the case, which effectively spelled the end for *The Little Review* as well as for publication of *Ulysses* in English. Joyce was downcast over the verdict, but that was when Sylvia Beach came to his rescue, asking if she 'might have the honor' of publishing *Ulysses* under the auspices of Shakespeare and Company.

Ford Madox Ford considered John Quinn the only American gentleman – perhaps because Quinn was gentleman enough to support *The Transatlantic Review*. As Quinn's health declined, so did the magazine. Nevertheless, the shaky enterprise held together even after John Quinn died of cancer in July 1924. During the preparation for the July and August issues, Ford was out of Paris, ostensibly to solicit funds to keep *Transatlantic* afloat. In his absence Ernest Hemingway had full editorial control. When Ford returned he accused his assistant of stocking the latest issue with work by American cronies. Hemingway had done exactly that, but he resented Ford's editorial in the following issue: in effect, an apology for the contents of the Hemingway issue.

One of Hemingway's racetrack friends was a young American poet named Evan Shipman. 'Shipman,' said Gertrude Stein, 'was an amusing boy who was to inherit a few thousand dollars when he came of age.' Hemingway believed he would save *The Transatlantic Review* with his inheritance when he came of age – but he was not of age. He would also finance a review for the Surrealists when he came of age, Masson believed. When Shipman did come of age, Gertrude Stein sardonically remarked: 'Nobody who had known him then seemed to know what he did do with his inheritance.'

Meanwhile Hemingway had lined up a new patron, appropriately named Friend. Krebs Friend had worked with Hemingway on *The Cooperative Commonwealth* in the Chicago days: he had been badly shellshocked during the war and was now married to an heiress, forty years his senior, who thought it would be therapeutic for Friend to publish a literary magazine and contribute his own poetry to its pages. Even as *The Transatlantic Review* faltered for lack of money, Ford – to

Hemingway's disgust – high-handedly demanded financial guarantees from the new patron. Ford had the feeling of being mistreated by one and all – 'a green baize door that everyone kicks on the way in and out' – and needed to maintain a show of authority and strength. The failing magazine could not survive the continued clash of temperaments and editorial in-fighting. *The Transatlantic Review* had published enduring work by such important contributors as H. D. (Hilda Doolittle), John Dos Passos, William Carlos Williams, Djuna Barnes, Gertrude Stein and James Joyce. By January of 1925 the magazine quietly expired just as the first half of the Twenties came to an end.

*

When one literary journal folded, another sprang up in its place: *Gargoyle, Broom, The Boulevardier, Tambour, transition* – or, as William Carlos Williams explained, they were all one continuous little magazine under different names. Few survived more than a year, several folded after a single issue. *This Quarter* followed *The Transatlantic Review* as the most influential publication of the expatriate colony. The editor was Ernest Walsh, and the magazine was backed by his much older paramour, Ethel Moorhead. A poet-editor's liaison with a woman of wealth, usually older than himself, had become almost *de rigueur* for founding a literary journal.

Miss Moorhead had met the dashing but destitute Walsh at the Hôtel Claridge: Walsh was in the bar, hopelessly in arrears with his hotel bill, but he could not leave the Claridge because the management had confiscated his luggage. In the course of their conversation (Miss Moorhead paid for the drinks) she remarked on his flushed and underfed appearance and Walsh merrily informed her he was consumptive. (Hemingway called him The Man Who Was Marked for Death.) 'I'm fine,' said Walsh, 'I've got another five years to live.'

There were those of the Montparnasse crowd who believed Ernest Walsh conned his way in Paris through Irish charm and the sympathy he aroused by his doomed look. The tubercular condition was genuine enough; Hemingway had witnessed one of Walsh's hemorrhages and reported, 'It was very legitimate, and I knew that he would die all right.'

Miss Moorhead drew from her inheritance in Scotland to finance *This Quarter*. Whenever a new publication was launched Ernest Hemingway was certain to be part of the apparatus: he volunteered advice and assistance, suggested the magazine publish Gertrude Stein, and offered a long ambitious story of his own, 'The Big Two-Hearted

Robert McAlmon (left, photographed by
Berenice Abbott) ran Contact Editions;
Ernest Walsh (below) was the editor of
This Quarter.

River'. Also, Hemingway arranged for Walsh to approach James Joyce for excerpts from his work in progress; and finally, he managed to repay in part a debt to his mentor Ezra Pound with a contribution to the first issue entitled 'Homage to Ezra'.

The fate of *This Quarter* depended upon the mercurial relationship between its co-editors, Ethel Moorhead and Ernest Walsh. To keep Walsh on the shortest possible leash, Miss Moorhead was given to threats of removing Walsh's name from the masthead. On one such occasion Walsh raged through their hotel room and in his fury flung a vase of water at his patron-mistress. The tempestuous and unstable situation was further complicated when a slim young beauty 'with a profile like a knife' joined the staff as editorial assistant.

Kay Boyle had been drifting in a vacuum between an unsuccessful marriage to a Frenchman in the provinces and her ambition to become part of the Paris literary scene. When her husband became unemployed, Kay Boyle decided she might escape domestic misery by applying for a job at Shakespeare and Company: she came to the door of the famous bookshop on the rue de l'Odéon, but hesitated at the threshold, too shy to approach Miss Beach in person. For the rest of the day she drifted about Paris in limbo, browsing through the quayside bookstalls, reading in the lonely company of swans beside the lake in the bois de Boulogne. On another aimless excursion through Paris she was passing the Café de la Paix where she recognized a friend sitting with a group on the *terrasse*. She joined the group and met Ernest Walsh: Kay Boyle also had been consumptive, they had a subject of mutual interest. Eventually Walsh sent her to his own lung specialist in Paris, then asked her to assist in the production of his new magazine, *This Quarter*.

The inevitable triangle of complications arose when Walsh became enamored of his young assistant while remaining completely dependent on Miss Moorhead for sustenance. The ménage-à-trois became all the more involuted when Ethel Moorhead developed a lesbian attraction to the young rival for Walsh's affection. The tension between Miss Moorhead and Kay Boyle took its own peculiar form: the older woman would sometimes observe the younger at her toilet or lying naked in the bath. 'I can't understand,' she once remarked, 'you're really not beautiful.'

Walsh's tubercular condition grew worse. The household of three was obliged to move from hotel to hotel when the consumptive's fits of coughing alarmed the management. They edited *This Quarter* on the run. Finally the journal was published long-distance from the South of France. The complex threesome settled near Monte Carlo, Kay Boyle pregnant by this time with Ernest Walsh's child.

Back in Paris, Ernest Hemingway saw the proofs of *This Quarter* through the printers, who did not read English. He wrote to Robert McAlmon: 'Walsh now that he is dying is getting to be a pretty nice guy. I wonder if it would have the same effect on the rest of us. Somehow I think not. I can picture Ezra [Pound] for instance.'

Ernest Walsh suffered a final massive hemorrhage and died in a hospital in Monte Carlo. Ethel Moorhead stayed on with the pregnant Kay Boyle – but she allowed *This Quarter* to expire with Ernest Walsh.

*

While covering the 1922 Lausanne Conference for the *Toronto Star*, Ernest Hemingway met the correspondent Lincoln Steffens. Steffens was greatly impressed with Hemingway's short-story 'My Old Man' and asked if he might personally send it off to his friend Ray Long, at *Cosmopolitan* in New York. It was the season of autumn rains in Paris, so Ernest contrived for Hadley to meet him in Lausanne for a quasi-vacation for them both. When Hadley arrived she was so tearful and distraught her husband was unable to piece together what had happened. Hadley had thought Ernest might want to work at his own writing during the Swiss sojourn, and as a surprise had brought along his manuscripts. A valise containing the sum of Hemingway's first year's work in Paris had been stolen at the gare de Lyon.

Hemingway hurried back to Paris to confirm the full extent of the disaster: worse, every carbon copy had accompanied its original in the missing suitcase. Only two stories survived: 'Up in Michigan', which had been tucked away in a drawer after Gertrude Stein had declared it too sexually explicit, or *inaccrochable*, and 'My Old Man', which had been returned with a rejection from *Cosmopolitan*.

At 27 rue de Fleurus the crushed young writer received considerable sympathy, and an excellent lunch, from Alice Toklas and Gertrude Stein. Miss Stein thought some good must come of the tragedy since Hemingway would be obliged to reconsider his youthful oeuvre from point zero. But Hemingway himself was badly shaken. Miss Stein's words were small consolation to a man who had just learned that a hard year's work had disappeared. No loss in his young life had been as traumatic since the time Agnes von Kurowsky wrote announcing her engagement to another man.

Soon after Ernest rejoined Hadley in Switzerland, they were invited to Rapallo by Ezra Pound, who was spending more and more time in the sun-bathed village on the Italian Riviera as his own sanctuary from the cold rains of a Paris winter. In Rapallo, Hemingway met Robert McAlmon, a young poet Pound had discovered and wanted to encourage – not so much to write poetry as to set up as a publisher. McAlmon was that *rara avis*, a poet with money. He had entered into a marriage of convenience with Winifred Ellerman, known by the pseudonym Bryher, a pen name she signed to her own poetry. She was the daughter of Sir John Ellerman of the British shipping line fortune: the marriage arrangement allowed Bryher to live independently from the Ellermans as 'Mrs McAlmon', and McAlmon to pursue his true infatuation, the Dôme-Rotonde-Coupole café life in Paris. 'I knew all too well,' wrote McAlmon, 'that Paris is a bitch and that one should not become infatuated with bitches, particularly when they have wit, imagination, experience and tradition behind their ruthlessness.' Ellerman money permitted McAlmon to continue his affair with the ruthless, imaginative bitch, Paris. Hemingway referred to him as 'McAlimony'.

Both McAlmon and Hemingway were known for their charm, which either one could turn on or off, according to his mood. The source of McAlmon's winning manner was difficult to trace – except for his convenient habit of picking up the check – since he had none of the physical attributes of the tall, good-looking, athletic Hemingway. The two expatriate Midwesterners got along well enough in one another's company, but each sniped at the other behind his back.

Everyone knew and took advantage of McAlmon's lavish allowance from Sir John: Ezra Pound thought the largesse could be put to better use than the paying of bar bills all over Montparnasse. Back in Paris he urged McAlmon to begin a series of publications called Contact Editions, to be printed on Bill Bird's ancient press on the quai d'Anjou, with Shakespeare and Company as mailing address. Despite the often punctured friendship between Hemingway and McAlmon, Contact Editions was to publish Hemingway's *Three Stories and Ten Poems* as one of its initial offerings. When the slim booklet came out in a limited edition of three hundred copies it generated little interest outside the English-speaking colony in Paris, a group of expatriate literati already familiar with Hemingway's work. One review copy did fall into the hands of Edmund Wilson for the first favorable comment on Hemingway's writing by an important critic. Otherwise, in the New York publishing world, *Three Stories and Ten Poems* went unnoticed and unreviewed except for a brief mention by Burton Rascoe in the *New York Tribune*. Ernest Hemingway had made his debut as an original talent of large expectations – but the applause was from a distant shore, and muted.

*

When Hadley became pregnant, Ernest Hemingway went immediately to Gertrude Stein to announce in the tone of defeat and self-pity he sometimes affected: 'I'm too young to be a father.' In the childless world of the Stein-Toklas household he had a sympathetic audience: Gertrude Stein had never been interested in wives or mothers or the customary domestic arrangements. The reluctant father-to-be was offered a glass of eau-de-vie.

The Hemingways returned to the US for the birth of the baby, a· boy they nicknamed Bumby. Ernest was now obliged to consider his enlarged responsibilities as a family man, so he accepted a salaried job with the *Toronto Star*. Being a paid hireling on the newspaper for which he had worked as a freelance reporter in Europe was a depressing comedown, Toronto an impossible city after Paris. He soon clashed with his iron-willed editor, thus ending the brief period of middle-class respectability in Canada. The Hemingways, with Bumby in tow, returned to Paris, this time to a flat at 113 Notre-Dame-des-Champs, close to the separate establishments of Hemingway's two tutelary saints, Ezra Pound and Gertrude Stein. Miss Stein and Alice Toklas became the unlikely godparents to Bumby, Alice to provide suitable garments in wool and needlework for their infant godson. Ezra Pound continued to instruct the new father in literary craftsmanship, while in turn receiving lessons in the art of boxing.

The whine from the buzzsaw in the courtyard sawmill drove the young writer once again to the isolation and quiet of a good café in which to work. His new sanctuary was the nearest bistro in the quarter, the Closerie de Lilas, where poets and artists had met since the time of Baudelaire. From the café table where he worked he could look out upon the equestrian statue of one of his favorite military figures, Marshal Ney. (Hemingway was unusually superstitious and thought the coincidence of having the gallant marshal nearby brought him luck.) Beyond this piece of statuary was the extravagant fountain at the place de l'Observatoire: mythical ladies in bronze bearing the universe on their bare shoulders, turtles rising from the basin squirting water at the heads of raging horses (the bronze toes of the ladies delicately out of range of the squirting turtles) – the conglomerate display bathed in a green Parisian patina. Fortunately this sculptural extravaganza had far less effect on the sober Hemingway style than the lonely nobility of Marshal Ney.

From the fountain at l'Observatoire the young author took a single-minded promenade through the double line of chestnut trees leading directly to the far end of the Luxembourg Gardens. Feeling 'belly-empty hollow-hungry' after a morning's work, he carefully avoided the enticing restaurant smells from nearby boulevard St-Michel: his goal, the Palais du Luxembourg where Impressionist and Post-impressionist paintings were housed for a cooling-off period, awaiting posterity's final word and official recognition by the Louvre. It was at the Palais du Luxembourg that Hemingway made his curious attempt to understand how painters like Cézanne created landscape, so that he might learn to do the same with words. On the return trip home the hungry young author occasionally lingered in the park near the Medici Fountain just before the guard closed the gates for the night, to kill a stray pigeon with a homemade slingshot. He would carry the dead bird home for supper, tucked inside his jacket.

In other matters of economy, Gertrude Stein offered her advice. She taught Ernest to cut his wife's hair. Miss Stein's idea of saving was that Hadley buy clothes for comfort and durability – like the heavy shapeless garments she herself wore – so that the money could be invested, as hers was, in paintings.

After Bumby was born, the Hemingways could be seen trudging through the Luxembourg Gardens, Ernest in baggy suit with elbow patches carrying Bumby on his hip, Hadley in makeshift dress following silently like an Indian squaw.

During this period of marginal living at freelance writing – a rare check from the German magazine *Der Querschnitt*, an occasional win at the Auteuil racetrack – Hemingway met Harold Loeb. Loeb had published a novel, *Doodab*, in New York and had been a boxer in college – two dangerously competitive accomplishments to bring to a friendship with Ernest Hemingway. Furthermore, Loeb represented the ease and affluence of the Loeb-Guggenheim families at a time when the Hemingways were struggling to survive on 'next to nothing a year'. (Loeb's cousin was Peggy Guggenheim, not yet an art collector but

Hemingway's first wife, Hadley, and their son Bumby.

already a collector of artists: she came to Paris as soon as she came into her inheritance, anxious, as she put it, to lose her virginity.) Loeb was an editor of *Broom*, a magazine of the arts which proposed 'to make a clean sweep'. The little magazine was edited in New York and Paris, printed in Berlin for $150 per 3,000 copies at the prevalent mark-dollar exchange rate. *Broom* was one of the few little magazines Hemingway did not help edit, but he did become friendly with its Paris editor, Harold Loeb. In the beginning the two men were the closest of café companions, fellow writers and boxing partners.

Through Loeb's mistress, the dancer Kitty Cannell, the Hemingways came to know Pauline Pfeiffer, a fashion editor on the Paris staff of *Vogue*. Pauline Pfeiffer was to play an important role in the life of the Hemingways, but a role altogether inconsistent with her first impression of the young couple. It was Hadley she liked, was friendly with, and felt sorry for. She thought Ernest was a disagreeable boor. She knew the Hemingways had little money, but her ideas concerning a woman's wardrobe were the reverse of Gertrude Stein's: she considered Ernest a brute not to allow Hadley to dress well. Pauline took it upon herself to give the neglected wife advice on the new fashions that made Paris the style capital of the world.

This Quarter n.º 2

EZRA POUND
JAMES JOYCE
CARL SANDBURG
W. CARLOS WILLIAMS
ROBERT McALMON
ERNEST HEMINGWAY
EMANUEL CARNEVALI
KAY BOYLE
CARLO LINATI
AND MUSICAL SUPPL

BY
ANTHEIL

Edited
in Milano
by
Ernest Walsh. Ethel Moorhead

CHAPTER EIGHT
The Twenties Look

Before the war Gabrielle (Coco) Chanel was shared by two wealthy lovers in a ménage-à-trois that shifted from Arthur Capel's country estate and hunting lodge to Paris, where Chanel was installed in a ground-floor apartment of her own in Etienne Balsan's *hôtel particulier*. For the Frenchman Balsan, Coco was the charming partner he could display at Maxim's and Delmonico's, a conquest as decorative in public as she was appealing in private. The Englishman 'Boy' Capel saw her as more than a casual cocotte. The slim, dark-haired Auvergnate dressed so simply, yet exquisitely, in a way that belied her humble origins. No one would have believed what Chanel all her life took such pains to obscure: she had grown up in rural poverty; she had made her way to Paris on the music-hall circuit, then into the *beau monde* with the help of lovers like Balsan and Capel.

Chanel had a flair for design and the ambition to go into business, so Capel set her up in a millinery boutique near enough to the Hôtel Ritz to assure a well-to-do clientele. Her hats were successful: Chanel proved to be in her element among the exclusive labels and discriminating buyers of the place Vendôme. Her aspirations extended beyond the millinery trade: Coco Chanel intended to become dressmaker to society. While still designing hats for her boutique, she observed one evening a theater audience of women as elaborately costumed as the Molière characters on stage, and murmured a prophecy and a promise to Capel: 'That can't last. I'm going to dress them simply, and in black.'

*

The Ballets Russes had set the style for the previous age with its exotic display of orientalism beginning with the startling production of *Sheherazade.* The sets and costumes by Leon Bakst were an important

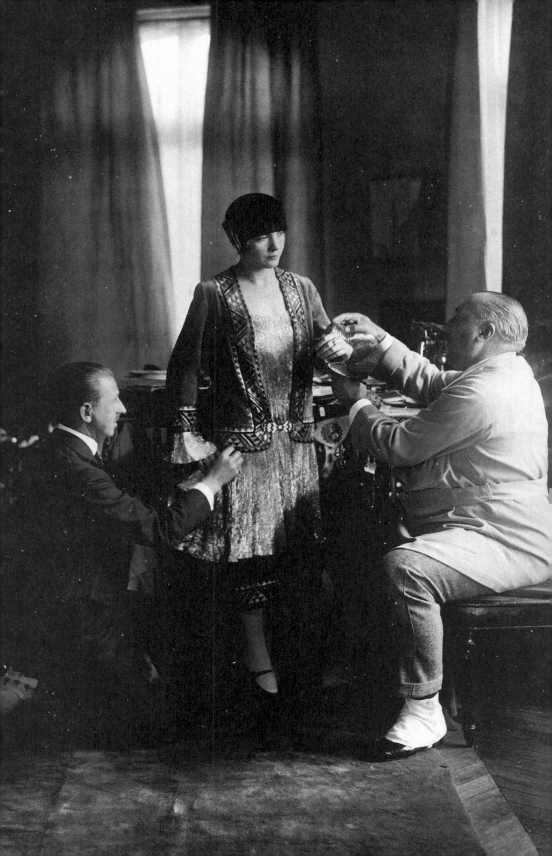

influence on the leading fashion designer of the prewar years, Paul Poiret, when he introduced the striking theatrical colors of Bakst: Persian blues and greens, the hard flat orange known as tango. (These vibrant strokes of color may have led Proust to put into the words of Baron de Charlus: 'Only women who do not know how to dress are afraid of colors.') Poiret introduced the harem-inspired *jupes-culottes*, turbans, aigrettes, ropes of pearl – to be accompanied by sensuous perfumes of his own manufacture with names like Mahardjha, redolent, or at least suggestive, of the East.

But high fashion was completely disrupted by the great European conflict. The textile industry had collapsed in the devastated north; demand for original creations had so diminished in wartime Paris that leading couturiers simply closed their doors and donated their delivery vans to Misia Sert's private ambulance service. Immediately after the Armistice in 1918, the beehive of Parisian designers, cutters, fitters, models and *vendeuses* hummed once again: the woolen mills in the north were rebuilt by state priority; the silk factories near Lyon were back in production – silk competing now with a strange new artificial fabric that would revolutionize the stocking industry, rayon.

Women of society turned first to Poiret, Worth and Molyneux for the lavish wardrobes denied to them during the four years of austerity in dress. The *Gazette du Bon Ton* offered advice to women attending functions at military hospitals: 'We must make ourselves as beautiful as we can for the wounded.' Again, Paul Poiret was the most sought-after couturier: the instant revival of his prewar harem wear coincided with the revival of interest in the Ballets Russes. But as Chanel pointed out, such costume-exotica could not last.

At the beginning of the Twenties American suffragettes had just won their voting rights (Frenchwomen had already gained the vote in 1919), and fashion would reflect the spirit of liberation, rejuvenation, and experiment. Before the war Poiret had succeeded in banishing the antique whalebone corset – but he had then made women into awkward geishas by putting them into long ankle-clinging hobble skirts. Freedom of movement became an essential consideration in designing for the new woman. Shop girls wore silk stockings for the first time, and experimented with Ambre perfume and Fleur de Pêche, skin cream of crushed almonds, and depilatories. Women smoked openly, extending long ivory cigarette holders or dangling a *mégot* between lacquered fingernails.

Paul Poiret (right) fitting a jacket with the help of his tailor Christian, October 1925.

By 1922 there were eighty feminist societies with some 60,000 members throughout France: the best-selling novel of that year was *La Garçonne* whose nineteen-year-old protagonist deliberately plans to have a baby out of wedlock and bring the child up herself, independent of the despicable society of men. The novel stirred protest and scandal, but President Poincaré dared not suppress the book for fear of being made ridiculous – the only official action taken was to expel Victor Margueritte, the author, from the Légion d'Honneur.

The new heroines were social outlaws like Lady Duff Twysden and Nancy Cunard of the lean and hungry look, or Zelda Fitzgerald, the I-don't-care girl of the Jazz Age. These were the models for characters in novels, and models for the way women in the Twenties wanted to look and dress. No one saw more clearly than Coco Chanel that women had emerged from the foyer into the larger world of independence and possibility – she had done so herself.

*

The shifting uncertain world of fashion was a challenge to Chanel's best instincts and ideas. At first Capel may have backed Chanel's millinery enterprise as a way of indulging his attractive and determined mistress with a gift of money he could as well afford to offer as a trinket from Cartier's. It was soon evident that Chanel was not only a gifted originator of design, but a businesswoman of insight and inspiration: if she wanted to establish her own *maison de couture* – *pourquoi pas?* The shrewd peasant side of her character, and her worldly dealings with men, gave Coco Chanel an outsized respect for the power of money. Capel's investment in her was a means of making a beginning; after that, she would create a name and fortune of her own.

Just before the war Coco established the house of Chanel on rue Cambon, where it would remain a landmark throughout the Twenties and beyond. From her headquarters in the vital heart of the *quartier d'élégance* she set out to challenge the reigning prince of fashion, Paul Poiret, in his own domain. In the wake of Cubism, Chanel created cubes and rectangles out of a bare meter of fabric; she did away with the curved trace of bosom and buttocks, lifted hemlines, eliminated showy detail. The Chanel line was austere but graceful, and if not as lushly feminine as the Poiret costume, her clothes appealed to the modern, independent, and – like herself – career-minded woman. In the severity of her design, Chanel pursued what she called *le luxe dans la simplicité*.

Poiret sighed, and saw the world of Chanel as linear and flat, her direction a deluxe impoverishment: 'Until now, women were beautiful and architectural, like the prow of a ship. Now they all resemble undernourished telephone operators.' Slowly, but with devastating effectiveness, Chanel began to encroach upon Poiret terrain by designing for defectors from his exclusive clientele, le Tout-Paris.

But just as Coco Chanel's business venture began to show enormous promise, her personal life collapsed. Hard-edged as she was in the daggers-drawn fashion world, her shrewd gift of assessment failed her in affairs of the heart. Against every indication, she made up her mind that Boy Capel intended to marry her. Instead, the British aristocrat became engaged to Diana Lister, a socially acceptable Englishwoman of his own rank and background. In the thoughtless manner of the rich, Boy suggested to Coco that he might introduce her to his fiancée – so that his mistress might bestow her blessing on the match.

No sooner had Chanel recovered from the shock of Boy's engagement than she was plunged into grief over news of his death. In December 1919 Boy Capel was killed in a driving accident near St Raphael. Chanel had become half-reconciled to Boy's marriage, but his death – the loss of the only man she had ever loved – was a blow from which she could not recover. Coco Chanel lapsed into lethargy and black depression: even her bedroom was draped in black, the color she had made fashionable. Boy Capel had left her a legacy of £40,000. She would never be without money again; she was wealthy, and alone.

An intimate friend, Misia Sert, one of the most influential figures of the prewar social and cultural scene, offered the exuberance and solace of her high-spirited company. Misia lured Coco out of her shadowy cloistered life into the light. Her husband, the painter José-Maria Sert, took charge of redecorating Chanel's town house at 29 rue du faubourg St-Honoré: he changed the color scheme of the somber bedroom to pink. Misia's example as patron of the arts and social hostess to le Tout-Paris inspired Chanel to open her own salon to that variegated parade of artists, poets, princes, and the publicity-minded.

Jean Cocteau became a regular at 29 rue du faubourg St-Honoré: a talented poet-painter-cinéaste and gregarious wit, who could be wickedly diverting after a stressful day of fittings and fits of temper in the rue Cambon. Twice Chanel saw Cocteau – financially and supportively – through disintoxication cures for his addiction to opium. She also saw him through the great loss of his life (just as Misia had done for her) when his young protégé Raymond Radiguet, author of *Devil in the Flesh*, died at the age of twenty in 1923. By this time Chanel had become involved with the poet Pierre Reverdy who had been co-founder with Apollinaire of the arts journal *Nord-Sud* and was one of the emerging Surrealists. As both lover and patron to Reverdy, Chanel sponsored the publication of a volume of his poetry, with watercolor illustrations by Pablo Picasso.

This was Picasso's period of following the lead of Jean Cocteau as social butterfly – Picasso's 'unreliable period', in the words of Gertrude Stein. Chanel's salon was a favorite visiting place for the painter who was being courted by wealthy collectors and entertained by the lion-hunters of the nouveau riche. 'Picasso is still doing beautiful work,' Juan Gris wrote to Kahnweiler, 'when he has time.'

Another member of the Chanel circle was Picasso's friend Max Jacob, who had once been appointed Superstitions Consultant to Paul Poiret (to advise on which colors brought *bonheur* or *malheur* to the wearer). A religious mystic since his conversion to Christianity, Max Jacob suggested to Chanel that she should trim her hair in the manner of Jesus Christ, then launch the new coiffure in her own persuasive way.

Chanel did in fact wear her hair clipped short in advance of the rage for bobbed hair and the even more boyish shingle-cut. To accommodate the new fashions in millinery – the bell-shaped cloche hat that fit the head like a helmet, cloth or jeweled bandeaux across the forehead, turbans and matador caps – shorter hair styles for women were inevitable. Cropped hair had already enjoyed a brief success in France just before the war when Antoine the hairdresser convinced Eve Lavallière to appear on stage with her hair cut daringly short. Even the dancer Caryathis preceded Chanel in shedding the crowning glory of the previous age when she clipped her long tresses and left them, as a reproach, on the pillow of an indifferent lover. The ultimate in shorn hair was Genica Athanasiou's appearance as Antigone in the 1922 Jean Cocteau production: Cocteau had persuaded her to shave her head bald and pluck her eyebrows to conform to his conception of the Greek heroine.

Antigone was a landmark theatrical event in other ways: the music was composed by Arthur Honneger, the sets designed by Picasso, and the costumes were by Chanel. 'I asked Mlle Chanel for the costumes,' Cocteau announced, 'because she is the greatest designer of our day and I cannot imagine the daughter of Oedipus badly dressed.' Little attention was given to Cocteau's play at the minuscule experimental theater l'Atelier, but Chanel received considerable publicity from her first venture in costume design. Man Ray took photographs of the costumes, Georges Lepage did a series of drawings of the Chanel designs for the French *Vogue*, and a review of the play was headed, 'Chanel Goes Greek'.

Chanel had passed through her Russian phase the year before at a time when Russians and all things Russian were à la mode. She engaged ruined countesses, Russian saleswomen and fine-boned Slavic models to launch her exclusively Russian line. This was a temporary aberration, a move away from the classic Chanel pattern: the blouses were loose-fitting in the muzhik-peasant style, ornamentation and embroidery reappeared – excess she had ruthlessly eliminated with her simplified Cubist line. The Baltic Period at 31 rue Cambon lasted not much longer than Chanel's interest in the exiled Russian, Grand Duke Dimitri Pavlovich.

During the time Misia Sert was introducing Chanel into café and salon society, Coco met Dimitri at a party given by Marthe Davelli. At 29 the Grand Duke was eleven years younger than the great lady of fashion, but in the tradition of penniless aristocrats in exile, he made obvious his interest in the older woman of means. Marthe Davelli observed the rapprochement and took Coco aside to reveal what must have been obvious to Chanel, that Dimitri was her lover. Dimitri's taste for champagne and Charvet neckties was getting to be more than Marthe Davelli could afford. Would Coco be interested in adopting the distinguished and handsome Russian nobleman? The scenario might have been written by Colette.

Chanel had inherited a grand duke as escort and lover: she was fond of him, but Dimitri could never be more than a casual if decorative substitute for her late great love, Boy Capel. Like the affair with Pierre Reverdy whom she met during her Russian interlude with Dimitri, or a brief liaison with Stravinsky in 1920, attachments were a temporary distraction from genuine loss. Reverdy drifted out of Chanel's life to become a religious contemplative at a monastery outside Paris. Inevitably, Grand Duke Dimitri, having placed himself and his title on the open market, took leave of her as well.

A gaggle of American heiresses had invaded Paris in a sometimes frantic scramble for titled European husbands. The transaction was a cold-blooded one. (Boni de Castellane spoke of the *chambre de penance* when he referred to the bedroom where he slept with his wealthy American wife: 'She will never know how much I loved her for her money.') Thus the heiress Audrey Emery became the duchess of a no longer existent duchy by pledging her fortune in marriage to Grand Duke Dimitri Pavlovich. If Chanel was hurt by Dimitri's mercenary change of heart, she hid her wounds well – even from Misia.

To fill whatever vacuum these dead ends left in her, Chanel turned to her work, a total commitment to the dressmaking trade. She was there at the beginning, cutting paper into patterns as if creating paper dolls; her hand was in at every stage from fabric-cutting to an occasional turn at the stitching and hems. For the spring and fall salon presentations, Chanel selected the models herself and taught them an unaffected manner of display that would appeal to the 'undernourished telephone operator' as well as to the comtesse de Noailles.

Chanel was well aware of the snob appeal of haute couture, but this was a snobbism that could be exploited beyond the confines of the faubourg St-Honoré. She anticipated the mass-marketing of couturier-label garments, the ready-to-wear boom; she had already accepted the challenge of dressing not just the *beau monde* but *tout-le-monde*.

Out of such ugly-sounding substances as rhodoid, galalithe and nacrologue, Chanel began to design and market inexpensive costume jewelry, the ideal accompaniment to her plain-spoken elegance in dress. There was no pretense that these baubles were anything but colorfully artificial: it became as acceptable to pin a Chanel costume jewel to an evening dress as to wear one in daytime. The trinkets could be discarded at the next turn of fashion with no great heartache.

The first of the grand couturiers to make perfume an adjunct to his fashion line was Paul Poiret. Chanel became a contender in this field when she discovered Ernest Beaux, the half-French son of the *parfumier* to the court of the Czar. At his perfume center in Grasse, Beaux had been experimenting with a product of extraordinary subtlety whose redolence endured throughout an evening, yet did not reek of the obvious source odors. With Beaux's formula, and the assistance of a master chemist who had defected from Coty, Chanel launched the product that was to make her name a byword for perfume.

Once again her timing and instinct were exact. Even the design for the flask was an inspiration: a simple square-edged bottle, plain in the

Chanel evening gown in black *mousseline de soie* – autumn 1925.

way of a well-cut gem. By eliminating the Art Nouveau flourishes from the label, Chanel N° 5 – in plain black letters on white – quietly announced itself a classic.

*

Misia and José-Maria Sert were the constants in Chanel's life: they were there to distract her from brooding despondency; she could confide in Misia and be entertained by José-Maria. Privately, Chanel had little appreciation for José-Maria's artistic talent – he was society's pet decorator and muralist of the period – but she was amused by him and comforted by his exuberant generosity. Early in the Twenties the Serts took Coco on a motor tour of Europe: Sert insisted on paying for every trifle during the trip, took great pains to engage Coco's interest in art, was tireless in the role of good companion. The relationship between Coco and Misia was more complicated. At that time, two people seen constantly together, openly affectionate, were invariably believed to be lovers. Theirs was an intense, almost rival-sibling friendship that endured from one decade to the next – a lifetime alliance based as much on competitiveness as affection. The large irony in their shifting ambivalent friendship was that Misia, having married three times, was envious of Chanel's lovers; Chanel, for all her passionate affairs, would have wanted marriage.

During the continental tour with Misia and José-Maria, Misia introduced Coco to Sergei Diaghilev at a café in Venice. It was doubtful if the great entrepreneur even noticed the dark beauty sitting quietly at Misia's side other than to murmur, 'Enchanté.' Diaghilev had no great interest in women: Misia was an extraordinary exception. He was troubled, and needed to detail his current fiscal difficulties to his dear friend, since Misia had always been his close confidante and occasional savior. (Once when an opening curtain was inexplicably delayed for one of his ballet performances, Diaghilev suddenly appeared in Misia's theater box: 'Do you have 20,000 francs? The costumer refuses to allow the curtain to go up until he is paid.' Misia immediately sent her chauffeur for a checkbook.)

Diaghilev's present dilemma was this: the London season had been brilliant, but a financial disaster: the company was in frightful difficulties. He needed to restage the ever popular *The Rite of Spring* but could not afford to engage the large orchestra required for Stravinsky's score. Throughout Diaghilev's troubled monologue Misia's companion remained silent.

Jean Cocteau and Sergei Diaghilev backstage at the Ballets Russes.

When Diaghilev returned to Paris, still despondent, he received an unexpected visitor at the Hôtel Continental. He could not place her, or remember her name. It was Coco Chanel, to present him with a check for 300,000 francs. The plans for *The Rite of Spring* could now be successfully consummated – with the proviso that Chanel's gift remain anonymous: Diaghilev was never to speak of the money to anyone, or to remind his benefactor of her generosity.

Pavlova, Diaghilev, Bakst, and Stravinsky, caricatured in the *Tatler*.

CHAPTER NINE

The Baltic Tide

Before the Russian Revolution the favorite café of Menshevik and Bolshevik conspirators had been La Coupole, on the boulevard Montparnasse at place Vavin. Political outcasts like the fiery intellectual Leon Trotsky sat at its tables fanning the hopes of fellow exiles, while Lenin, awaiting his hour, preferred to play chess at a corner table. Military and social collapse in czarist Russia made possible the Communist upheaval and eventual takeover: civil war sent a new swarm of émigrés to the west, particularly to Paris. Meanwhile the former colony of conspirators was traveling in the opposite direction. The socialist theories they had spun and disputed across the café tables of Zurich and Paris were suddenly in force; the exiles could return to Russia in triumph, prepared to direct the new Bolshevik regime.

In Paris the revolutionaries were replaced by the aristocracy, but aristocrats stripped of their privileges and wealth. 'We were all suddenly poor,' remarked the composer Igor Markevitch. 'You wrote a check on the Imperial Bank, but no roubles came.' Grand dukes worked as headwaiters, czarist colonels became doormen (hoteliers thought the Russians wore their uniforms of braid and epaulets with such distinction), and a great many became taxi drivers, like the 'Colonel Taxovich' in Nabokov's *Lolita*: 'There were thousands of them playing at that fool's trade.' It was thought chic to engage a former lady-in-waiting to the Czarina as companion to a nouveau-riche dowager; Russian princesses were in demand as governesses. The former director of the Naval Academy was happy to find part-time employment with a translation service. Prince Youssoupoff, the assassin of Rasputin, dealt for a time in antiques and paintings (he was sued for fraud concerning several questionable Rembrandts), then opened a fashion house that went bankrupt.

Ambassador Malakoff had been named by the transitional Kerensky government as Russian ambassador in Paris, but when Kerensky was overthrown by the Bolsheviks there was no longer any government to represent. Western nations had not yet recognized the USSR. Malakoff was shunned at embassy receptions and was no longer welcome at the French Foreign Ministry, yet he stayed on at the empty Russian Embassy on rue de Grenelle where he continued to serve as minister-without-portfolio between the French government and the Russian émigrés. 'I resemble a newspaper one leaves on a chair to show that it is occupied.'

But the Bolsheviks left no newspapers on their chairs in Paris. La Coupole was still the preferred haunt of displaced Russians, but White refugees now sat brooding in the wicker chairs so recently abandoned by the Reds.

*

Seventeen-year-old Boris Kochno, born to the vanquished aristocracy, had escaped Russia by way of Constantinople with only a few volumes of poetry as baggage – and a newspaper photograph of Sergei Pavlovich Diaghilev, the ballet impresario. In Paris the young refugee and his mother were taken in by the painter Sudeikin and his wife Vera, who happened to be close friends to Diaghilev. (The friendship was subject to the impulsive temperament and constant intrigue of Russians living abroad: Diaghilev had only recently introduced Vera Sudeikin to Igor Stravinsky, suggesting that she 'be kind to him, for he is quite moody' – she was kind to him, and the two immediately became lovers.) For Boris, the compelling interest of being in Paris was the hope of meeting the great director of the Ballets Russes.

Sudeikin knew how wary Diaghilev was of having prodigies thrust upon him (although Kochno was neither dancer nor musician, a prodigy in no way other than showing a sensitivity to music and dance that Diaghilev himself possessed), so he contrived a scheme whereby the young man would simply appear at Diaghilev's hotel with a message from the painter. Since Diaghilev was attracted to young men, Sudeikin sensed he would be charmed by this one. Boris was carefully coached in how best to approach the unpredictable *maître*. The young man memorized a list of answers to questions Diaghilev would surely put to him.

At 3 rue Castiglione, between the place Vendôme and the rue de Rivoli, Kochno found the ultra-smart Hôtel Continental. He was surprised to be allowed by the desk clerk to proceed directly to

Diaghilev's suite. As it turned out, Diaghilev was expecting a visitor at precisely that hour, so he had left instructions with the front desk to send the party to him without delay. The valet Beppe met Kochno at the door, then told him to wait. In a moment the great man appeared, his thick figure swathed in a dressing gown, a monocle in one eye, a single forelock of white combed back in his dark hair. He welcomed the young man with unexpected warmth.

Boris Kochno was completely disarmed. None of the careful rehearsal by Sudeikin had prepared him for this cordial encounter. As soon as he launched into the first prepared phrase, Diaghilev changed the subject to Russia, bombarding him with questions in Russian about the country from which Kochno had just fled. A persistent nostalgia for Mother Russia was the fate of every émigré, and Diaghilev was not immune to the deprivation felt by his fellow exiles. While Kochno dredged up recollections of Moscow and St Petersburg and searched for names that would be familiar to the former director of the Imperial Theaters (Diaghilev was of the same social background as Kochno, descended on 'the wrong side of the blanket' from Peter the Great, but had lost his post when he fell out of favor with czarist administrators), Diaghilev stood chewing his tongue, as he did when he was deep in thought. He removed his monocle and stared into the middle distance as if suddenly Russia were as near and vivid as the young man standing before him. Abruptly Diaghilev asked Boris his age.

'I have just turned seventeen.'

He then took Boris's hand and said, 'We will meet again.'

At the next meeting Boris Kochno was appointed secretary to the Ballets Russes. The appointment was vague, his duties undefined. Diaghilev seemed to prefer answering the telephone himself, attending to his own mail. Finally the young man found the courage to ask, 'But what is my role?' In French Diaghilev informed him, 'A secretary simply makes himself indispensable.'

From that moment Boris Kochno made himself indispensable to Sergei Pavlovich and to the Russian ballet.

*

The dispersed Russian nobility often made way-stations of Zurich, Berlin, New York before seeking ultimate sanctuary in Paris. A young and adaptable composer like Vernon Dukelsky could find America compatible and even make a career for himself – under the name Vernon Duke – composing musical comedies for the Broadway stage.

Eventually he would make his way to Paris to enter into the magic circle surrounding Diaghilev. Sergei Prokofiev, despite his American success with *The Love of Three Oranges*, found the United States uninhabitable from the beginning. A constant irritant was that his reputation as avant-garde composer did not advance as swiftly as that of Stravinsky, back in Paris. The American critics kept referring to Prokofiev as 'the pianist', because of his concert tours, and to his *frère-ennemi* Stravinsky as 'the composer'. This no doubt helped Prokofiev decide to make Paris his home base.

'To settle in Paris,' said Prokofiev, 'does not mean that one immediately becomes Parisian.' Prokofiev resisted becoming Parisian with all his Russian soul. He lived with his wife and mother near the Invalides, out of the center of things, critical of the new French music. The Parisian spirit that was beginning to influence Stravinsky's life and music had little effect on Prokofiev: his debut with the Ballets Russes was the music for *Chout*, purely Slavic in style, the theme derived from Russian folklore. Although Stravinsky was Diaghilev's preferred com-poser – or, as Nijinsky commented: 'Diaghilev cannot exist without Stravinsky, nor Stravinsky without Diaghilev' – it was to Prokofiev the impresario turned for the music to *Pas d'Acier*, the all-Soviet ballet. In Diaghilev's judgment, a spectacle that celebrated a Sovietized Russia would be closer to Prokofiev's heart than to Stravinsky's – but the choice aroused Stravinsky's jealousy, for a change, of his rival's success.

Much about the west was compatible and stimulating to Stravinsky; life in Paris suited him, and he became a French citizen. He was introduced into the gadfly social life that circulated in and around the arts, and felt at home in the salons of Coco Chanel and the Princesse de Polignac. Prokofiev directed all his energies into his work, as if to fend off the insidious influence of so seductive a city. He was rigid in his habits, a slave to routine: each day he walked around the dome of the Invalides for a pre-apéritif stroll that lasted exactly twenty-six minutes. His final composition for the Ballets Russes was *The Prodigal Son* in 1929, after which the prodigal son himself returned to the Soviet Union to make his peace and accept his place under the new regime.

'Neither Stravinsky nor Prokofiev ever won a beauty contest,' remarked Diaghilev, who was a connoisseur of male beauty. Stravinsky was short, with thick Slavic features, fussy and self-conscious in his dress. He exercised daily, was muscular and fit, yet something of a hypochondriac. Health foods had not yet become a fad, but Stravinsky

Sergei Prokofiev (left, drawing by Henri Matisse) and Igor Stravinsky.

often put himself on a bizarre regime of his own design: raw potatoes and tomatoes taken with oil and lemon. Once, at the restaurant opposite the Orthodox Russian Cathedral on rue Daru, Stravinsky ordered his famous raw repast in the company of composer Nicolas Nabokov. Nabokov could not finish his *cotelettes Pojarsky*; Stravinsky scooped the remainder of Nabokov's cutlet onto his own plate, doused it with sour cream, and devoured the morsel saying, 'I want to astonish the raw potato in my stomach.'

To arouse astonishment was one of the composer's foremost accomplishments, as if he could hear Diaghilev's 'Astonish me!' each time he undertook a composition. His *Rite of Spring* caused the kind of excitement and outrage that made the Ballets Russes so consistently astonishing. (Diaghilev was well aware of the value of controversy over any new presentation: he could always count upon Stravinsky to break through the barriers of musical sound.) Prokofiev responded to each of Stravinsky's triumphs in predictable fashion: there was no music whatsoever, he declared, in *Firebird*; of the oratorio *Oedipus Rex* he made the sarcastic comment, 'The libretto is French [by Cocteau], the text is Latin, the subject is Greek, the music is Anglo-German, and the money is American – true cosmopolitanism.'

The tandem relationship between Diaghilev and Stravinsky – each of whom thought he manipulated the other – was a curious association of opposites yet a mutually inspiring partnership. Ironically, it was the *ancien régime* and not the new order in Russia that had produced these two revolutionaries whom the political revolution left untouched.

Stravinsky's unappealing features and unimpressive stature did not prevent him from being something of a dandy and a womanizer. His friendship with the dressy Bakst may have influenced Stravinsky's acquired taste for modish men's-wear, and the brief liaison with Coco Chanel (kept discreetly from his wife Catherine) certainly enriched his wardrobe. Chanel indulged both his vanity and hypochondria by purchasing scarves from Hermès and providing him with an astrakhan coat when he complained of catching colds in drafty rehearsal halls. The affair with Chanel took place just before the fateful introduction to Vera Sudeikin.

The two radical innovators of twentieth-century music and dance, Stravinsky and Diaghilev, were nonetheless conservatively religious – Diaghilev in spirit if not in practice – and remarkably superstitious. Stravinsky had remained faithful to the Russian Orthodox Church of his youth, and regularly attended mass at the Russian cathedral on rue Daru. As a further precaution against evil or malchance he pinned amulets and religious medals to his underwear. For Diaghilev, even the short voyage across the English Channel was a dread experience, for he was haunted by a gypsy's unnerving prediction that he would die upon water.

*

'I am a charlatan first of all,' was Diaghilev's description of himself, '– but a charlatan with style. In the second place I am a great charmer; and thirdly, I have no end of cheek.' Neither musician, nor dancer, nor painter, nor businessman, Diaghilev managed to be all of these, a genius in bringing all the arts together on stage, and in business substituting charm for money.

Except for charm, style and cheek, less might be said of those other charlatans swept to Paris on the Russian tide.

Dr Sergei Voronoff announced in January 1920 that he intended to establish a monkey farm in the South of France, indirectly seeking subscriptions from the public and the approval of the French government. He had already achieved official recognition as a distinguished scientist by the Collège de France for his singular experiments with monkey glands. These glands, grafted onto sheep, were said to increase the size and strength of the sheep, and a subsequent improvement in the quality of the wool. From sheep, Dr Voronoff moved on to humans. Many believed he could rejuvenate the aged with his monkey-gland treatment, and he soon acquired a well-to-do clientele hoping for a return to youth via the Voronoff injections.

Another doctor, Ivan Manoukhin, working at the Red Cross Hospital in Kiev, claimed to have cured over 8,000 cases of tuberculosis by applying X-rays to the spleen. The treatment was meant to re-activate or restore the gland, and thus cleanse the blood of tubercular bacilli. At the outbreak of the Russian civil war, Manoukhin came to Paris to set up a private clinic in the affluent Passy district. (Generally speaking, there were two separate Russian colonies in Paris: the impecunious tended to settle in the 15th arrondissement, whereas the wealthy – Baron Sergei Jastrebzoff, Baronne Héloise d'Oettengen, Princesse Nathalie, Grand Duke Paul – were to be found in the 16th arrondissement, Passy, on the Right Bank.)

News of Manoukhin's unorthodox treatment reached Katherine Mansfield, then living in Switzerland. The short-story writer had been a desperate consumptive since 1917 when a spot was discovered on her lungs. By 1918 she had embarked on a restless journey in search of a place in the world where she might practice her art and prolong her life: doctors advised her she could not survive more than four years, under the best of conditions. Naturally the story of Manoukhin's success with X-rays inspired a new surge of hope. Of her yearly allowance of £300 from her father, she wrote, 'I have saved £100 for this *last chance*.'

Katherine Mansfield moved to Paris, staying first at the Victoria Palace Hotel at 20 francs per day, then, as her funds ran low, at the Hôtel Sélect at half the rent. After the first consultation – through an interpreter, since Manoukhin spoke little French and no English – the Russian specialist announced that he could cure her completely. There would be an initial session of fifteen *séances* at 300 francs per *séance*, or 4,500 francs in all – a sum in line with the chic Passy address. Then the patient should seek a change of climate, rest for a time, and return for a series of ten additional treatments. In January 1922, Mansfield put herself into Dr Manoukhin's hands and submitted to his radiation bombardment of the spleen.

Despite whatever suspicions she harbored about Manoukhin's cure, she was fascinated by the Russian doctor – as she was by all things Russian. He had at one time been Maxim Gorki's physician, and this link to Russian literature was a further attraction; Manoukhin was able to introduce Katherine Mansfield into the literary branch of the Russian émigré colony. Her own work had been influenced by the stories of Anton Chekhov, and through Manoukhin she met Alexander Salzman, friend to Chekhov's actress-widow. She also met the writer Ivan Bunin, something of a sour encounter, for Bunin did not share her enthusiasm for Chekhov.

Since Manoukhin had put her on a fattening diet, Katherine had gained weight by April, but that was the only indication of progress. X-rays at that time could not be effectively focused or controlled. She was beginning to suffer the after-effects of radiation sickness: neuritis, heart strain, a constant sensation of burning and nausea. While Katherine Mansfield agonized through those first fifteen *séances*, she wrote in a letter: 'I have the feeling that M. [Manoukhin] is really a good man. I have also a sneaking feeling (I use the word "sneaking" advisedly) that he is a kind of unscrupulous impostor.' She did not return for Manoukhin's concluding series of ten X-rays, for in the interval she had transferred her hopes and allegiance to another Russian in exile.

Katherine Mansfield spent her last
months in the care of an exiled guru from
Russia, Georgei Ivanovitch Gurdjieff.

Through the mathematician Piotr Uspenski (P. D. Ouspensky) Katherine met a charismatic guru from Armenian Russia, Georgei Ivanovitch Gurdjieff, founder and director of the Institute for the Harmonious Development of Man. Gurdjieff had traveled to Paris via devious trade routes: he was a dealer in carpets and diamonds who had fled the revolution along with a contingent of his followers from the original Institute he had established in St Petersburg; he escaped Russia by way of Georgia, then crossed into Constantinople with a shipment of caviar.

In Paris Gurdjieff rented the Dalcroze School of Eurhythmics for his disciples, an appropriate setting for the ritual dance program that was part of his philosophy of enlightenment. The Institute was at first financed by the profits made from selling gems and rugs smuggled out of Russia: 100,000 francs. In the autobiography *Meetings with Remarkable Men* Gurdjieff offers to explain his financial dealings in answer to a rhetorical question posed by himself. The chapter is devoted to a recitation of travels in the Caucasus and Turkestan trading in carpets and antiques, then in Paris by the manipulation of oil shares and an investment involving an unspecified cabaret in Montmartre which Gurdjieff sold at a large profit. As a sideline, Gurdjieff acted as agent in the sale of icons, cloisonné and other family treasures brought out of Russia by White refugees.

In Turkestan Gurdjieff had studied the religious dances of the Sufis and had lived the communal life with nomad tribes in Asia Minor: from these experiences had evolved his theory of 'the harmonious development of man'. A dramatic figure with his shaven skull, Mongol eyes, and long black Cossack mustache, Gurdjieff naturally attracted rumors – that he was a holy lama, or that he had been the Czar's chief secret agent in Tibet. According to the Gurdjieff philosophy, enlightenment could be accomplished by conscious effort, self-knowledge, and voluntary suffering. Gurdjieff rejected the Cartesian notion of a universe split into mind and matter: by concentrating on mind and body as one, his followers sought escape from alcoholism, drug addiction, bodily ills, and self.

Along with his successful financial dealings, Gurdjieff enlisted the support of Lady Rothermere, wife of the British newspaper magnate, in order to acquire Le Prieuré (The Priory), a chateau near Fontainebleau. Here, just an hour from Paris, Gurdjieff established a permanent communal settlement for his disciples and himself.

Reactions to the Gurdjieff phenomenon were mixed, but those closest to Katherine Mansfield were almost unanimously opposed. D. H. Lawrence, also tubercular, considered the Institute a great hoax and Gurdjieff the worst kind of fraud. Katherine's husband, John Middleton Murry, was estranged from her at the time; the rift grew deeper because of her decision to become involved in Gurdjieff's occultism. But Gurdjieff, like Manoukhin, offered the desperate consumptive the promise of a cure – a complete cure before Christmas.

More than a restoration of health drew Katherine Mansfield to Gurdjieff, for she was determined to break with a life gone awry in several ways other than infected lungs. She had just written a will, and may have believed she was approaching death in any case, hoping to attain spiritual enlightenment before she suffered the body's final betrayal. She entered The Priory as would a religious penitent; she retreated from the world, then submitted to the Gurdjieff regime of self-denial, humility, and discipline.

At first Katherine stayed in the main house, referred to as the Ritz, where visiting celebrities were housed and where Gurdjieff himself lived. ('In every circumstance in life,' wrote the master, 'try to combine the useful with the agreeable.') In time, Gurdjieff transferred Katherine Mansfield to a bare unheated room in the workers' dormitory. She was assigned to the kitchen force where she scraped potatoes and peeled onions until her fingers bled. Her laundry was stolen; she suffered from the cold and damp of her gelid cell – yet she was happy. Her letters from this period reflect the uplift of her mood along with incessant references to the cold. 'It is intensely cold here – colder and colder ... I simply live in my fur coat. I gird it on like my heavenly armor and wear it ever night and day.'

It was Gurdjieff's belief that Katherine would improve if she regularly inhaled the breath of cows, so a loft was furnished for her above the cattle stalls in the barn where she shared the bovine breathing space and sometimes drank milk fresh from the milking pail. She was delighted with her private hayloft in the great barn (surely warmer than her room) and particularly loved the Gurdjieff cows. In her leisure time – routine was fixed and rigid at The Priory – Katherine studied Russian. As much as anything in her new life, she was enamored of the Russianness of Gurdjieff and his commune of disciples.

Meanwhile Gurdjieff was caught up in a project to build a dance pavilion in The Priory grounds from a converted airplane hangar. Here the ritual dances were to be held, with the master looking on from a raised dais, a kind of throne decorated with Persian carpets. (Edmund Wilson had observed the dance exercises during which the dancers were required to remain at intervals in immobile postures, and commented: 'They were like trained zombies.') With Christmas approaching, the dance hall was scheduled to be inaugurated as a backdrop to the holiday festivities.

Members of the community, including Katherine, devoted long hours to completing the dance hall in time for the New Year. She decided to invite John Middleton Murry for a husband-and-wife reunion, and he arrived in time to celebrate New Year's Eve with her. The visit was more than a reunion: there was the prospect of a reconciliation, certainly an acceptance by her husband of Katherine's decision to live at The Priory. It appeared to Murry that his wife's spirits were greatly improved, and perhaps the Gurdjieff regime would have a favorable effect on her tubercular condition. But on the night of 9 January 1923, Katherine became overexcited, flushed, hyperactive – she seemed to want to show Murry how happy she had become. On the way to her room she ran ahead of him up the stairs. Halfway up she turned to him with a strange look, then suddenly began to vomit blood. When she could speak she announced quite calmly, 'I think I'm going to die.'

Two doctors came to attend her immediately: hot water bottles were applied to her cold form, but she was dead. Murry, who had come to celebrate the New Year with his wife, stayed on to attend her funeral. The service was held at Fontainebleau, and Katherine Mansfield was buried in the cemetery there.

Her last letters attest to a happiness at The Priory beyond any happiness she had known in her life, yet it would seem certain her stay at the Gurdjieff Institute hastened her death. In her notebooks were written words and phrases for which she wanted to learn the Russian equivalents: *I am cold. Wood. Smoke. Matches. Flame. Strong. Force. To light a fire. No more fire. Because there's no more fire.*

CHAPTER TEN

The Hive

Refugees of one diaspora or another – Lipchitz, Zadkine, Soutine, Chagall – followed their troubled paths to the new ghettos of Montparnasse. The displaced painters and sculptors sought light and cheap living space: at La Ruche on the rue Dantzig they found both, and the reassuring company of fellow artists of predominantly Eastern European origin. The ambience was decidedly Russian, the samovar a focal point of social life ('Tea,' said Stravinksy, 'is the center of all our nostalgias') – or vodka and slivovitz when there was money. Ambulant peddlers went from pavilion to pavilion selling pumpernickel bread and sausages with horseradish.

Of the several *cités* of marginal artist-studios in the 13th and 14th arrondissements, La Ruche was the most original. This housing project for refugee artists was the accomplishment of an academic sculptor of no merit or distinction other than his benevolence. With the commission money from the King of Rumania (for portrait busts of himself and his queen), Alfred Boucher bought a parcel of *terrain vague* at the dead end of rue Dantzig, a piece of wasteland adjoining the slaughterhouses of Vaugirard. Construction of the queerly assembled *cité* took place not long after the Paris Exposition of 1900. Boucher purchased several pavilions scheduled for demolition, then arranged for the buildings to be reassembled on his rue Dantzig property. The large circular wine hall designed by Eiffel, using the same girder-structure as his famous tower, became the centerpiece of Boucher's reconstituted ensemble. With its unintentionally Cubist roof and octagon shape, the wine hall resembled a beehive – thus the name La Ruche.

The two-storey central unit was converted into twenty-four triangular studios so narrow the tenants referred to them as coffins. Outbuildings left over from the Exposition were also re-erected on the site and divided into small flats, or larger studios meant for sculptors. In this piecemeal way and through imaginative scavenging, Alfred Boucher realized his dream of 140 studios and flats, a turbulent hive of working artists, situated on the grim periphery of a slaughterhouse.

For his own coffin, with an interior balcony that served as a shelf-like bedroom, Marc Chagall paid 150 francs per year – 'And one was not even obliged to pay', he declared. The altruistic Père Boucher wandered through the garden of La Ruche with his pet donkey Jeannette, saluting his artists, greeting them by name. He was not driven to collect even the lowest fifty-franc rents from such tenants.

During the war years La Ruche had been requisitioned by the state as a hostel for refugees stranded in Paris. These temporary residents chopped down the trees around the cité for fuel – La Ruche had been assembled without heating facilities, and there was only a single source of running water for each structure, on the ground floor. Since there were no chimneys, tenants removed windowpanes to accommodate makeshift stovepipe outlets.

When the painters and sculptors trickled back to their studios after the war, the beehive had become a ruin. The aging Boucher lived in a ground-floor flat, cared for by his niece. Wearing now the ribbon of the Légion d'Honneur in his buttonhole, he seemed unaware of the sad state of his dream as he shuffled along the littered walkways between pavilions, greeting his 'bees'.

Many artists nurtured at La Ruche – housed by the benevolent Boucher, promoted by the dedicated Zborowski – had achieved some eminence as members of l'Ecole de Paris. Several were successful enough to afford the comfort and status of respectable neighborhoods far removed from the screaming beasts and foul miasma of the Vaugirard stockyards. For some, even the desperate ugliness of the district slaughterhouses was an inspiration. Chaim Soutine painted the halved carcases of beef as if smearing the canvas with caked or flowing blood of the beasts themselves. In Chagall's lyrical fashion the bellowing oxen became airborne: they were dream cattle floating in the sky of a remembered village called Vitebsk.

The courtyard around the octagonal ruche echoed with Brancusi's hammerblows and Zadkine cutting stone, the unlit central staircase reeked of turpentine and spilt ordure. The tight little studios circled the stairwell like wedge-slices of Brie. Chagall locked himself into his narrow triangle, humming to himself as he painted in the nude, ignoring the stones Soutine chucked at his window. The grotesque

La Ruche – the *cité d'artistes* on the rue Dantzig.

Marc Chagall during his years at La Ruche.

Soutine was to be avoided: he was more likely to want money than company. Soutine shared the cheapest fifty-franc cell with Kremegne, the only one of the painter-tenants at La Ruche who could abide Soutine's ugly face and the rank odor that trailed after him. For days Soutine smelled of the herrings he had filched from somebody's open coffin-studio; two of the fish rotted as he painted them, a third was snatched away by a rat. Chagall automatically turned his paintings to the wall when Soutine banged at the door, for fear that Chaim's filthy overcoat might brush against a still wet canvas.

When there was no food, the painters could venture out into the larger hive of Montparnasse to eat at Marie Wassilieff's *cantine* on the avenue du Maine. Before the war Marie had been awarded a grant by the Czarina to attend l'Ecole des Beaux-Arts in Paris, but when support from Russia was cut off after the revolution she became hostess and earth-mother to the bohemian branch of the émigré colony. Marie Wassilieff had given up painting, but she earned a fluctuating livelihood creating stuffed-animal sofa cushions for Paul Poiret and creating caricature puppets for the puppetmaster Gaston Baty. During the Red scare after the revolution, when posters appeared on kiosks of a slavering Bolshevik with a dagger between his teeth, Marie was arrested and tried in a French court for having been the mistress of Trotsky. To this charge she replied: 'I am the mother of a Frenchman!' – which struck the right note of patriotism. The *procès* was swiftly set aside.

At the Wassilieff *cantine* one was sustained by soup, entrée, a glass of white wine, and one cigarette – all for fifty centimes. A special cauldron of vegetable soup was kept to one side: Marie dispensed the nourishing *potage* free of charge to the truly indigent.

The abject poverty continued for those at La Ruche who remained undiscovered, like Kremegne. Soutine attempted suicide. When Kremegne found him hanging by a rope, he cut him down, revived him, and never spoke to him again. Granowsky, dressed as a cowboy, screamed from his minuscule balcony: 'Moi, génie – moi, génie!' But declarations of genius went unheard except by other frustrated geniuses in the hive, or by the marauding butchers from the Vaugirard slaughterhouses. Much of the time the butchers and artists mingled peaceably enough despite a natural antipathy. They drank together at the Café Dantzig, though sometimes the butchers drank up their pay, then went on a rampage through the grounds of La Ruche shouting obscenities at the painters and decapitating sculptures in the ruined gardens.

After the revolution in Russia, Marc Chagall made a frustrating attempt to return to his native Vitebsk – he was even appointed local minister of art by the Commissar of Fine Arts himself, Lunacharsky, who had been a fellow tenant at La Ruche. Later Chagall was put in charge of a school for orphans, refugees from famine and civil war: 'I was to teach them to be painting geniuses in twenty-four hours.' The school failed, and Chagall's paintings came into conflict with collectivist attitudes toward art. In 1922 the disillusioned painter was again obliged to flee his homeland.

When Chagall reached Paris a year later he discovered his studio at La Ruche had been occupied by refugees during the war, then given over to a new tenant. He was homeless again, but at least homeless in Paris. For this half-assimilated Frenchman, haunted by dream scenes of a distant *shtetl*, the only way to recover the past was by painting it. All his prewar paintings were missing – stolen, destroyed, or sold for a few sous. Several were later found in the garden behind La Ruche: the wartime concierge had used them as roofing for a rabbit hutch: they kept out the rain because of the oil paint on them.

A nucleus of the prewar Russian group lingered on at La Ruche alongside a new wave of indigent artists seeking shelter in the humble studios. Others, like Chagall and Soutine, moved on. By 1923 Soutine had been plucked from obscurity and his wretched life at La Ruche by the American collector, Dr Alfred C. Barnes, who had invented the trademark pharmaceutical Argyrol. Through Barnes, Soutine had become so affluent he was installed in a rented villa beside the Parc Montsouris. Chagall now frequented the studio of Moïse Kisling: Kisling had grown successful with his gauzy nudes of Kiki, the era's favorite model – his studio on the rue Joseph-Bara was the new hub of social life, a center for painters, dealers, models attracted by Kisling's generosity and warmth.

La Ruche continued, although a commercial garage replaced one of the pavilions, a private apartment building encroached on the communal terrain on the other side of the hive. Throughout the Twenties Boucher – so aptly named, in a district of butchers – roamed the grounds of La Ruche like an absent-minded parish priest offering his benediction to the faithful. If his 'bees' had changed, he seemed not to notice: they were still painters and sculptors; vodka parties still spilled over into nude wrestling matches in the mud where once the trees had been.

CHAPTER ELEVEN

A Musical Offering

I t was inevitable that the young composer Igor Markevitch should come to the attention of Sergei Diaghilev. Just as Kochno had made his approach to the *maître* through Sudeikin, Markevitch was placed in Diaghilev's line of vision by the intermediary Alexandrine Troussevitch, an under-secretary to the Ballets Russes. When the sixteen-year-old musical prodigy was presented to Diaghilev, the impresario made a comment of dismissal: 'He has the look of having just been snatched from the nursery' – but in Russian Diaghilev issued the command: 'Tell him to be at the Grand Hotel with his music tomorrow afternoon at 5.'

Diaghilev did not keep that first appointment with Igor Markevitch. The period of 1927–28 was one of stress and distraction for Diaghilev: he had lost a series of choreographer-dancers by defection and marriage; there were the usual financial pressures, including unpaid hotel bills that he sidestepped by changing hotels. He was not above thrusting the ballerina Alice Nikitina into the corpulent arms of Lord Rothermere in the hope that the newspaper magnate would then be happy to pour funds into the empty coffers of the Ballets Russes – or encouraging the Armenian oil millionaire Gulbenkian in his pursuit of Spessivetseva for the same reason. (Occasionally these matchmaking schemes backfired so thoroughly that Diaghilev lost both ballerina and patron.) The twentieth anniversary of the Ballets Russes approached, a celebration planned by the company only filled Diaghilev with horror: anniversaries reminded him of his own advancing age, birthdays were hateful events.

Also at this time the Ballets Russes had revived Stravinsky's *Petrouchka*, with Lifar dancing the role Nijinsky had made famous in the golden age of the Ballets Russes before the war. In a Machiavellian backstage intrigue, Nijinsky had managed to slip out from under

ch. Bérard

Backstage after a Ballets Russes performance of
Petrouchka: (l. to r.) Alexander Benois, Sergei Grigoriev,
the dancer Tamara Karsavina, Diaghilev, the by then
hopelessly schizophrenic Nijinsky, and the dancer Serge
Lifar. Igor Markevitch (above, drawing by Christian
Bérard) was present on this occasion but not
photographed.

Diaghilev's influence and relentless surveillance to marry a member of the troupe, Romola. By 1919 Nijinsky had lapsed into hopeless schizophrenia, unable to dance or even to function without Romola's aid. It was Diaghilev's belief, or hope, that if Nijinsky could attend the performance of *Petrouchka* – one of his greatest roles – the experience might shock or recall the dancer to a semblance of sanity. While Romola was away in America, Diaghilev arranged personally to bring Nijinsky to the Opéra where *Petrouchka* was being performed. Nijinsky was installed in Diaghilev's own box: the maestro attempted to elicit some remark or sign of recognition from his former protégé, but Nijinsky did not respond – he was unable to react to the ballet or even to the memory of his own great art.

Igor Markevitch was present the night of the *Petrouchka* revival and the Nijinsky-Diaghilev reunion. It would seem an inauspicious occasion to attract Diaghilev's attention, but the young man was included in the backstage entourage when Nijinksy was photographed with Diaghilev, Karsavina, Grigoriev, Benois – only Markevitch, just beyond the range of the camera lens, does not appear in the haunted photograph.

Alexandrine Troussevitch had known all along that Diaghilev would be attracted to the young composer with his striking borzoi profile, strangely resembling another of Diaghilev's lost loves, Leonide Massine. Although he had failed to show up at his first rendezvous with Markevitch, she was familiar with the Baron de Charlus side of Diaghilev's character: he would assume indifference in the beginning, then play his cat-and-mouse game with a young boy who interested him.

Another appointment – arranged, again, by Alexandrine – took place at Colombin's, the *chocolatier*. In this elaborate charade of coquetry, Diaghilev plied the young man with a sick-making collection of sweets, an extravant *goûter* intended for a nine-year-old. When Diaghilev was ready to hear Markevitch play, he announced, 'We are going to Mlle Chanel's where we can work quietly.'

The music salon at Chanel's *hôtel particulier* was smothered in the odor of tuberose. Diaghilev led Igor to the massive polished Steinway and directed him to play a composition. On those first youthful and derivative pieces Markevitch played, Diaghilev commented: 'I have told you to prepare Tomorrow for me, and you are thinking only of Yesterday.'

Shy as he was at sixteen, Igor was nevertheless capable of a ready return: 'I'm not interested in yesterday or today but what is forever.' The spirit behind this remark caused Diaghilev to study the young man all the more closely through his monocle.

Markevitch then sang several melodies he had written to poems by Apollinaire. 'There,' conceded Diaghilev, 'you have come upon some happy inspirations. In two or three years we must collaborate on something worthwhile.' The impresario was looking at his watch as he said this.

Finally Markevitch played his most recent composition, the finale to his *Sinfonietta*. Throughout this presentation Diaghilev pulled at the flesh of his neck, an habitual gesture of thoughtful agitation.

'Why didn't you play that straight off?'

'It is only a fragment,' explained Markevitch. 'The work is still unfinished.'

'Play it for me again.'

Markevitch obliged the maestro by repeating the composition.

'But what led you to write music like that?'

The young man then told of his arrival in Paris the year before, his reactions to the swirl of sound and color seen from his window on the square des Batignolles. He described the emotional impact of an afternoon when he sat transfixed by the panorama at the place du Tertre, fascinated by the movement around him – so fascinated that his tram, number 31, passed several times before he thought of returning home. A theory of motion in life that could be translated into music was beginning to dawn on the sixteen-year-old.

Suddenly Diaghilev realized that the light in the salon had faded. '*Mon Dieu*, I have barely time to dress for the theater.' He led Markevitch away from the piano and to the stairs. As the impresario and the boy with a portfolio of music under his arm made their way down the grand staircase, a lovely perfumed apparition was just coming up.

'Ma chère Coco,' Diaghilev called to her in passing, 'here is a child who promises great things.'

*

Through Diaghilev the young Igor Markevitch was given a passe-partout for the interlocking circles of patrons and patronesses of French society who supported the Ballets Russes and commissioned works of music from promising composers. After meeting Coco Chanel – then her equally influential friend, Misia Sert – Markevitch made his debut chez 'Tante Winnie' at her imposing mansion on the avenue Henri-Martin.

American-born Winnaretta Singer, now the Princesse Edmond de Polignac, was the woman most likely to consider the young man's possibilities and promote his ambitions, for she took particular interest in composers and was herself a musician of ability and sensitivity. To the embarrassment of Markevitch, Diaghilev presented him in these terms: 'This young man is less mild than he appears, and is more impertinent than his music.' It was perhaps the most effective way to bring Igor Markevitch to the attention of the Franco-American princess.

Behind Winnaretta's imperious façade was a shy and self-conscious woman with a need to penetrate the façades of others. She was drawn to the personage behind the mask, and to impertinence in music as well as in character. The Princesse de Polignac had financed a number of avant-garde compositions, and was prepared to do so again. Markevitch was made welcome to her entourage and almost immediately received a generous commission to write his *Partita*, a concertante that brought the young composer his first success.

Invariably Diaghilev drew his young men into the limelight with one hand, and jealously clung to them with the other. Igor was the latest in a series of protégés, all of whom were principal dancers except for Kochno and himself. Fokine, Nijinsky, Massine, Dolin, Lifar and Balanchine were all great talents enlarged by Diaghilev's efforts and influence, but whose lives and devotion he considered his exclusive property. Kochno and Lifar were Diaghilev's trusted palace guards, two constants in his ménage, but the others had found ways of escape into personal and professional independence – two of them, Nijinsky and Massine, intrigued behind Diaghilev's back to form liaisons with young women, members of the watchful magician's own dance company. There was no fear that Winnaretta would capture the affections of young Markevitch: the older woman's amorous interests lay elsewhere.

*

A share in the famous Singer sewing-machine fortune elevated Winnaretta Singer to the aristocracy: she was able to marry the Prince Louis de Scey-Montbéliard in what appeared to be a mutually advantageous wedding of wealth and the bluest of blood.

Winnaretta was no naive arriviste with a copy of the *Almanach de Gotha* in her steamer trunk. She had been brought to Paris at the age of two; as an adolescent she studied with the academic French painter Felix Barrias until music became the love of her life. She installed a massive pipe organ in her townhouse in Passy so that she might practice the chorale-preludes in Bach's *Das Orgelbüchlein*. A first investment in the arts was her purchase of Manet's *La Lecture*; she came to know the artist, who died when Winnaretta was eighteen. She visited the blind Degas in his testy declining years. Commissions to fin-de-siècle musicians Chabrier and Fauré brought her into contact with Proust, the Comtesse Greffulhe, and one of Proust's models for the Baron de Charlus in *Remembrance of Things Past*, Robert de Montesquiou.

Winnaretta's quiet opulence, culturally acceptable credentials and shrewd generosity made her salon the equal of any French social circle in the rarefied air of the faubourg St-Honoré and faubourg St-Germain. Her acceptance of the prevailing sexual deviations of the day made her equally acceptable to the night-blooming Proustian set. When she discovered that her own lesbian tendencies had overcome any hetero-sexual interest she might have imagined for Prince Louis de Scey-Montbéliard, the two parties to the misalliance decided on divorce.

While Winnaretta carried on her discreet and alternating liaisons with Baronne de Meyer, Dame Ethel Smyth, Romaine Brooks, or Violet Trefusis (the former lover of Vita Sackville-West), her brother Paris followed more closely the tradition of the Singer family patriarch. Isaac Merritt Singer had fathered sixteen illegitimate progeny by three common-law wives in addition to his six legal offspring (Winnaretta and Paris among the latter) and provided for all out of the vast profits from his sewing machine. Paris lived openly with Isadora Duncan as her 'Lohengrin'. He was the father of one of her two children (Gordon Craig was father of the other) who drowned in the Seine when Isadora's chauffeur-driven car rolled off an embankment.

Robert de Montesquiou was able to convince Winnaretta that whatever her sexual inclinations, divorce was a great disadvantage to a woman in society. Soon after, she met the Prince Edmond de Polignac through the awkward circumstance of having been 'some American woman' who outbid him at an auction for a Monet he coveted. Later they met formally, and the woman with the Dantesque profile and nasal voice the Prince had 'vowed to eternal damnation' became an immediate friend and eventually his wife.

The Princesse de Polignac, *née* Winnaretta Singer (inset), and the harpsichordist Wanda Landowska.

The couple shared a love of the arts, especially of music, and together they were a happy complement as host and hostess of the grand salon on avenue Henri-Martin. Since the Prince de Polignac was homosexual, their affections were not at trial in the marriage bed: they could indulge their divergent passions while maintaining great respect and genuine affection for one another. Edmond was 59 when they married, Winnaretta was 28. Robert de Montesquiou – miffed at not being invited to the small private wedding – called the alliance a marriage between the sewing machine and the lyre (Edmond played the harpsichord), or a wedding of the dollar and the sou.

The Prince died before the 1920s arrived, and just as Montesquiou had counseled, a widowed Princesse de Polignac became a substantial and altogether legitimate cornerstone of French society. She was homosexual, but in an age and in a city where sexual inversion excited little notice even when publicly flaunted. Her most intimate friends and frequent guests were either homosexual or bisexual, and she may have preferred lesbians to all others, but her salon and the recipients of her largesse were mixed.

While the Duchesse de Clermont-Tonnerre regretted the age of candlelit dinners in gold lamé rooms, when Proust drank seventeen cups of coffee in her drawing room to calm his asthma, entertainments chez Polignac began to take precedence over the fading salons of the old guard. Madame Marie-Louise Bousquet still received in a suite of oblong rooms with walls done in red velvet (which Dolly Wilde called the *chemin-de-fer* because of the resemblance to first-class carriages in French trains); the Vicomtesse de Noailles, the Comtesse Greffuhle, Comte Etienne de Beaumont were still at home to one another, but the rituals and privileges of the aristocratic rich were an anachronism in a democratic age.

A global conflict that had begun with the assassination of a prince and ended with the defeat of a kaiser and the overthrow of a czar had created a renewed sense of *liberté-égalité-fraternité*. The *beau monde* now included Picasso, Colette, Stravinsky, and Cocteau – a mélange with origins in music hall, poet's garret and atelier. The Princesse de Polignac spared neither money nor taste nor ingenuity in maintaining a guest list of distinction, but not just distinction of lineage. Artistic accomplishment, or the promise of artistic gifts, was as important a *laissez-passer* to the music salon on avenue Henri-Martin as blood rank or money.

There were exceptions to Tante Winnie's hospitality and open-handedness. When Vera Sudeikin asked her why she never invited Chanel, Winnaretta replied, 'I don't entertain my tradespeople' – but the real reason may have been that Chanel was a competing patron with her own salon in the same Right Bank milieu. Or the Princesse might be reluctant to support members of rival salons – such as Virgil Thomson, who was a favorite of Gertrude Stein – but only as a diplomatic precaution after a careful assessment of territorial rights. In her own domain she was preeminent, 'the irreplaceable Maecenas', as Poulenc called her. She sat a perpetually firm seat, 'determination,' according to Harold Nicolson, 'in every line of her bum'.

The twentieth-century revival of baroque music had not yet come about, except in the music room of Winnaretta's mansion. It seemed to her the days of the great orchestral works were over, so she encouraged composers like Stravinsky to write works for small orchestra that could be performed in her own salon.

Winnaretta loved ancient music, but she was neither deaf nor indifferent to the new. At the turn of the century she had made possible Ravel's *Pavane pour une Infante défunte*, and in the Twenties Satie's *Socrate* was first heard chez Tante Winnie. Try-outs for the avant-garde ballets *Le Renard* and *Les Noces* were held at Winnaretta's soirées before Diaghilev arranged for formal rehearsals on a theatre stage. Some of the most advanced compositions of Manuel de Falla, Igor Stravinsky and the young French musicians known as Les Six were performed in the Polignac music room. Through a member of Les Six, Darius Milhaud, Winnaretta met Cole Porter, whom she commissioned to write a jazz ballet, *Within the Quota*.

Naturally the patron was pleased when the *Concerto pour piano* she had commissioned from Germaine Taillefaire (the only woman composer of Les Six) was inspired by the Brandenburg Concertos, and she was equally pleased when Markevitch's *Partita* and Stravinsky's *Sonate pour piano* showed the influence of Bach, but she had learned to bestow only money, never inspiration, on those she wished to support.

Winnaretta's milieu represented a cross-pollination of socialites, sybarites, musicians, balletomanes, and the sexually restless. Their rivalries, feuds and outbursts of temperament appeared to leave the famous hostess unperturbed. In truth, she was extremely sensitive to public scandal. Her own outré behavior took place offstage, in the town house on avenue Henri-Martin or at the Palazzo Polignac in Venice.

If Stravinsky was jealous of Markevitch and Prokofiev of Stravinsky and finally, to make the circle complete, Stravinsky of Prokofiev – because of his commission to write the music for *Pas d'Acier* – Winnaretta was apparently unmoved. She distributed her largesse where she would, and with majestic assurance. Secretly Winnaretta must have deplored the hypocrisy of many of her guests and grantees, but her disapproval was likely to show in the form of dry wit, or not at all. She gave little away except money. When the gossiping audience at one of her concerts threatened to drown out the music with their whisperings, or if an ensemble of baroque instruments drove her guests to the lavish offering of the buffet table long before *The Musical Offering* was over, Winnaretta's only reaction might be to instruct the musicians privately to play the same piece again. She would then ask her naive *invités* which composition they preferred, and pretend to take their replies seriously.

Dedicated to creating an interest in baroque music, the Princesse inevitably sought out the leading exponent of the eighteenth-century repertoire, Wanda Landowska. The Polish harpsichordist sorely tested Winnaretta's forbearance by having an affair – a seduction for the love of seduction – with Violet Trefusis, now in exile in Paris, and Tante Winnie's own favorite of the moment. Here was a formidable challenge to Winnaretta's innate diplomacy and generosity of spirit – but generosity and diplomacy did prevail. The salon and its princess survived all subterranean intrigues and surface outrages. Possibly the spice of sexual adventuring lent an extra ingredient to that recipe for patronage the Princesse de Polignac subscribed to: social standing, independent wealth, and a need to know and sustain the creatively gifted.

Behind the glacial façade of a Victorian *grande dame*, Winnaretta displayed an unexpected wit and enjoyed a private sense of fun. To tease and possibly embarrass her, the mischievous Cocteau had inserted a slighting reference to *machines à coudre* in one of *Six Poèmes de Cocteau* set to music by Maxime Jacob. Immediately after the performance a straight-faced and sincere hostess praised Cocteau for his excellent verses. When a rival patron of impeccable bloodlines but declining fortune complained, 'My name is as good as Polignac,' Winnaretta replied: 'Not at the bottom of a check.'

CHAPTER TWELVE

The Left Bank of Lesbos

I f the spirit of Lesbos pervaded the important salons of the 1920s, the lesbian aura was never more evident than at 20 rue Jacob, in the faubourg St-Germain. Surely the most uninhibited of the Sapphic muses was Natalie Barney, a wealthy American who had resided in France since the turn of the century. Never as attractive as many of her conquests, Natalie was nevertheless an attraction – to men as well as to a veritable harem of women – her great mass of hair held loosely with pins, and liable to flow freely as the pins fell. White was her color: soft white flowing gowns by Lanvin and Schiaparelli, a white fox fur piece draped from her shoulder. She was forthright in her pursuit of feminine partners, a determined hedonist, a lover obsessed with conquest.

As a child, Natalie had hovered in the vicinity of the studio where her adored mother, the portraitist Alice Pike Barney, painted some of the loveliest ladies of Washington society, and where Natalie was once called upon to massage the stiffened flesh and muscles of a weary sitter. This was her first erotic experience: she became adept at the art of massage, her touch described as hypnotic, a comforting and arousing debut to a seduction. 'Men have skin,' Natalie wrote, 'but women have flesh – flesh that takes and gives light.'

Natalie was so fascinated by her beautiful mother that she lay at night in torment until she received her bedtime kiss, a scene reminiscent of Proust's nightly anticipation of that same maternal benediction and prelude to sleep. Whatever the impulses and origins of her deviant sexuality, Natalie became a confirmed and unswerving lesbian, flamboyant in her unorthodoxy. Since France had no legal sanctions against homosexuality, Paris was almost a predestined choice of sanctuary, the one place where Natalie Barney could so naturally be herself.

Because of her daily riding in the Bois de Boulogne dressed in masculine attire, with black bow tie and bowler, she became known as the Amazon. Natalie acquired this title more formally when she became the Amazon in Rémy de Gourmont's *Lettres à l'Amazone*: Gourmont's odd passion for this notorious lover of women is more exalted than explained in his *Lettres*, but Natalie was flattered to be called Amazon, a role and title she assumed with pride. For her part, Natalie was devoted to the grotesque French recluse. Gourmont was slowly dying of lupus, a degenerative disease said to have been exacerbated by his allergy to the dust between the pages of the books he pored over at the Bibliothèque Nationale. The platonic friendship Natalie offered Gourmont was his only sustaining pleasure in the last years of his life.

To another platonic friend, Gabriele d'Annunzio, she explained, 'You are interested in women only from the waist down, while my interest in men is only from the neck up.' This would explain her attraction to Bernard Berenson as well, though Berenson in conversation with the writer Harold Acton claimed to have made love to Natalie Barney. This would not seem likely since Natalie signed her letters to him: 'You and I, BB – friends as only those who have not been lovers remain.' Berenson surely wanted matters otherwise, for he signed his letters, 'Yours as much as you will', and, 'I kiss your feet.'

Like the Princesse de Polignac, Natalie Barney was one of the principal personages of the Belle Epoque who then emerged from the chrysalis of wartime France to flourish in the same grand style during les Années Folles. Also like Winnaretta, Natalie was as French as an American can be. She was perfectly bilingual. Her verses – love poems for the most part – were written in French, for she spoke and wrote in French more often than in English. Natalie cultivated French writers almost exclusively until the wave of literary Americans arrived in France. She then had the privilege of introducing one culture to the other.

It was Ezra Pound's initial interest in Rémy de Gourmont that brought him to the door of 20 rue Jacob. Gourmont's writings went into eclipse during World War I; then the works were revived and reached an even larger public than the author had known in his lifetime, due in large measure to Pound's efforts. In exchange for knowing Gourmont through Miss Barney, Pound brought English and American writers to Natalie's salon. James Joyce, ever on the alert for a possible benefactor, allowed himself to be introduced to Miss Barney by Pound, though he detested salons in particular and society in general. (Natalie was of no material help – she offered her *convives* a generous hospitality and a background of culture, seldom cash – but Joyce met others in her circle who were helpful in the way he most needed.) Literature was the dominant note at Natalie's afternoons, rather than the music that permeated Winnaretta's mansion on the opposite bank.

Affecting a cape, boots and cocked hat – or dressed as a shepherd, Renée Vivien as her shepherdess – Natalie would take part in the performances at her own soirées. She arranged for Sapphic pageants or poetry readings, her guests in separate sets: those who came purely for lesbian frolics, those who sought culture exclusively. Transvestite playlets or masquerade balls took place in the drawing room until architects warned Natalie that the floor of her 300-year-old mansion might collapse. On mild summer evenings the gatherings were held outdoors in the rear garden sequestered by the walls of houses on rue Visconti and rue de Seine: 'a curtain of ivy over the walls, a huge tree in the courtyard which hung over the house – a lovely rambling garden with its eighteenth-century temple', as described by Natalie's intimate friend Bettina Bergery. The mock Greek temple was called the Temple à l'Amitié, a Mediterranean motif suggestive of the isle of Lesbos and altogether appropriate to the pageants performed on its steps.

Although Mata Hari's prewar belly dances were presented to an all-female audience in the enclosed courtyard, not all the garden rites were restricted to so exclusive a gathering. To a mixed audience Paul Valéry might read his *La Jeune Parque* or Colette preview her 1922 play *La Vagabonde*, with Paul Poiret playing opposite her. Before Virgil Thomson fell in with Gertrude Stein he was a member of Natalie's salon, and played and sang his own music at the Temple à l'Amitié.

Refreshment at these entertainments was likely to be tea, with cake and sandwiches – only at the end of the Twenties did Natalie see fit to serve champagne. She finally conceded to gin and whisky 'when the Americans came', but drink was not the object of attending Miss Barney's afternoons or soirées. She shared with the Princesse de Polignac and Gertrude Stein a distaste for the bohemian habitués of café terraces. 'I suppose Miss Barney has at some time been in a café,' said Richard Aldington, 'but she is not the kind of person you would think of inviting to such a place.' Aside from offering her home as a place of sexual rendezvous, Natalie Barney was imbued with higher-minded motives than entertaining the cabaret set.

She was at home to those whom society generally excludes: sexual rebels and cultural revolutionaries. Ezra Pound, who shared Natalie's literary interests, could feel as comfortable at the Temple à l'Amitié as Romaine Brooks, the painter who shared Natalie's erotic tastes. The house and its quaint garden – where little sun penetrated, the fountain choked with sea-green plants – was a very special sanctuary for a varied collection of soul mates. Sylvia Beach might gently tease Paul Valéry for his need to frequent Miss Barney's salon, but the poet admitted he wanted to hear the muted sounds of distinguished repartee after a day's grueling thought-work, and the friendly clink of teacups in a crowded drawing-room.

Whatever good works were accomplished at 20 rue Jacob, the guiding deity of Miss Barney's crowded establishment was Eros. Natalie could never resist a beautiful face and form: she claimed to have been the lover of over forty women – and without being pressed would name names. In her *Souvenirs indiscrets* Natalie tells of her first glimpse of the demimondaine Liane de Pougy riding in her carriage in the Bois de Boulogne. Immediately Natalie determined to seduce one of the most famous courtesans of the Belle Epoque – to save Liane, as she expressed it, from a life of degradation at the hands of men. Against all odds, the young American upstart did seduce the worldly Parisienne: the two women enjoyed a clandestine love affair while concurrently Liane followed the métier of *grande horizontale* for her socially prominent gentlemen.

Another of Natalie's early conquests was the lovely, ephemeral Renée Vivien. Theirs was one of the grand passions of the period just before the Great War; but Natalie was an inconstant lover, forever collecting new women to add to her indiscreet souvenirs. Renée suffered from what she considered a series of betrayals. She died, it was said, of love for Natalie – but it would seem that Renée Vivien was already marked for death before she met Natalie, languishing in the midst of life, gradually expiring from an anorexia of the spirit.

The American painter Romaine Brooks was another of Natalie's on and off favorites for many years: theirs was as close as any to a stable and continuing relationship, perhaps a reminder of the intimacy and excitement of Alice Pike Barney's atelier – for Romaine was also a portrait painter, specializing exclusively in portraits of women. Romaine had weathered a torrid love affair with the Princesse de Polignac, and with Natalie managed to make the transition from lover to intimate friend that Renée Vivien had failed to do.

Although Romaine detested large gatherings, she consented to serve as co-hostess at Natalie's Friday afternoons, or at a Persian dinner (a small boy out of sight behind the skylight scattered flower petals on the guests below), while Natalie flirted with every pretty young thing in sight. Once pressed by Natalie to converse with a neglected guest,

Natalie Barney and a room in her Temple
a l'Amitié.

Romaine protested: 'How can I talk to her, she has such ugly arms?' Romaine affected masculine dress, her medium-cropped hair tucked into a modified top hat. She painted Natalie in a variety of elegantly transvestite costumes. Besides appearing in Romaine's portraits, Natalie was the model for Evangeline Musset in Djuna Barnes's *Ladies Almanach* and Valerie Seymour in Radclyffe Hall's long-suppressed *The Well of Loneliness*.

When Oscar Wilde's niece Dolly appeared at one of Natalie Barney's masques disguised as her uncle, Janet Flanner remarked that her sad equine face was the image of Oscar Wilde's, looking 'both important and earnest'. Dolly resembled her uncle in other respects, breaking the sexual taboos of the age, risking all in compromising entanglements. She too fell in love with the Amazon of rue Jacob. Natalie was a drug whom Dolly – already addicted to alcohol and cocaine – could not resist: on one occasion she slit her wrists on Natalie's account. After she again attempted suicide by taking an overdose of sleeping pills, Natalie sent her housekeeper Berthe to sit the rest of the night at Dolly's bedside. Finally Natalie bought the impoverished Dolly Wilde a ticket to London, to rid herself of a cast-off lover.

As soon as Dolly was dispatched, Natalie went to her favorite *patisserie*, Rumpelmayer's, as a solace and celebration to the end of an affair. While enjoying a rich *mousse au chocolat*, Natalie looked up to see Dolly Wilde enter Rumpelmayer's like a ghost returned to haunt her. Dolly's face was running with tears: she had changed her mind, she simply could not leave the city where Natalie dwelt. When she sat down, Natalie joined her in a good cry – the reunited lovers wept together into the *mousse*.

Despite her consuming passion for women, Natalie found time for sporadic and capricious support of art and artists. As a reaction against the male-dominated Académie Française, Natalie founded an Académie des Femmes, to offer support to women in pursuit of literary careers.

Another of her projects was establishing bursaries to subsidize individual writers, like Valéry. Ezra Pound suggested a venture to relieve T. S. Eliot of his onerous job at Barclay's Bank so that he might devote full time to poetry. Miss Barney was to offer the initial donation, the remaining funds to be subscribed through a society known as Bel Esprit. According to Ernest Hemingway, who was recruited away from Gertrude Stein's rival salon, you either had *bel esprit* or you did not.

Pound solicited Hemingway's help in collecting subscriptions. The imprint on the society's stationery was a logo of the Temple à l'Amitié in Natalie Barney's garden, symbol of the spirit behind the enterprise. Hemingway accepted his fund-raising obligation with little enthusiasm, but he admired Pound and was willing to assist in the altruistic scheme despite a supercilious attitude about Greek temples in Left Bank gardens and saving poets from banks. When the society collapsed (Eliot escaped his bank job by other means, with the help of an English patron), Hemingway took the money he had put aside for Bel Esprit to the racetrack at Enghien, where he wagered all on a drugged horse in a steeplechase, and lost.

Of Natalie Barney's own verse, Ezra Pound gave mixed notices. Her writing, he thought, was the product of mental laziness, full of unfinished sentences and broken paragraphs, lit by an occasional sublime comment: the style was elaborately Edwardian. Pound reviewed her 1920 *Pensées d'une Amazone* as a favor, but got at the heart of the Amazon's weakness by quoting one of her own lines: 'Having got out of life, oh having got out of it perhaps more than it contained.'

But Natalie Barney devoted far more energy and enthusiasm to her collection of *intimes* than to her collections of verse. She was completely loyal to her friends, and all-forgiving. When Paul Valéry became a member of the Académie Française in 1925, and once in that exalted circle dropped out of Natalie's, she resisted the impulse to comment. Besides, there were so many others for whom she could play devoted hostess: Ford Madox Ford, Djuna Barnes, Anna de Noailles, Sherwood Anderson, Isadora Duncan, Sinclair Lewis, Marie Laurencin, the Princesse Marthe Bibesco – and once, briefly, Marcel Proust. The journalist Morrill Cody said that visiting Natalie Barney's salon may have been a bore, but was part of one's education. With his lips poised over Natalie's fingers, Anatole France murmured: 'I kiss your hand with sacred terror', but André Gide declined even that formal gesture. 'Miss Barney', said Gide, 'is one of the few people one ought to see – if one had time'.

*

Since Gertrude Stein and Natalie Barney presided over rival Left Bank salons, it would seem that neither would 'have time' to see the other – in fact, they were wary acquaintances and sometime friends.

Gertrude could hardly refuse an invitation to Natalie's subaqueous garden to hear a tribute to herself read by Ford Madox Ford on the steps of the Temple à l'Amitié. (A similar speech was delivered at a Sylvia Beach soirée by Edith Sitwell, meant as a eulogy to Gertrude Stein, during which Gertrude's name was not once mentioned.) Both Gertrude and Natalie were inordinately fond of chocolate. The two might take tea at Rumpelmayer's together, but there was no intimacy between them, certainly no weeping into the *mousse au chocolat*. Natalie once said of Gertrude and Alice: 'I am afraid the "bigger one" who gets fatter and fatter will devour her [Alice Toklas]. She looks so thin.' Yet Natalie's notes to Gertrude reflect an admiration almost obsequious in her characteristically florid style. It would seem Natalie Barney's eagerness for a stronger relationship with Gertrude Stein resembled Bernard Berenson's invocation to Natalie: 'Yours as much as you will.'

But of the three Sapphic patrons of the 1920s, Gertrude Stein was the only one who remained monogamous. It was not Gertrude who was likely to devour Alice: in many respects Alice had the stronger will, and in private was dictator of the ménage. In public Alice assumed the role of diplomat-companion, screening Gertrude from wives, discouraging hangers-on, seldom venturing a remark as long as Gertrude held the floor. Alice's subservient position was only the outer face of her relationship with Gertrude. The devotion of one to the other was unassailable, their alliance a commitment for life. When the ladies of the rue de Fleurus visited 20 rue Jacob, it was not to fall in with Natalie Barney's promiscuous pairing-off.

Alice might go off to the kitchen to chat with the housekeeper, Madame Berthe. The two excellent cooks compared notes on the rue de Buci market, where to go for beetroot and the best price for butter. (Madame Berthe's recipe for Rumanian sauté of veal and mixed vegetables appeared in the *Alice B. Toklas Cookbook*.) Meanwhile, Gertrude sat impassively in her heavy clothes whatever the weather, knees apart and feet planted solidly, like a monument to herself. She might or might not acknowledge the presence of someone brought forward to meet her. A curt nod of the head was as much of a greeting as a new acquaintance was due – this was Natalie Barney's circle, and not her own. Gertrude Stein's head, nodding or not – already sculpted by Jo Davidson and Jacques Lipchitz – was impressive. By the mid-Twenties her hair had been trimmed close to the skull by Alice, for Gertrude had much admired the short-cropped hair style worn by the Duchesse de Clermont-Tonnerre. When she had worn her hair in a bun at the top of her head, as in the Lipchitz bust, Hemingway said she

Gertrude Stein *chez elle* on the rue de Fleurus. Picasso's portrait hangs on the wall behind her.

looked like an Italian peasant; with her hair cut short as a man's, she resembled a Roman emperor.

This was the period when Gertrude Stein's reputation was spreading beyond the boundaries of the Left Bank arrondissements. After the years of being almost alone in taking herself seriously, homage was being paid to her by the literati of England and America. The mockery and tittering over her lines had grown fainter, though she was still called the Mother Goose of Montparnasse.

In 1925 Robert McAlmon published *The Making of Americans* in his Contact Editions, the first serious effort to bring her work to the reading public. Since both author and publisher were capable of misunderstanding an understanding, each accused the other of bad faith. Gertrude was particularly sensitive to the uses of publicity – having been a successful promoter of the arts, and herself, all her life – and resented McAlmon's slack way of publicizing and distributing *The Making of Americans*. McAlmon thought Miss Stein high-handed about finances and author's copies, for someone who had an independent income. Actually, Gertrude's income from a trust fund came to approximately $150 per month, a more than adequate sum on which to live in franc-depressed Paris, but hardly in a class with Natalie Barney's wealth or the fortune at the disposal of the Princesse de Polignac. At any rate, McAlmon had begun to sour on the geniuses he published: he denigrated the work of James Joyce and Ernest Hemingway, and published his own collection of tales, *The Hasty Bunch* – a title given to him by James Joyce – almost as a counter-revolutionary gesture. In a moment of weakness, Gertrude Stein did once confess to McAlmon: 'Sometimes I wonder how anybody can read my work when I look it over after a time. It seems quite meaningless to me.'

Through McAlmon, the poet William Carlos Williams met Gertrude Stein while on a sabbatical from his medical practice, living in Paris and writing poetry. Williams was not one of the writers who came to sit at the feet of Gertrude Stein. Brusque and outspoken, he replied to her question about what to do with her accumulated manuscripts: 'If they were mine, having so many, I should probably select what I thought were the best and throw the rest in the fire.'

After a stunned silence, Gertrude said, 'But of course, Doctor, writing is not your métier.'

'But Doctor Stein' (Gertrude had studied medicine at Johns Hopkins), 'are you sure writing is your métier?'

Of this Gertrude Stein was certain: writing was not only her métier, she was a genius at it. Genius was a word she used frequently, perhaps carelessly. 'It takes a lot of time being a genius, you have to sit around so much doing nothing.' But doing nothing was not just doing nothing: 'A genius is a genius, even when he does not work.' She could count the geniuses of her time on fewer than the fingers of one hand – or Alice, speaking for Gertrude, could count them: Alfred North Whitehead, Pablo Picasso and Gertrude Stein. Considering the centuries outside her own, Gertrude once announced to Robert McAlmon: 'Yes, the Jews have produced only three originative geniuses: Christ, Spinoza and myself.' Provocative statements were her forte. If Gertrude Stein's experimental writings did not excite sufficient controversy, her grandiose proclamations would.

The argument in the art world had less to do with genius than with the question: was Gertrude Stein an important talent or an incredible fraud? T. S. Eliot, turning down her work for the *Criterion* in England, wrote: 'It is very fine, but not for us.' In a malicious chapter about Gertrude and Alice in *A Moveable Feast*, Hemingway grudgingly admitted: '*Melanctha* was very good...she had also discovered many truths about rhythms and the use of words in repetition that were valid and valuable and she talked well about them.' There was some evidence that Gertrude Stein had discovered an ingenious mode of expression, but that what she expressed was unreliable. In the literary enclave of London, Edith Sitwell was a lukewarm defender: she thought Gertrude 'was verbally very interesting', then added, 'the more so as she invariably got everybody wrong'.

That she had got everybody wrong was a near-unanimous opinion of the painters Gertrude no longer saw. Reassessing her value to the Fauvist and Cubist era before the war, Matisse declared that Gertrude Stein 'understood nothing' about art, and Braque said: 'For one who poses as an authority on the epoch it is safe to say she never went beyond the stage of tourist'. Her former friends became her severest critics, as if they had forgotten how important Gertrude Stein was to them in the beginning. Their paintings hung first on the walls of her atelier, and only after being displayed at 27 rue de Fleurus were these works well and truly acknowledged by the world at large. In a sense, Gertrude Stein discovered their discoveries with them: she was one of the first to buy and champion the paintings of Matisse, Braque and Picasso.

Her bitterest quarrel with Picasso erupted over the death of Juan Gris in 1927. Gertrude accused Picasso of not having truly loved the painter; Picasso maintained that he had loved Gris as much or more than Gertrude ever had. Both had forgotten or ignored how they turned away from Gris after the war. Gris had gone on painting in the Cubist manner which no longer interested Gertrude; he was something of an embarrassment to Picasso, who shunned his company as a reminder of the obscurity they had shared at the Bateau Lavoir. But Gertrude Stein had the last word by proclaiming her affection in the literary portrait, *The Life and Death of Juan Gris*.

Another falling-away was with Ernest Hemingway, who no longer played the devoted pupil eagerly seeking Gertrude's literary advice. The pupil was becoming better known than the instructor, an intolerable situation for Gertrude. Still, Hemingway 'made the necessary appearances ... and waited dismissal with most of the other men friends when that epoch came and the new friends moved in'.

In the second half of the decade the new friends moved in. These were a group of painters known as Neo-romanticists, including the Russian émigrés Pavlik Tchelitchev and brothers Eugene and Leonid Berman; Kristians Tonny from Holland, and Frenchman Christian Bérard. Mixed with the painters were two poets: Georges Hugnet – who had established his own publishing outlet, Editions de la Montagne – and the surrealist René Crevel. Gertrude referred to the group as 'the young men of 26', for most were 26 when she met them. 'It became the period of being twenty-six. During the next two or three years all the young men were twenty-six years old. It was the right age apparently for that time and place.'

An American, Bravig Imbs, joined the entourage. He was another of the aspiring novelists working for the Paris edition of the *Chicago Tribune*; he also had ambitions to become a great composer, and studied with the avant-garde composer George Antheil. 'His aim was to please,' was Gertrude Stein's summary of Imbs's character, but if his aim was to please Gertrude he simply followed in the tradition of the young men of 26. The adulation of this new circle of friends was remarkable even by Gertrude Stein's high standards. The young men were in frantic competition for her attention and favor.

Although Gertrude sporadically collected the work of her newly-discovered painters, it was difficult to know if she took their Neo-romanticism seriously. Gradually, or abruptly, she rid herself of the collection when the paintings 'began to disappear into the walls'. In Gertrude's opinion, the great moment of painting had passed – easel painting had become a minor art. She may have been justified in her analysis, at least in the case of her own entourage. Tchelitchev, Bérard, and Eugene Berman were to achieve wider fame as theatrical designers; 'Bébé' Bérard became a standby of the Cocteau set, designing costumes and settings for the masked balls given by titled socialites.

Never was Gertrude as gossipy, malicious and manipulative as with the young men of 26. She incited or approved of their petty quarrels and professional jealousies. While Alice sat sphinx-like with her embroidery and her private assessments of the young men, Gertrude delighted in baiting them, then watching them conspire for the limelight and compete for her attention. She shushed, but tacitly approved, Hugnet's snide comments about the others; she encouraged Tchelitchev's jealousy of Bérard and listened with relish to Bravig Imbs's colorful account of Tonny hurling insults at Bérard.

Gertrude Stein was not much attracted to music, but Alice Toklas loved dancing, so they had attended a performance of Stravinsky's *The Rite of Spring*, as much for the scandal it had aroused as for the music itself: 'one literally could not, throughout the whole performance, hear the sound of music.' A measure of Gertrude's musical taste was that she preferred *The Trail of the Lonesome Pine* to any other piece of music, and played it over and over on a wind-up gramophone. Nevertheless, she had heard of George Antheil by way of Bravig Imbs, and was aware of his *succès de scandale* with a score for Léger's film *Ballet Mécanique* first performed at Shakespeare and Company. Gertrude informed Sylvia Beach she would like to meet the young composer. When Gertrude Stein expressed a desire to meet a young poet or painter or musician it was the same as a royal summons. Antheil went along to the rue de Fleurus willingly enough, but he brought along a friend and fellow composer, Virgil Thomson. Alice did not much care for either of these two young Americans, but Gertrude became interested in Thomson when she discovered he had read and liked her *Tender Buttons*. Antheil received a limp handshake goodbye and was never invited back – he moved on to Natalie Barney's salon the following year. When Virgil Thomson proposed to set Gertrude Stein's poem *Susie Asado* to music, and when he was seen bearing a golden yellow grapefruit – 'The first of the season' – to 27 rue de Fleurus, he had become a member, at age 30, of the young men of 26.

CHAPTER THIRTEEN

Etudes

Invariably there was an older figure, an established and knowing presence, to whom the fledgling writers, painters, and composers turned when they arrived in Paris. For Virgil Thomson the lodestar was Gertrude Stein. 'Gertrude and I got along like Harvard men,' he declared, an echo of Hemingway's statement that he and Gertrude were just like brothers. Thomson got on well with older women, and even managed to charm the initially hostile Alice Toklas. Before the decade was out, Virgil Thomson and Gertrude Stein would collaborate on the opera *Four Saints in Three Acts*, but by the time Thomson was setting her words to music, he and Gertrude were no longer on speaking terms.

In 1921 Virgil Thomson was a member of the touring Harvard Glee Club, and after singing with the choral group in Paris he fell in love with the city and stayed on. 'I had become a Parisian instantaneously,' he wrote. 'Paris was where I felt most at home.'

At first Thomson was able to survive by piecemeal journalism: he wrote about music and musical events for *The Boston Transcript*, then became a freelance correspondent for *Vanity Fair*, *The New Republic*, *American Mercury*, and *The Dial*. While Gertrude Stein might encourage her followers and admirers in a number of ways, she was not inclined to distribute largesse in the form of commissions. Nonetheless, Thomson found financial support on the opposite bank of the Seine, from Mrs Christian Gross, wife of the First Secretary of the American Embassy. Heiress to a sugar fortune, Mrs Gross was known to be extraordinarily naive in the uses of money. When she purchased the necklace of Catherine the Great from Cartier's, she concluded the transaction by asking shyly if she could pay at the end of the month. She was fond of music and interested in musicians: she offered Thomson a commission of $500 for a composition of his own choosing, and the young composer

Virgil Thomson and Gertrude Stein, 1927.

set to work. Before he could deliver the piece in completed form, Mrs Gross seemed to have vanished. Later Thomson discovered she had left her vast apartment on avenue Charles-Floquet, abandoned her diplomat husband, and eloped with a Mexican. Luckily she had not waited until the end of the month to pay Thomson his commission.

By 1924 another older woman came to Thomson's aid: Louise Langlois, who at forty was already living in semi-seclusion in her boulevard St-Germain apartment. Marcel Duchamp – himself something of a recluse now that he had given up painting for chess – shared her twilight world with an occasional rubber of bridge. She was cared for by a Russian companion who always addressed her as *princesse*. 'Ever jealous, ever rewarding,' Louise Langlois granted Thomson a monthly stipend of 4,000 francs so that he could continue his music without financial pressure.

During his first years in Paris, Virgil Thomson lived in the still gaslit rue de Berne, part of a warren of streets named for European cities spoked out behind the gare St-Lazare. His furnished flat had the rare convenience of a working piano. There were no complaints from other tenants over the late-night practice and composition on the piano: the house was otherwise occupied by prostitutes.

Thomson spoke for many of his generation when he said: 'We had all had music teachers who had been formed in Germany or by Germans, and it was time to get out of that.' To study in the Paris of Debussy, Ravel, and Satie – where Stravinsky and Prokofiev continued to extend musical frontiers – was the immediate goal of young Americans with a need to express new music.

An extraordinary teacher of harmony and counterpoint, Nadia Boulanger, was one of the principal reasons why Paris was so important to young composers. At the American Conservatory of Music, opened in Fontainebleau in 1921, Mlle Boulanger (daughter of a Frenchman and the Russian Princess Mychetsky) helped form and launch the first wave of modern composers America had produced. Virgil Thomson studied with her as early as 1921, and Aaron Copland was the first American to enroll in her class at Fontainebleau. From 1926 until 1929 Roy Harris studied with her, and considered those formative years in Paris 'the best thing I ever did'. Harris had been driving a truck before he came to Paris: his will was as strong as Mlle Boulanger's, and there was a clash of temperaments, but no lack of respect on either side. It was through Nadia Boulanger's efforts that Harris's *Concerto for Piano*,

Clarinet, and String Quartet was given its first performance in Paris. Nadia not only put her students through a rigorous training in musical theory and composition (it was her formal French lycée approach to instruction that Roy Harris rebelled against, and then Nadia would resort to Russian tantrums or tears), but she inspired them to create daring new work of their own, then arranged for this experimental music to be heard in concert. When Igor Markevitch studied with her he was only sixteen, the only student in her class at l'Ecole Normale de Musique still wearing knee pants, half in love with his exciting and excitable teacher trying to hide her femininity behind a pair of authoritarian pince-nez.

In the spring of 1926 a landmark concert of all-American chamber music was presented in Paris under Nadia Boulanger's direction. Included among the works by Thomson, Copland, Walter Piston, Herbert Elwell, and Theodore Chanler was a composition by the only one of the important young American composers not to have been a member of the 'Boulangerie', George Antheil.

At 22 George Antheil was short and delicate-looking, his light hair worn in Fauntleroy bangs, but he made up for his sweet-natured appearance by an unexpected bravado and a series of musical compositions each more outrageous than the last. He went farther than most in his deliberate attempt to *épater le bourgeois*: when playing for a concert of his own music he carried a pistol in an inside pocket of his evening jacket; before he sat down to play he took out the revolver and placed it on the piano top.

Antheil's idol was Igor Stravinsky, whose music was so important an influence on his own work that Honneger remarked, on first hearing a piece by Antheil, 'I prefer my Stravinsky straight'. Antheil and Stravinsky met while both were traveling in Germany: the unusual young American and his outré compositions impressed the Russian; Stravinsky even went to the trouble to arrange a first concert for Antheil in Paris, and notified him by cable to Hungary – but Antheil had fallen in love with a Hungarian girl and kept putting off his return to Paris until six months had passed. The concert was canceled. When Antheil finally did come back to Paris with Böske, Sylvia Beach was so completely charmed by the young couple she allowed them the use of the small flat above her bookstore, which Antheil entered, when he had forgotten his key, by swinging to the upper storey by way of the Shakespeare and Company sign.

Americans in Paris: (right, l. to r.)
composers Virgil Thomson,
Herbert Elwell, Walter Piston,
Aaron Copland. Their mentor in
Paris was Nadia Boulanger
(below).

George Antheil (opposite) entering his room above Shakespeare and Company the ha

Antheil also attracted the attention of Ezra Pound, who urged the composer to write two sonatas for his mistress, the violinist Olga Rudge. Pound was an amateur bassoonist and, along with an incredible range of diverse interests, had become a first-time composer of a short opera on François Villon. At the premier of *Villon*, Antheil played the score for harpsichord, an instrument ill-suited to his sense of dynamic percussion. So impressed was Pound by the original direction taken by Antheil that he wrote *Antheil and the Treatise on Harmony* to explain his music to the uninitiated.

Although Gertrude Stein had snubbed him, Antheil did find a warmer reception at Natalie Barney's salon, where his *First String Quartet* was presented: 'What they made of it I often wonder,' said Antheil, 'for this particular little quartet was by no means a mild number.'

Audiences at an Antheil concert usually made known 'what they made of it'. The Ballets Suédois offered Antheil the opportunity to play three of his short piano sonatas as a curtain raiser (in front of Léger's Cubist curtain) to their October 1923 ballet performance. Rioting broke out almost as soon as Antheil appeared on stage – a calculated ploy by the Ballets Suédois, in order to stir up a burst of publicity for the rest of the program. The Surrealists in the audience took Antheil's side, but not in a civilized enough manner to prevent their being arrested by the police. Satie, too, tried to applaud above the hissing and clamor, then called out, 'What precision, what precision!'.

Antheil's most famous – or infamous – work was the *Ballet Mécanique*, performed in 1925 at the Salle Pleyel under the direction of Antheil's student, Bravig Imbs – for the composer was out of Paris at the time, and the music was registered on piano rolls. James Joyce attended the concert, and although he was not a lover of modern music offered the opinion that the composition was much like Mozart, and even requested to hear the second roll played again. A full-scale performance of the *Ballet Mécanique* included eight pianos as well as an airplane motor: the roaring propellor was said to have blown off the wigs of women in the audience, but more likely only their hats were dislodged. Again, the police were obliged to subdue the riot.

By 1926 a reaction had set in. There was some truth in the claim that George Antheil had been made too much a *cause célèbre*, and nothing bored the restless public of the 1920s more than last year's riot. In his autobiography, Antheil admitted he may have gone too far too fast as

Bad Boy of Music. Audiences were not staying around long enough to hiss, or stage a free-for-all. For the Antheil–Copland concert of 10 May 1926, Irving Schwerke offered a wry comment by way of review in the Paris edition of the *Chicago Tribune*: 'The hall, which held a large audience at the beginning of the concert, held a small one at the end.'

When Antheil returned to the US in 1927, his Carnegie Hall concert was a failure: his career as a composer – except for Hollywood film music – went into decline. For a time he wrote a column of advice to the lovelorn, out of a theory he had evolved concerning the secretions of the endocrine glands.

SALLE du CONSERVATOIRE

2, rue du Conservatoire — Paris

Mardi 11 Décembre à 21 h.

OLGA RUDGE
violoniste

GEORGE ANTHEIL
compositeur

Donneront le programme suivant:

I
1 Plainte pour la mort du roi Richart Cœur de Lion XII siècle *Gaucelm Faidit* air déchiffré par Ezra Pound du manuscrit R. 71 superiore, Ambrosiana
2 Gavotte *J. S. Bach*
3 Sujet pour violon (resineux) *Ezra Pound*
Olga RUDGE

II
Ire Sonate pour violon et piano *G. Antheil* allegro moderate;-andante moderato, funèbre, presto
Première audition, l'auteur au piano violon, Olga RUDGE

III
Concerto en la majeur *Mozart* allegro-aperto, adagio, rondo,
Olga RUDGE et George ANTHEIL

IV
2me sonate pour violon et piano *G. Antheil* allegro - mechanico
Première audition, l'auteur au piano violon, Olga RUDGE

Prix des billets : 25, 15, 10 et 5 francs

DIRECTION : Bureau International des Concerts, C. Klesgen & E. C. Delaet, 47, rue Blanche, Trudaine 20-62

On trouve des billets

Salle du Conservatoire, 2 bis rue du Conservatoire; Durand & Cie 4, place de la Madeleine; Bureau Musical, 32, rue Tronchet Guide-Billets, 20, avenue de l'Opéra; Roudanez, 9, rue de Médicis; C. Klesgen & E.-C. Delaet, 47, rue Blanche; Typographie François Bernouard, 73, rue des Saints-Pères.

Five of Les Six, grouped around the pianist Marcelle Meyer (kneeling on chair), with the bespectacled conductor Jean Wiener and their early spokesman Jean Cocteau (standing far right). The composers are (l. to r.) Germaine Tailleferre, Darius Milhaud, Arthur Honegger, Francis Poulenc, and Georges Auric (seated right).

CHAPTER FOURTEEN

The Ox on the Roof

During the first theatrical season after the war, Jean Cocteau and Darius Milhaud concocted a circus-ballet, opera-bouffe called *Le Boeuf sur le Toit*, presented by the Fratellini Brothers at the Théâtre des Arts. 'Cocteau's little joke' enjoyed a certain success, especially with his own crowd of Right Bank socialites and Left Bank intellectuals. Also, Darius Milhaud's score, the antics of a troupe from the Cirque Médrano, and a pastiche of colorful sets by Raoul Dufy, enlivened an otherwise bleak February of 1920.

Le Boeuf might have disappeared from the jargon of the Twenties as soon as it faded from the stage if Milhaud had not had the idea to bring together Moysès, the barman who catered to the theatrical crowd, and Cocteau of the bird-like countenance and wire-brush hair, stage-manager to society. (Picasso spitefully remarked to Gertrude Stein that Jean Cocteau was getting to be very popular in Paris, 'so popular that you could find his poems on the table of any smart coiffeur'.) Milhaud suggested that writers and artists had their own cafés and bars, why not a cabaret devoted to musicians and composers?

Cocteau advised Moysès to rid himself of the customers who patronized le Gaya, but to keep Jean Wiener at the jazz piano. Wiener was later joined by Clément Doucet, whose father had invented a complicated harmonium that reproduced the sounds of piano, organ, violin and flute: fewer than one hundred models were ever sold; only Clément Doucet, the demonstrator-salesman, had ever managed to play the instrument.

Since Dada was the current rage, the cabaret was rechristened Le Boeuf sur le Toit. The décor was spartan and Dada-inspired: Dadaists left souvenir sketches on the wall, and the centerpiece, flanked by bottles behind the bar, was Picabia's communal-effort *L'Oeil cacodylate* (cacodylate being the salts used in the treatment of venereal disease), inscribed by leading, and casual, Dadaists of the day. Marcel Herrand sang their theme song, 'Dada-Dada': 'Mangez du chocolat, buvait du lait d'oiseau ...' ('Eat chocolate, drink bird's milk ...'). As Cocteau promised, Les Six and their friends assembled at Le Boeuf sur le Toit: Milhaud, Poulenc and Auric joined Wiener for nightly jam sessions that attracted jazz enthusiasts to the cabaret, which became suddenly and almost inexplicably the in-café of the decade. The rue Duphot bar became so crowded that Moysès was obliged to move to larger but still cramped quarters at 28 rue Boissy-d'Anglas.

A 1925 guidebook spoke of Le Boeuf as 'the work of Jean Cocteau, its godfather: the wildest fantasy within the finest of established traditions. At the Boeuf one encounters the artistic trend of the moment, the literary trend of the moment, and, briefly, the *trend* of the moment, whatever it may be.' Tourists began to arrive, for the ambience and the 24-franc table d'hôte dinner; by midnight the late-shift newsmen had poured in, along with the theater crowd and Cocteau's own eclectic following. Businessmen, illustrators, circus performers, editors – le Tout-Paris in force – made the ritual pilgrimage to Le Boeuf. In that mélange, the Grand Duke Dimitri Pavlovich, the Dayang Muda and King Ferdinand of Rumania were minor royalty compared to Cocteau, who reigned supreme from midnight until dawn, beside him the eighteen-year-old novelist Raymond Radiguet, his crown prince.

Le Boeuf was the place to top off a night's café crawl: Robert McAlmon told of the evening he met Sari, a sixteen-year-old model, at the Dôme. 'It's no fun to be sixteen,' she said, 'and know too much about life.' McAlmon took her to Le Boeuf for gin fizzes and dancing: there, under Cocteau's suffering eye, she danced with Radiguet on the cramped dance floor. At nineteen, Radiguet made the comment: 'What I would like to know is at what age one has the right to say , "I have lived"?' The two teenagers, in the decade that knew too much about life, left together.

Radiguet was constantly slipping away from Cocteau for heterosexual rendezvous; even, it was said, with Cocteau's own patron and beloved friend, Coco Chanel.

The first time Radiguet visited Cocteau at 10 rue d'Anjou, the valet Cyprien announced: 'Il y a un enfant avec une canne.' The young author carried a cane with him always, wore a monocle, and supposedly shaved his head with an oyster shell. Cocteau received the 'child with a cane' in his cluttered room, carefully observing as he invariably did any visitor's reaction to his collection of jewels, postcards, pressed flowers, crystal ball, skull and blackboard. It was Cocteau who urged and finally forced Radiguet (by locking him in his room at the Hôtel Foyot) to complete his first novel *The Devil in the Flesh* at the age of twenty. The author did not survive his twenty-first birthday. A case of typhoid fever was mis-diagnosed as grippe, and he was treated with injections of *eau-de-mer*. He was said to have died in the arms of his Polish mistress at the Hôtel Foyot; in another version, chez Cocteau, who fed him all the alcohol he wanted 'so that he might go out unconscious, the way he had come into the world'. Actually, Radiguet died alone, in a private clinic, under the care of Diaghilev's personal physician, Dr Dalimier. After the death of Radiguet, Cocteau was called Le Veuf (the Widower) sur le Toit, but the Widower soon consoled himself in the company of such luminaries as Barbette, of the Cirque Médrano. Barbette was the sensation of several theatrical seasons at the Alhambra and the Casino de Paris: the transvestite performer from Round Rock, Texas, whose real name was Vander Clyde, did a graceful tightrope act as a lovely nymph in tights and ostrich feathers.

Only a few months before Radiguet's death in 1923, the dying Marcel Proust declared plaintively from his sickbed: 'If I could only be well enough to go once to the cinema, and to Le Boeuf sur le Toit.'

Fashion is a mysterious phenomenon: Moysès made the classic mistake of moving Le Boeuf to a third locale, still in the 8th arrondissement, only a few blocks away. Although Le Boeuf sur le Toit survived long past its heyday in the Twenties, the overflow trade did not follow Moysès to the rue de Penthièvre. Cocteau may have been responsible for putting the ox on Moysès's roof in the first place, but it is impossible to explain how the beast got down again.

*

Frequently among the congested patrons at Le Boeuf appeared a curious figure in stiff collar and *chapeau melon*, carrying an inevitable umbrella. If Cocteau served as spokesman and publicity agent for Les Six, the anachronistic Erik Satie – as privately remote as he seemed publicly accessible – was their honored patriarch. Georges Auric, Louis Durey, Arthur Honneger, Darius Milhaud, Francis Poulenc, Germaine Taillefaire, all had one thing in common: their devotion to the older Satie.

They had become known as Les Six 'because', said a music critic of the day, 'there were six of them'. Satie called them Les Nouveaux

Erik Satie.

Jeunes, and apparently reciprocated their affection – but he was a temperamental mentor whose moods and motives were difficult to fathom. Nevertheless, he led the way for these 'new young' to innovate and experiment in musical composition. Among themselves they were quite different in character and tastes: Poulenc and Taillefaire derived much of their music from the eighteenth-century baroque; Honneger was a devotee of Richard Wagner. Les Six might share a concert stage at the Salle Huyghens with Satie – the hall donated by a painter, the stove an instrument of suffocation no one could regulate – or gather round him at Le Boeuf, but not one of the young composers had ever crossed the threshold of Satie's humble quarters in Arceuil, nor had anyone else. For a quarter of a century the composer had lived in that unlikely suburb, the working-class periphery of Paris, in a grim building known as Four Chimneys. He might allow a friend to accompany him as far as the door, but no one was ever invited inside.

Satie had not always been a solitary or a semi-recluse. Before the war he had lived with the painter Suzanne Valadon, whom he called Biqui, but even this interval of bohemian domesticity disturbed the internal rhythm of his soul. He called upon the police – 'A woman,' he reported, 'has been forcing her attentions on me' – to have her evicted from the premises and from his life.

The Chat Noir was Le Boeuf sur le Toit for a previous generation, and Satie's eccentricities were celebrated even when he worked there as second pianist: he carried a hammer in his pocket for protection. 'I never take a bath,' he announced. 'You can only wash properly in little bits.' He used pumice stone instead of soap because 'it goes farther than soap'. By the early 1900s he had broken with the past – his own, and the musical past – and discarded the corduroy uniform of Montmartre for the dark suit of the bourgeoisie: false collar, *cravate*, pointed goatee, and pince-nez – an aspect that placed him at the turn of the century, while he composed music for the century ahead.

There were those who said his bizarre, often macabre, humor was meant to attract attention. Surely he did not endear himself to the occupants of an air-raid shelter when he entered during an alert, in his funereal garments, and announced, 'I have come to die with you.' His feuds were based on enmities and injuries known only to himself. He was much loved, but was an unpredictable and difficult friend. Maurice Sachs, chronicler of the Twenties, said of him: 'In spite of Satie's gentle mien, he could be terrible. His modesty hid bitterness, misery, fears, nerves, and loathings.' Georges Auric was astonished and shocked when Satie broke with him, for a reason or reasons never explained. He never spoke to Auric again. In these circumstances Satie's paranoia was most evident: friendships would come to an immediate end because of imagined insults or gestures only Satie would interpret as slights.

When Satie determined to drop out of the circus atmosphere of Montmartre-Montparnasse, he shut himself into the cell at Four Chimneys, incommunicado, as removed as on another planet from the pretensions and megalomania of fashionable bohemian life. He did not remain aloof from the Parisian hurly-burly consistently or for long. Le Boeuf sur le Toit was a favorite place of rendezvous, or Milhaud's apartment where Les Nouveaux Jeunes frequently met; or he might be seen in his fussily old-fashioned attire at the salon of the Princesse de Polignac. (When Satie presented *Socrate* chez Tante Winnie, he told the audience: 'Those who do not understand are asked to assume an attitude of submissiveness and inferiority.')

Regularly he took the trolley-bus into the heart of the great city from his dismal lodgings in Arceuil. Satie especially enjoyed an outing when it rained, for he loved the wet. (On one excursion he deliberately exposed his chest to the elements, and contracted bronchitis as a result – but this was when he was young, and was possibly a ploy to escape military service.) He acquired a collection of umbrellas, and was never seen without one.

A favorite haunt was the bookshop Shakespeare and Company. Sylvia Beach was charmed by the little man in black, with his pointed beard and sparkling but malicious eyes: he was invariably a delightful presence, even when he did not speak. She wondered why he would want to browse among her stacks of books in English, a language he did not read. He called her 'Mees', the only English she had ever heard him utter.

Satie's humor – refuge or subterfuge – extended to the music he composed. The early titles of piano pieces – *Trois Morceaux en forme de poire* and *Aperçus désagréables, pour quatre mains* – anticipated the playful taunting of the Dadaists. One of the reasons Satie's music was not always taken seriously at the time may have been because of titles like *Valse au chocolat aux amandes* and *Les Véritables Préludes flasques (pour chien)*. When Stravinsky turned down a commission to write a musical sequence on *Sports et divertissements* because the money was insufficient,

Satie accepted the assignment without a qualm, except that he thought he was being overpaid. He had little respect for the established musicians of his day, or the day before: he despised Wagner, and once said of Ravel, a sometime friend: 'Monsieur Ravel has refused the Légion d'Honneur, but all his music accepts it.' His mocking 'Conservatory Catechism' included such ironic commandments as: 'Dieubussy alone shalt thou adore, and copy most perfectly; Melodious never shalt thou be, in deed nor in consent', concluding with the injunction: 'Perfect harmony shalt thou not desire, except in marriage alone.'

Religion was a convenient secondary target for his barbed wit, yet Satie had at one time been interested in the arcane revelations of Joseph Péladan's Rosicrucianism, and composed an organ piece based on the theme of the Rosy Crucifixion.

At 51 Satie wrote the music for Cocteau's Cubist ballet *Parade*, which in 1917 set the world of music, and several other worlds, upside-down. Guillaume Apollinaire wrote the program notes for the opening performance; Picasso was engaged by Diaghilev for the sets and costumes. Cocteau wanted the sounds of everyday life interspersed with the music, and Satie provided a score for typewriter, ship's siren, the running spiel of a circus barker, and other sound effects, one of which resembled machine-gun fire, to the outrage of the audience – 1917 was the dreadful year of Verdun. Although Diaghilev had salted the audience with Russian soldiers on leave from their service with the French army (ostensibly to support their fellow nationals of the Ballets Russes), reaction was riotously negative, the whistling and verbal abuse drowning out the scattered applause. Cocteau overheard one spectator remark to his wife: 'If I had known it would be silly, I would have brought the children.'

When the critic Jean Pouieh wrote a damning review of *Parade*, Satie saw fit to reply on a postcard calling Pouieh *un cul* (buttocks, backside), and an unmusical *cul* at that. Pouieh sued for slander. The legal point was that the defamation was not delivered in a sealed letter, but on a postcard that anyone could read, therefore public. The judge ruled in favor of the critic, despite testimony for the defense by Braque, Léger, Derain and Apollinaire. Cocteau, enraged by the decision, made a scene in court – he was roughly hauled off by the police, and claimed to have been beaten up. On appeal, Satie was fined but did not have to serve the originally imposed prison term.

Satie did not write another ballet score for seven years after *Parade*, but he had become a legend to the younger generation of composers because of the radical break with tradition *Parade* inspired. When the ballet was restaged after the war, its reception was the reverse of the debut performance, a reaction so tepid that Diaghilev – perpetually concerned with the revolutionary – decided its time had passed, and *Parade* was dropped from the repertoire.

In 1924 Satie wrote *Relâche* for the Ballets Suédois, Diaghilev's arch-rival. This was a Dadaist production, including an entr'acte film by René Clair and Picabia – the title itself was a pun: *relâche* meaning the theater is temporarily closed. Since the opening was delayed, and a genuine 'Relâche' posted on the theater doors, the first night crowd – accustomed to the double-dealing Dadaists – thought the notice was a stunt and attempted to break into the empty theater. The police had to be called; they had to be called again for the legitimate opening night. Once more the audience reaction was an uproar of counterbalanced booing and applause: Satie had achieved another *succès de scandale*.

But the composer had only a month to live. The years of steadily drinking the roughest *clochard* wines had ravaged his liver, though he gave no apparent sign of his infirmity and drank as much as ever to the last. One January evening in 1925 Satie complained to friends that he did not have the strength to return to Arceuil that night. This was an unheard-of event, a rare admission. Man Ray found a room for him at the gathering-place of the Dadaists, the Hôtel Istria. Next day it was obvious that Satie was gravely ill. He was admitted to the Hôpital Saint-Joseph, rue Pierre-Larousse. His friend and patron, the Princesse de Polignac, was notified; she and the Comte Etienne de Beaumont made arrangements for the composer to have a private room: they would pay all medical expenses. Those friends who had not been excluded from his touchy *amitié* gathered regularly at his bedside. Although he had abandoned the Catholic faith of his childhood, nuns hovered over him. To make his friends happy he even allowed a priest to visit. His feelings about the Church were reflected in the statement: 'Why attack God? He may be as unhappy as we are.'

As he lingered through the first months of 1925, Satie's medicine was laced with opium, he was given champagne. On a warm summer afternoon a small band of Satie's friends arrived at l'Hôpital Saint-Joseph to visit the failing composer. But Satie's room was empty, the hospital bed freshly made. A nun appeared and led the group down a

R E L A C H E

Relâche, rose de feuille — feuille de guêpe, cul de lampe, etc..... ● ●
Relâche est un passage à niveau, un table — ou l'amant-chaise! Et puis l'aime; la vie sans lendemain, la vie rien pour hier, rien pour demain
Les phares d'automobiles, les colliers des femmes, la publicité, la musique, l'abit noir, le mouvement, le bruit, plaisir de rire, voilà Relâche.
Relâche a été fait comme l'on abat maquillé les cartes. ● ●
Relâche a les plus belles jambes du jarretières noires et blanches. Relâche, ni en arrière, ni à gauche ni à droite.
pas tout droit ; Relâche se promène dans la vie

rose ; guêpe de taille — taille de
passage à nivache ; Relâche est lamen-
Relâche est la vie, la vie comme je d'aujourd'hui, tout pour aujourd'hui,

de perles, les formes rondes et fines, l'automobile, quelques hommes en le jeu, l'eau transparente et claire, le

neuf dix-sept fois de suite sans avoir ● ●

monde, ses bas sont champagne, ses c'est le mouvement sans but, ni en avant
Relâche ne tourne pas et pourtant ne va
avec un grand éclat de rire, ERIK SATIE,

BORLIN, ROLF DE MARÉ, RENÉ CLAIR, PRIEUR et moi avons créé Relâche un peu comme Dieu créa la vie
Il n'y a pas de décors, il n'y a pas de costumes, il n'y a pas de nu, il n'y a qu'espace, l'espace que notre imagination aime à parcourir ; Relâche est le bonheur des instants sans réflexion ; pourquoi réfléchir, pourquoi avoir une convention de beauté ou de joie ?
Il faut risquer les indigestions si l'on a envie de manger ! ● ● ● ● ●
Pourquoi ne pas se ruiner ? Pourquoi ne pas travailler quarante-huit heures de suite si c'est notre plaisir ? Pourquoi ne pas avoir quinze femmes et pourquoi une femme n'aurait-elle pas cinquante-deux hommes si cela peut lui plaire ?
Relâche vous conseille d'être des viveurs, car la vie sera toujours plus longue à l'école du plaisir qu'à l'école de la morale, à l'école de l'art, à l'école religieuse, à l'école des conventions mondaines

FRANCIS
PICA-
BIA.

Page from program for *Relâche* with drawings by Picabia.

corridor to the chapel. There the body of Erik Satie was laid out, his mouth hanging open, flies crawling over the composer's motionless face. Satie had died quietly during the night. The painter Valentine Gross had brought flowers; she placed them around the body and upon his chest, the blossoms arranged to hide the mouth gaping open in death.

The funeral took place in Satie's adopted quarter of Arceuil. The mayor of this dreary suburb wore his tricolor sash at the head of a file of mourners that included the composers Satie had called Les Nouveaux Jeunes, except for Durey; but Auric, with whom Satie had broken, was there. Also attending the funeral were Ravel and Albert Roussel, Cocteau and his mother, Valentine Gross, Picabia leading a scattering of Dadaists and Surrealists, neighbors, and the tenants of Four Chimneys. Satie's family was represented by his brother Conrad, who would have the responsibility of opening the sealed premises at 22 rue Cauchy.

When the time came to make inventory of the deceased's possessions – prior to public auction, required by French law – Conrad Satie took with him Milhaud, Jean Wiener, and other friends of the composer, to the incredibly ugly building where Satie had lived for nearly thirty years. Brancusi took a photograph of the desolate staircase leading to Satie's flat: there was a crude water-closet in the entryway that opened to a single airless room. The little committee was overwhelmed. Satie's appearance had been old-world, but fastidious always – yet he had lived in this cave of a room in the most wretched conditions. A blanket of dust lay over the room like a shroud, dust 'thick enough to make a goldfish sneeze'. A bed and chair made up the composer's furniture: even these surfaces were piled with velveteen suits of a vanished era; hats, umbrellas, cigar boxes, ancient newspapers, scraps of writing in a minuscule lycée script. The writings were in different colored inks, legible but indecipherable, possibly compositions, projects, notes to himself. The ancient piano was heaped with discard, its broken pedals fastened with cord. Unopened packages and letters lay scattered about the room. Behind the piano someone found the score for *Jack in the Box*, music for a projected ballet, missing for years.

Erik Satie was buried in the cemetery at Arceuil. Diaghilev produced *Jack in the Box*, with sets by Derain, not many months after Satie's death.

CHAPTER FIFTEEN

1925

The festive spirit was alive along the quays between the pont Alexandre III and the pont d'Alma, but visitors to the International Exhibition of Decorative and Industrial Arts were obliged to step gingerly through mud and plaster around the unfinished pavilions and to listen to the inaugural address – 'Our children will live in beauty...' – against the sounds of saws and hammer blows. On opening day the Art Déco Exposition of 1925 was a skeletal ensemble, still under construction. Of the foreign pavilions, only the Danish House was ready to be viewed by the public. Several national pavilions would not be completed until a few days before the end of the exposition.

The vast fair celebrating the decorative arts had originally been scheduled for 1915, but with the intervention of the war, plans were sent to the archives. Pavilions designed for ten years before were erected as the new look of 1925. Because of tariff feuds between England and other European nations, the contribution from Great Britain was small and inconsequential. Six years after the Great War the enmity between France and Germany still smoldered: Germany was not invited to show, thus the influential Bauhaus style was missing and left a large hole in an exhibit billed as 'international'. The United States declined to participate.

By 1925 much of the show reflected the past rather than the future. A reaction to the Art Nouveau style had taken place as early as 1900: by the end of World War I the designers Paul Follot, Maurice Dufrène, Clement Mère, and the sculptor Armand-Albert had helped create what came to be known as Art Déco. Like the couturiers of the 1900s, the designers were influenced by the vivid colors and oriental motifs used by Leon Bakst for the Ballets Russes; but Art Déco included elements of the inescapable French passion for Louis XV furnishings, and celebrated the elongated oval and stylized patterns of the Art Nouveau it hoped to replace.

Nevertheless the Exposition was a spectacle that appealed to the public, impressed by the Lalique glasswork fountains as ornate as crystal chandeliers, the cascades of water pumped from the Seine and at night the fountains lit from within by neon. Neon was coming into widespread use, and André Citroen managed to obtain permission for the giant letters CITROEN to appear down the sides of the Eiffel Tower in gaudy neon. Visitors could travel from exhibit to exhibit in a miniature railway that could achieve a speed of 100 kilometers an hour, but a dangerous derailment occurred when the train approached that speed. Each of the pavilions – when completed – was set in its private garden; the quayside trees had been spared the axe, and were a natural part of the site, but constructions were in lath and plaster. There were no buildings of any substance that an Alfred Boucher might buy up, as Boucher had done after the 1900 Exposition, to reconstruct in the style of La Ruche as a permanent *cité* for artists. Even the wrought-iron entryway between the Grand Palais and the Petit Palais, a massive gate of Edgar Brandt ironwork, was not iron but, as a measure of economy, plaster painted to resemble iron.

The most successful building at the exhibit was the work of architect Pierre Patou, Le Pavillon d'un Collectioneur, from a design for the *hôtel particulier* of Emile-Jacques Ruhlmann, containing Ruhlmann-designed furniture. Ruhlmann was the modish decorator of the period: his elegant furnishings were sought after by the wealthy, but he showed no penchant for mass-produced furniture at prices within reach of the general public. Ruhlmann employed the finest craftsmen to create objects and décor in ivory, tortoise-shell, lizard skin, and shagreen. Ruhlmann's opulent interiors and Patou's theme of majestic simplicity – Patou had also designed the ten massive entryway columns to the exposition at the place de la Concorde – set the tone for other decorators like André Groult, Jean Dunand, Jean Dupas, and Eileen Gray (an Englishwoman designing in Paris), who exhibited their Art Déco ceramics, silver leaf, floor-to-ceiling murals, and elaborate lacquered screens catering to the carriage trade, destined to furnish townhouses in Passy.

Against this backdrop of luxurious design and exotic materials, the couturier Paul Poiret was inspired to make a dramatic gesture. Mass-production of ready-to-wear garments had badly disrupted the exclusive

The Eiffel Tower with its special illuminations for the Exposition des Arts Décoratifs, 1925.

dressmaking trade, and Poiret had failed to take up the challenge of Coco Chanel by appealing to a wider clientele. In what he hoped would be an abrupt reversal to his declining fortunes, Poiret outfitted three large river barges tied up at the quayside, perhaps the most original site at the Exposition outside the row of chic boutiques lining the pont Alexandre III. Poiret's three *péniches* were called: *Amours*, the nightclub-restaurant of the miniature fleet; *Délices*, which housed a complete theater; and *Orgues*, the display vessel for objets-d'art, luxury furnishings, and fabrics created in Poiret's Atelier Martine. Interiors of the barges were the work of Raoul Dufy, who also designed Poiret's fabrics. Overwhelmed by creditors, the couturier had plunged even deeper into debt to stage this riverside extravaganza to save the House of Poiret.

All the theatrical elegance of the Belle Epoque was personified in Paul Poiret as he stood on the deck of his flagship *Orgues* dressed in *smoking* and top hat, offering champagne to the remnants of his upper-crust clientele. But the socialites were outnumbered by a file of window-shoppers strolling from one beautifully appointed barge to the next: they had come to look, not buy. Nothing in Poiret's champagne manner and the seigneurial hauteur he had learned from his idol and predecessor Jacques Doucet hinted at impending bankruptcy or revealed a desperate captain of a sinking ship.

*

A nostalgia for Art Déco lingered in the bas-relief dancer on the façade of the Folies-Bergère and in the lounges and smoking salons of transatlantic liners, but the mannered style left little imprint in the world of art. That same year, 1925, an exhibit of more lasting significance took place at the Galerie Pierre: the first important group show of the Surrealists Paul Klee, Hans Arp and Man Ray – even Picasso, who denied the Surrealist or any label, did not object to being shown alongside his younger Catalan friend, Miró.

The poet André Breton was beginning to write extensively about this new theme in art called Surrealism, and to publicize its adherents in the way Apollinaire had explained Cubism and promoted Cubist painters a generation before. (It was Apollinaire who had first used the term *sur-réalisme*, in his program notes for *Parade*.) In one essay, Breton tried to include the unclassifiable Picasso with the Surrealist movement; Picasso relished the praise lavished on him by Breton, but resisted the connection.

Picasso had abandoned his Neo-classicism of the early Twenties, and he had given up designing theater sets for the Diaghilev productions – but he was far removed from the Surrealist bloc of collective thinking as he painted in solitude in his self-contained world. He did occasionally entertain the Surrealists at his studio on the rue La Boétie, for he enjoyed their spirited company and he remained a close friend of Miró. Their manifestos expressed with such revolutionary ardor might be stimulating or amusing, but Picasso did not sign them and was no party to the rigid dogma put forth by Breton and Louis Aragon. If the Surrealists wanted to cast him in the role of precursor – or present believer – Picasso made no public protest. Privately he shrugged. The show at the Galerie Pierre was principally in honor of Miró, whose painted dreams set against a lunar landscape were far more representative of the strange new art.

By this time Dada had splintered into factions and fragments: out of the shambles of that vociferous camp marched the fresh troops of Surrealism. Duchamp was perhaps the last practicing Dadaist (as he may have been the first), but he preferred life in America, a reclusive art – or no art at all, which was perhaps the ultimate in Dada. Picabia might still hope for a Dadaist revival – he had, with Brancusi, designed the bizarre set for *Relâche* the year before (and had driven onto the stage, with Satie beside him, in a miniature automobile) – but both Duchamp and Picabia were excluded from the Galerie Pierre show. Cocteau, who was usually the gadfly public relations agent for any avant-garde sect, condemned the Surrealists with a shudder: 'Ils sont tous les petits Nietzsches.'

Picasso, too, recoiled from the more outrageous visions expressed by the Surrealists. At a Max Ernst show he complained: 'Imagine a dove flying out of a stationmaster's derrière.' Picasso's indignation might have summed up public opinion toward the new movement; Gertrude Stein's personal opinion was that 'the surrealistes are the vulgarization of Picabia as Delaunay and his followers and the futurists were the vulgarization of Picasso'. Whatever reaction or outcry the Surrealists provoked, the movement survived, flourished, and prevailed. Unlike Dada – anarchistic, even about its own ideas – Surrealism would not expire from making a joke of itself. Surrealism profited also from the vogue for Freudian dream-symbolism that had overtaken Paris. Surrealism returned to the tradition of easel painting, a more acceptable remove from the stunts and gadgetry of the Dadaists – even though Man Ray's found-art objects harked back to the inventive humor of Duchamp exhibiting a shovel, a wine rack, or an unadorned toilet seat as ready-made sculpture.

Man Ray sought out the Dadaists (soon to become Surrealists) upon his arrival in Paris on Bastille Day, 1921. Protégé of Alfred Stieglitz, familiar of Duchamp and Picabia when they were in New York, Man Ray was immediately welcomed by the French Dadaists: he was to become the only American member of the group. His Rayograms, a technique of making photographs without a camera, were very much in the Dada-Surrealist mode; an early painting, *The Rope Dancer Accompanies Herself with Her Shadows*, was Dada in concept and title; and a 1921 portrait of Duchamp in his guise as Rrose Selavy (*c'est la vie*) made it inevitable that Man Ray would be invited to show and caper with the Dadaists.

The photographer, painter, sculptor, cinéaste set up shop in a tiny darkroom-studio around the corner from the Dôme, on the rue Delambre. Gertrude Stein, in *The Autobiography of Alice B. Toklas*, describes Man Ray's sanctuary: 'I have never seen any space, not even a ship's cabin, with so many things in it and the things so admirably disposed. He had a bed, he had three large cameras, he had several kinds of lighting, he had a window screen, and in a little closet he did all his developing.' Court photographer to the celebrated of Montparnasse, Man Ray did revealing portrait studies of Gertrude Stein, Alice Toklas, Brancusi, Stravinsky, the transvestite performer Barbette, Tristan Tzara kissing Nancy Cunard's hand, and eccentric portrait-commentaries like the photograph of himself – significantly taken in 1929 – with alarm clock, pistol in hand, his head in a hangman's noose.

Many of the photographic portraits are of Kiki, who moved in with Man Ray and his cameras, a jealous and tempestuous mistress. Kiki of Montparnasse had been a model since fourteen, when she blackened her eyebrows with matchsticks and fled her dread apprenticeship as a baker's helper to pose for an aged sculptor on the rue Mouffetard. Her outraged mother broke in on one of Kiki's nude modeling sessions and threatened to put her errant daughter into reform school. But the free-spirited Kiki simply drifted on into the demi-monde of pimps and painters, cocaine addicts and the down-and-out.

During Kiki's teenage tour of the lower depths, she and a girl friend, both broke, trudged through the snow to the rue Dantzig where her friend knew a painter who might put them up. As they climbed the

The photographer Man Ray (below) and his mistress Kiki of Montparnasse.

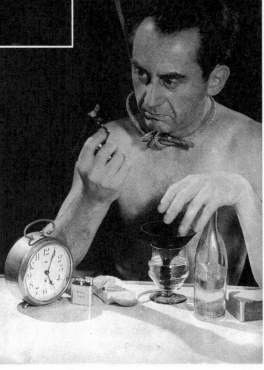

central staircase at La Ruche they heard voices coming from the painter's room, and realized he was with a woman. The two chilled and bedraggled ladies of the night waited on the staircase until 2 a.m., until Kiki wept with misery: her friend suggested they try the next building, where Soutine lived. In her memoirs Kiki wrote of the encounter with Soutine: 'He was so fierce looking that I was a little bit afraid, but my girl friend bucked me up.' Soutine took them in and 'spent the night burning up everything in his place to keep us warm. Ever since that day I've had a crush on Soutine...'

After Soutine, Kiki become the favorite model and vivid café companion to Kisling, Foujita, and Pascin. She could be as capricious and startling as the avant-garde Montparnos she frequented: her bawdy songs and outrageous behavior enlivened the café scene around the place Vavin. A beauty in no easily defined sense, she was of sturdy Burgundian stock, well-proportioned, nothing of the p'tite ma'mselle about Kiki. Hemingway admired her features – 'Having a fine face to start with, she made of it a work of art' – and Gargallo sculpted her head as a 1920s artifact: a hollowed-out bronze of incisive lines, the pointed ends of her bobbed hair against the cheekbone. Despite an apocryphal story (one she originated herself) that she chalked spirals of hair on her otherwise bald pubis before posing, she appears in Man Ray's nude studies with a triangle of natural pubic hair.

Kiki fell in love with Man Ray after attending the film *La Dame aux Camélias* with him; in her words, 'Now he's my lover.' She began to meet the Dadaists and Surrealists, and for her part saw no difference between them. Nor did she distinguish between the great and not so great who were received with equanimity in the miniature atelier-hotel room, to pose for the camera lens. While Man Ray photographed, Kiki would lie stretched out on the bed impatient for her lover to finish with his sitters and join her. Of his portrait studies, Kiki's favorite was the one of the Marquise Cassati taken through the sides of a glass bowl of leaves and water, the face having moved at the critical moment.

In the manner of Duchamp adding a mustache to the Mona Lisa, Man Ray repainted the enigmatic lady with what appeared to be her telephone number, 'PL 188-189', inscribed above her eyes. He assembled unlikely items in droll juxtaposition: mobiles of clothes pins and clothes hangers, an egg framed by a toilet seat (again, Duchamp's style), a photo of Mina Loy with thermometers as earrings, strings and sound holes painted on the lower back of a seated nude to create a human-cello effect. At his first one-man show in Soulat's gallery, Salon Dada, Man Ray exhibited his *Export Commodity* – a jar filled with ball bearings in oil – and *Inquiétude* – the dismantled works of an alarm clock in a glass case filled with tobacco smoke.

In 1923 he began experimenting with cinematic techniques: his three-minute Dadaist exercise *The Return to Reason* was deemed so unreasonable that it provoked a riot. This riot was the last mass reaction to the Dadaists and their piquant presentations; by 1924 Dada was dead and Surrealism had been proclaimed by manifesto. When Man Ray joined with the painters of the Rue Blomet Group at the Galerie Pierre in 1925, Surrealism was launched as the seminal movement of the last half of the Twenties.

The Galerie Pierre exhibit fell just short of riot: the manager Pierre Loeb feared that the floor would collapse, and had to call the police to clear the crowd. The show was a great personal success for Joan Miró who was being celebrated as the crown prince of Surrealism in the presence of the crown prince of Sweden, attending the opening. Afterward, at a cabaret party in Montmartre, the shy Catalan painter was applauded as he danced a stiff tango with a Scandinavian beauty from the prince's entourage, a head taller than himself.

*

The culmination of Miró's prewar Montroig period was a large painting entitled *The Farm*, which failed to interest dealers but acquired an underground reputation of its own when it was hung in a Montparnasse café. In 1925 the poet Evan Shipman hoped to buy it, but then learned that his friend Ernest Hemingway wanted to give *The Farm* to Hadley as a birthday gift. Shipman offered to roll dice for the privilege of buying the painting, and Hemingway won – though he did not have the purchase price of 5,000 francs. Meanwhile the dealer Jacques Viot had received another offer, three times as high as the asking price, but Miró honored the original option to buy. In a frantic scramble to borrow the money, Hemingway and friends went from the Dingo to the Dôme to the Closerie de Lilas soliciting loans. Even Jimmy Charters, the amiable barman of the Dingo, contributed. Thus Ernest succeeded in buying *The Farm*, bearing it home to Hadley in a kind of victory parade: 'In the open taxi the wind caught the big canvas as though it were a sail and we made the driver crawl along. At home we hung it and everyone looked at it and was very happy.'

For Hemingway, Miró had put into *The Farm* feelings about Spain 'and what you felt when you were away and could not go there' that he was trying to express in his own attempt at a first novel. He had just come from the celebration of the feast of San Fermín at Pamplona where he had introduced a circle of Montparnasse cronies to the aesthetics of bull-fighting, just as he had been introduced to the Spanish ritual-sport by Gertrude Stein. His companions included the humorist Donald Ogden Stewart, who had recently arrived in Paris with sufficient American dollars – in a new surge of inflated value against the failing franc – to underwrite trip expenses for wealthy-impoverished Pat Campbell and Lady Duff Twysden. Truly wealthy Harold Loeb paid his own way. The five friends were to become the principal fictional characters in *The Sun Also Rises*, Hemingway himself as the model for Jake Barnes, the first-person narrator and protagonist. The author exploited the tense relationships and outright hostilities the trip inspired, documenting the fiesta and earlier sequences of Montparnasse life in a fresh and unadorned style that would be the cornerstone of his reputation. Reactions by the living prototypes of the characters in the novel were mixed. Stewart discovered his own quips and taglines issuing from a fictional counterpart, Bill Gorton, but was probably less amused to be depicted as an amiable alcoholic. As Brett, Lady Duff Twysden's words and mannerisms were just as carefully recorded, but her complaint was, 'I never even slept with the bloody bullfighter.' In his minor and fatuous role as Braddocks, Ford Madox Ford must have been dismayed, but he kept his annoyance to himself.

Harold Loeb was made miserable by the portrait of himself as Robert Cohn. After he had done so much to further Hemingway's career – admired and respected him as a man and as a writer – to be mirrored as a weak, vain, shallow-minded romantic was a betrayal that soured the remainder of his young life. Hemingway had needed a character to represent everything the new code of the lost generation opposed – if not a villain, at least a disagreeable catalyst-figure – and Harold Loeb was his ruthless choice.

When Hemingway showed the first draft of the novel to Gertrude Stein, it was little more than travelogue and dialogue. 'Start over again, and concentrate,' was Miss Stein's advice. It was the time when Gertrude Stein admitted to a weakness for Hemingway, 'because he is such a good pupil... it is so flattering to have a pupil who does it without understanding it, in other words he takes training and anybody who takes training is a favorite pupil.' Hemingway rewrote *The Sun Also Rises* following Miss Stein's advice. Gertrude Stein and Sherwood Anderson were said to have formed Hemingway, 'and they were both a little proud and a little ashamed of the work of their minds'.

With the left-over energy from having created his remarkable first novel, Hemingway set about writing a lightweight parody called *The Torrents of Spring*. The casual spoof was written in ten days and was meant as an unflattering take-off of Sherwood Anderson's style in the 1925 novel *Dark Laughter*. It was the Hemingway method of casting off Gertrude Stein as well, since Anderson was 'part of her apparatus'. Never again would Gertrude Stein and Ernest Hemingway sit together – he at her feet, she below the Picasso portrait of her – discussing issues literary over crystal glasses of pure fruit *alcools* distilled by the shadow-companion Alice.

For all the innovation and effervescence of that vintage year, 1925 marked a season of erupting feuds, damaged friendships, tight lips and thin skins.

*

But 1925 was also a year of sudden new liaisons. Kitty Cannell – Harold Loeb's fiancée, another maligned character in *The Sun Also Rises* – ran into Pauline Pfeiffer, then working for the couturier Mainbocher. Pauline was leaving Paris to join the Hemingways in Austria for a skiing holiday *à trois* that surprised Kitty, who remembered when Pauline shared her distaste and suspicion of Ernest. The distaste, over a number of months, had turned to love.

Another beginning affair, which surprised no one, was the burgeoning romance between Chanel and the Duke of Westminster, known as Bend'or. The Duke, reputed to be the wealthiest man in England, was in Paris to escape the ignominy of his divorce trial which featured a detailed indictment of his extra-marital episode with one of many mistresses at the Hôtel de Paris in Monte Carlo.

Chanel could not have failed to notice the 'amiable giant' Bend'or lurking about the Théâtre des Champs-Elysées during the rehearsals for *Le Train Bleu* the year before, but she may have thought he was there to meet with one of the ballerinas Diaghilev sometimes thrust upon potential backers of the Ballets Russes. No, it was the svelte and dynamic designer of costumes for *Le Train Bleu* who had caught the Duke's eye. At first Chanel was too occupied with costuming to respond openly to Bend'or's interest – an extravagant courtship that included such gestures as sending out-of-season fruit and masses of flowers, with gems scattered among the strawberries, a diamond hidden in the petals of a rose.

Le Train Bleu was another concoction by Cocteau, this time depicting the seaside sporting life of the Côte d'Azur, with curtain and décor by Picasso and music by Milhaud. Chanel was obliged to create something altogether new to accommodate the gymnast-choreography: she succeeded so admirably that a vogue for sportswear came out of the ballet, along with a trend for sunning on the Riviera.

By 1925 Coco Chanel was at the peak of her popularity: this was the year of the Chanel-inspired 'little black dress', mass-produced in the way of automobiles or, as *Vogue* put it, 'the Ford signed by Chanel'. Coco was seen at the Longchamp and Auteuil races in the company of the Duke of Westminster, and went with him to Deauville for sailing parties on his yacht *The Flying Cloud*. Bend'or had become the perfect replacement for her one great love, Boy Capel. His influence was obvious in Chanel's new designs for jerseys, women's suits in English tweeds – garments suitable to the outdoor life the Duke fancied.

*

Another Duke, but of the Broadway stage musical, Vernon Duke – or Dukelsky, his family name when he left Russia for the United States – was introduced to Diaghilev by Chanel's friend Misia Sert. 'Ah,' said Diaghilev, 'a good-looking composer, how rare.' He was obliquely referring to his two adopted 'sons', Stravinsky and Prokofiev. When he asked the young man's age, he was delighted to learn that Duke was only twenty. 'I don't like men over twenty-five. They lose their adolescent charm and sleep with any woman who gives them the nod. Oh, so you can still blush?'

Despite Diaghilev's horror of jazz and its rhythms assimilated by American composers like Duke, he accepted a Vernon Duke score for the 1925 ballet *Zéphyr et Flore*, presented at the Théâtre de la Gaîté-Lyrique with choreography by Massine and sets by Georges Braque. Massine had just returned to the Ballets Russes under the cloud of having deserted Diaghilev for the ballerina Savina, and having formed his own rival company. Diaghilev no longer permitted Massine to call him Serge, but Duke was adopted as Diaghilev's 'third son'. The filial tie was short-lived. Vernon Duke had his one and only chance with the Ballets Russes for his music to *Zéphyr et Flore*: he was never asked to write another ballet.

Diaghilev resisted all other efforts to allow the American idiom to become incorporated in music for his ballet productions. When Cole Porter was presented to Diaghilev by the Princesse de Polignac, the impresario deliberately avoided the subject of musical comedy. Diaghilev wrote to Stravinsky, with whom Porter wanted to study, 'Cole is writing a ballet... beware!' George Gershwin was also in and out of Paris, the scene of his popular *An American in Paris*, and he too approached Diaghilev, who promised to 'think about' using his *Rhapsody in Blue* as a ballet score – with no real intention of doing so.

Vernon Duke was in the audience for a performance of *La Revue Nègre*, the 1925 black import from the United States, when he saw a familiar figure slumped in hiding, inadequately disguised behind a pair of dark glasses, several rows behind his own. The impresario who professed to despise the growing influence of jazz and the increasing horde of blacks invading Paris, could not resist the sensational Afro-American spectacle. Duke recognized Diaghilev by his 'chinchilla' streak, the dyed white forelock of hair.

Josephine Baker with her pet leopard.

CHAPTER SIXTEEN

Arrangement in Black and White

E ven those who were unable to attend performances of *La Revue Nègre* were aware of the star at the Théâtre des Champs-Elysées, Josephine Baker. The Ebony Venus of the show (but Josephine was the color of dark honey) appeared on a poster by Paul Colin plastered on every kiosk in Paris. Her slicked-down coiffure – with spit curl like a question-mark upside-down on her forehead – was imitated by whites and became a verb in French: *Bakerfixer*. Poiret designed a gown for Mademoiselle Ba-kair that brought pink briefly back in fashion, a gown so widely copied it became known as *la robe Joséphine*; her caramel coloring was the inspiration for the sun-tanning craze at Deauville and on the Riviera. The flat accents of Josephine's Americanized French, so repellent to Parisians, were suddenly chic.

As soon as Paul Colin met the troupe of *La Revue Nègre* at the Hôtel Fournet, his eye for a poster subject narrowed to the slim and sensual mulatto from St Louis – he also intended to be Josephine's first French lover, but she had already tumbled into bed with the first Frenchman she met, a waiter at the Fournet who had surprised her in her bath. At Colin's studio, the artist could only communicate with his model by means of sketches since neither spoke the other's language: the drawings indicated that Mademoiselle was to disrobe. It was the first, but not the last time, Josephine was to appear *au poil* in public – or in costumes so scanty they were more suggestive than if she danced in the nude: a few bits of feather at the Théâtre des Champs-Elysées, the celebrated skirt of uptilted bananas at the Casino de Paris.

At her first performance, slithering snakelike on the back of a huge black performer, Josephine and the jazz-dancers of *La Revue* created the first shock waves of the new phenomenon. The primitive rhythms and unrestrained dance movements were a recall to Rousseau's glorification of the noble savage, a theme perpetually revived by French intellectuals and strangely attractive to French sophisticates. Black was the color, jazz was suddenly the sound. When the *Revue Nègre* opened, the Jazz Age came to Paris. The French language attempted to assimilate *up-to-date*, *un jazz band*, *un cocktail*, and *le jazz hot*. 'Shimmy' was pronounced with the accent on the second syllable. 'The Three Pullman Porters' became 'Les Trois Garçons du Wagons-Lits'.

Monsieur Mezz (Mezzrow) was giving alto-sax lessons to the Paris Symphony and the new Pied Piper's magic flute was Sidney Bechet's clarinet.

An exhibition of the new dance, the 'Char-less-ton', attracted unprecedented crowds to Claridge's on the Champs-Elysées, just as The Charleston Boys were appearing at the Mimosa. So many Parisians wanted to learn the Black Bottom that Orrea Waskae, "Colored American *danseuse*', was teaching the dance to a class of sixty French dancing masters. The traditional *thé-dansant* became Americanized to *un dancing*; it was no longer chic to attend the *bals musettes* in the working-class districts of Paris: the expatriate colonies now patronized black cabarets like Le Bal Nègre, across the rue Blomet from the building where the Surrealists met. The popularity of the accordion, traditional accompaniment to the dances at the *bals populaires*, declined while the race was on to be the first to learn to play 'Constantinople' on the jazzoflute, an instrument shaped like a bicycle pump.

Zelli's and Le Boeuf sur le Toit were soon competing with a new nightclub, Bricktop's, where expatriate Americans mixed with denizens of La Butte, French café society, and celebrities of several worlds. Bricktop herself – the dusky Ada Smith, who dyed her hair orange to touch up her coloring – knew all her regulars by their first names. In Paris, black and white mixed as casually as bohemian and aristocrat: the cocktail was international, classless, colorblind. The fashionable invited the black performers Snakehips and Whispering Jack Smith to their parties, or Baby Darling from *La Revue Nègre*, with her new husband Mr Legitimus. Cole Porter caused few eyebrows to raise when he invited Bricktop to accompany him to the exclusive Paris Opera Ball, Bricktop wearing the same Molyneux gown as Princess Marina of Greece.

Bricktop was the renowned hostess to the Franco-American cabaret set and Josephine Baker was the supreme *vedette* of that world. To the French the uninhibited Josephine, with her gold-painted fingernails and tutu made of bananas, was a creature Baudelaire had invented, or, as Anna de Noailles called her, 'a pantheress with gold claws' – a symbol of primitive sensuality. For Americans she was the Folies phenomenon transported from home, descending on stage from a feathered ball with mirrored interior, half nude, the star of Jazz Age Paris.

Josephine's personality was soon stamped by the demands of show business: she learned how to exploit the legend, on stage and off. One theatrical affectation was to keep a snake she called Kiki as part of her ménage, often enough coiled around her neck, a device 'to separate the men from the boys'. She went walking with her pet leopard Chiquita, the beast's collar changed daily to match the costume of its mistress – Chiquita and Josephine stalking the Champs-Elysées, two lithe animals associated in the public eye as one.

*

During the jazz phase of the Twenties, patrons of Mitchell's, Florence's or Zelli's risked an encounter with the criminal element of Montmartre: purse-snatching and mugging were on the increase. As a measure of self-protection, many black musicians and performers carried arms – a tradition from an earlier age when even Erik Satie, working at Le Chat Noir, carried a hammer in his velveteen jacket.

At Florence's in 1928, Mike McKendrick and Sidney Bechet got into an argument, then carried their grievance into the street. Both drew pistols. In the gun battle that followed, neither man was wounded, but a passing Frenchwoman was struck by a stray bullet. Until that time blacks had been given considerable latitude, but French tolerance of black skin did not extend beyond the provisions of the *code civil*. Bechet was condemned to eleven months in prison; after serving part of his sentence he was released, then expelled from France.

The field for jazz players was narrowing and the welcome was not as ready as in 1925. As black musicians began to monopolize the nightclub circuit, the French imposed counter-measures to assure that half the members of any band would be French nationals. Since jazz was an American phenomenon, and not until the Thirties would France produce jazz musicians like Django Reinhardt and Stephane Grapelli, French jazzmen were impossible to find. A way of dealing with the new regulations was to employ French musicians to sit in during perform-ances, without playing a note, their instruments no more than props. Those clubs that could afford two bands arranged for separate French and American groups to play alternate sets.

Jazz pianist Henry Crowder came to Europe just as the tighter restrictions and declining employment for ensemble players became prevalent. He had escaped a hardscrabble existence in the American south by working his way north, playing piano at YMCAs – or scrubbing floors, washing dishes, when no other employment turned up – then joined a black jazz quartet known as The Alabamians. A small-time manager got The Alabamians a series of short engagements in Europe, but the gigs trickled out in Venice, the manager disappeared. While Henry was stranded in Venice he met Nancy Cunard, who at this stage of her free-floating life had taken up the banner of black rights. She was plain-spoken in her defense of racial equality, and was able to contribute large sums of money, as well as genuine sympathy, to the cause. Her interest in Henry was no doubt influenced by the color of his skin, but only in part. Nancy, with the insouciant defiance of the rich, took Henry as a lover.

This was 1928: Fascism was on the rise in Italy – the mood in Venice did not match the classic tolerance of France. Wherever Henry Crowder and Nancy Cunard were seen together, black and white fingers interlaced, the shocked Italians reacted. Restaurant personnel were hostile or blatantly insulting: the manager at Henry's hotel suggested that he leave. Finally Nancy took Henry to Paris, where the climate for mixed couples was far more relaxed.

*

Because of her striking appearance, and by deliberately flaunting her independence, Nancy Cunard had been attracting attention since her adolescent years. Nancy was heiress to the Cunard Line millions of her father, Sir Bache Cunard, and his California-born wife – twenty years younger than himself – Maude Alice Burke, Lady Cunard. When Nancy decided to ignore the mores imposed by upper-class British society, she was in her way following the lead of her mother, who had fallen in love with the conductor Thomas Beecham and lived with him in London.

Nancy was a beauty in the jazz-age mold: extremely slim as the fashion decreed, elegant, and to all appearances reserved. William Carlos Williams described her as 'straight as any stick, emaciated, holding her head erect, not particularly animated, her blue eyes untroubled, inviolable in her virginity of pure act'. A far less charitable summary of her appearance was offered by a boyfriend of Norman Douglas: 'She looks like an asparagus.' Despite the demeanor of distant ice maiden Nancy sometimes assumed, she was sexually attractive to men and women, and was herself attracted to both sexes.

During the war Nancy made a single attempt at conventional life by marrying Sydney Fairbairn, the dashing young military officer of the moment. Lady Cunard opposed the alliance, and the marriage may have been as much an act of defiance as an act of love. While Fairbairn was away at the front, Nancy realized that she could not endure the role of wife to him or to any man. She fled to the South of France, ostensibly to recover from a bout of Spanish influenza, but at the same time to agonize over her rash marriage. At the end of World War I Nancy announced to the demobilized officer that she could not remain as his wife: the couple separated but did not divorce until 1925.

While expressing disdain for all that the Twenties cult represented, Nancy Cunard was the archetypal Twenties woman. She bobbed and shingled her hair, wore the short skirts and boyish fashions as if she were the principal model for the new mode; she could be seen in all the stylish cafés and nightclubs with a changing sequence of escorts, extending her long slim cigarette holder like a symbol of rank. It was Nancy who paid for the drinks, and she could drink throughout a night of party-going with no apparent effect. 'I never saw her drunk,' admitted William Carlos Williams, '– I can imagine she was never quite sober.'

A characteristic of the age was the need felt by the wealthy to participate directly in the arts. At the urging of Wyndham Lewis and Ezra Pound – for reasons more to do with the Cunard millions than the Cunard talent – Nancy began to write poems. An older mentor, the author George Moore, encouraged her as well; as a result, a first collection of poems appropriately entitled *Outlaws* came out in 1921.

Nancy not only wrote, she was much written about. In Michael Arlen's *The Green Hat*, the 1924 best-seller, Nancy appears as the central character, Iris March. Arlen and Nancy had been lovers at the beginning of the Twenties, and a traumatic incident in Nancy's life of that period is used by the author as a key episode; Nancy went to Paris in 1920, in secret, to have a hysterectomy performed. By her account, the operation was to 'make a free woman' of her, thenceforth unencumbered by the risk of maternity – although she risked her life, and barely survived the primitive back-street surgery.

An incident in Nancy's variegated and unconventional love life served Aldous Huxley for a scene in *Eyeless in Gaza*: a dead dog falls

Nancy Cunard.

from an airplane onto a couple making love outdoors. Nancy admitted this had actually happened to her. She also appeared in Huxley's *Antic Hay* and *Point Counter Point*, and in Wyndham Lewis's novel *The Roaring Queen*. George Moore, rumored to be Lady Cunard's lover before Thomas Beecham, and to have been Nancy's natural father, was as attracted to the daughter as to the mother. When Moore visited Nancy in Paris he begged her: 'Tell me about your lovers.' On another occasion the elderly gentleman asked Nancy to show herself to him in the nude – 'At least let me see your naked back.' Nancy obliged to that extent, and Moore was able to describe Nancy's back in his 1926 novel, *Ulick and Soracha*.

Whether in fiction or in life, Nancy Cunard became the prototype I-don't-care girl of the 1920s, a model of slender stylishness, social defiance, and sexual liberty. Wealth made it possible for her to lead exactly the life she chose: to support the talented, buy her own way into print, purchase an impecunious lover. Though she invariably picked up the check at Zelli's, enjoyed Maxim's and Lapérouse, she was more at home at the obscure demi-monde establishment, La Perle. Dinner at La Perle was a plebeian 20 francs per person, the food excellent; but it was the outlaw ambience that drew Nancy. Here the working prostitutes convened before they moved into the streets or went on duty at their *maisons tolérées*. The restaurant was a display case of *papillons de nuit*: Nancy, a butterfly of another species, was equally attracted to the flame.

In 1924 Nancy attached herself to the Surrealist group evolving out of the waning Dada movement. Louis Aragon became her lover; Man Ray did a portrait study of her, and Tristan Tzara wrote *Mouchoir de Nuages* for Nancy. The Brancusi sculpture *Jeune Fille Sophistiquée* is Nancy reduced to her most elemental. Her Ile St-Louis apartment on the rue Le Regrattier was decorated with the Surrealist paintings of Chirico, Tanguy and Picabia, the apartment itself described in Aragon's novel *Blanche ou l'Oubli*. The literary Surrealists met at the Café Cyrano in the place Blanche, and Nancy became something of an embarrassment when she was Aragon's lover and sat in on the meetings: Frenchmen all, these anarchists of art were traditionally conservative in their attitudes toward women. Nancy drifted out of Aragon's surreal orbit when the movement took a hard political line and Aragon became a Communist – she was a revolutionary too, but in no political sense.

Like so many of her set, Nancy was caught up in the fad for Africana that swept Paris. Fetishes and tribal masks appeared alongside the Surrealist paintings in her collection. She began wearing primitive earrings and pendants, her slender arms encased in bracelets of carved wood and ivory. She loved to dance to the new syncopation imported from black America: her former lover Richard Aldington complained that Nancy was always going to 'nigger cabarets'. Her favorite nightspot was The Plantation, with its mural of a Mississippi steamboat and chalk drawings of darkies on a blackboard. It was at The Plantation that Crowder got his first job when Nancy brought him back to Paris, an ironic comment on his situation.

Crowder maintained that Nancy's wealth was not the reason he lived with her; nevertheless, the Cunard fortune was an irresistible buffer in the pianist's insubstantial existence. In the backlash that followed the Bechet-McKendrick shooting incident – Crowder had worked with McKendrick – gigs were scarce, and Crowder was out of work for months at a time.

Nancy may have preferred Crowder's dependence on her. Despite her generosity in public, she doled out her lover's allowance in a spiteful, sometimes sadistic, tease. She kept him on a tight tether, with enough cash to play craps with his fellow musicians at The Flea Pit. Meanwhile Nancy continued her own liberated life of flirtation and sensation, and managed to outrage Crowder by her lesbian escapades more than her affairs with other men, black and white. Wealth was the means to Nancy's flamboyant independence, but a way of keeping Crowder from emancipation. She seemed to want to own a black lover as part of her collection of African art. 'Be more African!' she shrieked at him, and on one occasion struck him across the face with her armload of African bracelets.

The deteriorating situation improved abruptly when Nancy founded the Hours Press in 1928. Here was a way for her to pour energy and time into the arts, as well as money; and by making Crowder her assistant, solve his chronic unemployment. William Bird had given up the Three Mountains Press and was willing to sell his seventeenth-century hand-press to Nancy for £300. Just as Virginia Woolf had warned her, out of her own experience with the Hogarth Press, hand-printing was dirty, tiring and frustrating work. Dirt, fatigue and frustration played no part in Nancy's silver-spoon existence, yet the Hours Press turned out to be the most satisfying endeavor Nancy had ever attempted. Not only did she achieve personal fulfillment by learning to become a master printer, but she even managed to turn a profit: the Hours Press doubled her investment within a year. Her old friend George Moore helped launch the press by offering the reprint of his novel *Peronnik the Fool*, and Ezra Pound submitted the unlikely treatise, *The Probable Music of Beowulf*. It was difficult to imagine where the profit came from with such items as Norman Douglas's *Report on the Pumice Stone Industry of the Lipari Islands*. The Douglas *Report* represented Nancy's debut as a printer-publisher, and in fact the task of setting the paper in II-point type was a disciplined way of learning the printing trade.

Henry Crowder seemed to share Nancy's enthusiasm for the Hours Press, but when she once too often flung at him the taunt: 'Why don't you get a job?' he surprised himself, and Nancy, with the reply, 'I will.' He found a job at Le Bateau Ivre, a way back to jazz piano and a way out of Nancy's world.

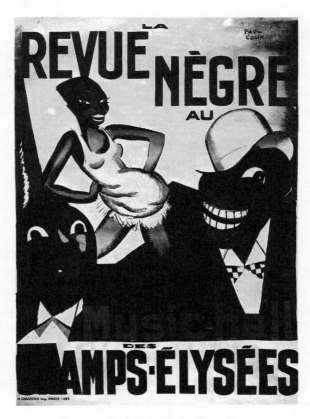

Poster by Paul Colin for *La Revue Nègre*.

CHAPTER SEVENTEEN

The Rich Are Different

In Harry Crosby's diary were the words: 'We who have known war must never forget war. And that is why I have a picture of a soldier's corpse nailed to the door of my library.' Crosby was determined to remember not only the war but his own close brush with death on the battlefield: dying was the morbid preoccupation at the center of his life.

He had been one of the gentleman-volunteers for ambulance service in World War I: for his heroism under fire and miraculous survival from an exploding shell, Crosby was awarded the Croix de Guerre. He returned to the US from wartime France with his citation, a hip flask given to him by his buddies in the Norton-Harjes Ambulance Corps, and a permanently-scarred psyche.

It was assumed Harry Crosby would go into banking or take his place alongside other returning veterans of the privileged class, with a seat on the New York Stock Exchange, for he was born into the highest circle of Boston's financial élite: his uncle was J. P. Morgan. But Harry was the family romantic – or n'er-do-well, as the van Rensselaer-Morgan clan would have it – and he immediately fell in love with a like-minded and rebellious socialite, Polly Peabody. Polly was married, with two children: the scandal of an adulterous liaison would have to be avoided, therefore J. P. Morgan arranged to have Harry Crosby employed by the family bank in Paris, safely removed from the attractions of Mrs Peabody. Paris was exactly where Harry most wanted to go – but not particularly to the Morgan bank and certainly not without Polly at his side.

In May 1922 Harry took up the tedious role of apprentice bank manager at number 14, place Vendôme, conveniently located opposite the Ritz Bar. He continued to maintain a long-distance courtship of Polly Peabody through extravagant multi-paged letters: if the family believed the charms of Paris would obliterate Harry's fascination with Polly, they knew nothing of the young man's determined and obsessive nature.

To escape the monotony of high finance, Harry spent as much time as possible at the bar of the Ritz – the Ritz Hotel, in fact, became his Paris headquarters. Ostensibly he lived at the Hôtel Metropolitan on nearby rue Cambon, but for a time he kept a room at the Hôtel Régina. Polly Peabody managed to get away from Boston for a brief clandestine holiday with Harry in this sanctuary on the place des Pyramides, overlooking a gilded equestrian Jeanne d'Arc.

Meanwhile he led the free-spending freewheeling existence of a rake abroad. He was as often at the baccarat tables as he was at his desk at the Morgan bank. He was an habitué of the clubhouses at Auteuil and Neuilly, for Harry was first and foremost a gambler. Death had passed him by at a millimeter's distance – could life be anything but a race, a gamble, a risk? He organized a reckless horse-cab race down the Champs-Elysées, and came in second. From the windows of the Ritz he tossed champagne bottles at the bizarre centerpiece of the place Vendôme, a column with wraparound hieroglyphics leading to a doll-like figure of Napoleon perched at the top. In the sound of the bottles merrily crashing against paving stones he may have sought release from the frustration over the distance between himself and the woman he loved.

When he could no longer support the enforced separation, Harry simply boarded the *Aquitania* bound for New York, without the fare in his pocket. He guaranteed his fare by wireless, then with his available cash bribed his way into first class. Harry might have served in the ambulance corps alongside *poilus* and American doughboys, but he did not travel tourist.

Neither Harry's family nor Polly's husband could prevent the inevitable. Peabody agreed to a divorce: Harry and Polly were married and returned to live in Paris in a flat on the rue des Belles-Feuilles in the same neighborhood as the Princesse de Polignac.

Polly's two children from the previous marriage posed a large problem: like many expatriates, Harry could not abide the presence of children or accept a mundane role as parent. He might on an impulse offer six-year-old Polleen a glass of champagne, otherwise he expected the children to be kept out of his sight. For Polly, this domestic purdah was impossible to maintain. Once when Harry found her playing with the children on the floor just as he entered the flat accompanied by friends, he was so outraged by the encounter that he steered his friends outside, then disappeared for days. When he did return – with no word spoken about his absence – he presented his wife with the gift of an expensive negligée, as much a hint of what he expected of her as a peace offering.

During the months Harry worked at the bank he often rowed to work in a canoe. The Crosbys had moved from the flat on rue des Belles-Feuilles to an apartment building on the Ile St-Louis, and there he kept the craft tied up at the quai d'Orléans. Mornings he and Polly set off rowing against the barge traffic until they arrived at the Right Bank end of the pont de la Concorde. Harry would step out of the canoe at the quai des Tuileries and walk on through the tidy gardens to the place Vendôme while his wife returned rowing upstream to the Ile St-Louis.

The code by which Harry Crosby lived was: never regret, never compromise, be in all things extravagant. His actions were determined by impulse: he must seize the moment at any cost; to hold back was to die of ennui.

On the last day of 1923 he bade the Morgan bank adieu. Banking was a denial of his need for total independence of action; he would answer to no one but himself henceforth, his life was his own to direct. In Harry's wide and eclectic reading he had come across a statement by Schopenhauer that he believed applied to himself: 'Social rules are made by normal people for normal people, and the man of genius is fundamentally abnormal.' Harry knew he was fundamentally abnormal and thought that he might, through writing, discover his genius. Meanwhile he and Polly could live on the interest from his share of the family wealth. With the Morgan-van Rensselaer fortune behind him, it was easy enough for Harry to declare: 'Money troubles are never fatal.'

As Harry's need to make himself into a poet grew into an obsession, Polly began to seek her own place in the arts. She changed her name to Caresse, a conceit that prompted a satiric letter from her cousin, signed 'Baiser' Beal. Thus newborn, Caresse studied sculpture with Antoine Bourdelle at the Académie de la Grande Chaumière where she met the other artist-teachers Noguchi, Léger and Giacometti. Harry was making his friends among the literary set: he went to the races at Chantilly with Hemingway and Dos Passos (both veterans of ambulance corps duty, like himself), and he wrote in his diary, 'I would rather have been Joyce than any man alive.' Another time he confessed: 'Today saw Joyce three times . . . and worked in me the same emotion as when Lindbergh arrived.'

Harry's older cousin was Walter Berry, a longstanding resident of Paris in the exclusive faubourg St-Germain quarter. Walter Berry was a bona fide member of Parisian society that included only the most distinguished Americans, or those with sufficient wealth and a title, like the Princesse de Polignac. (Marcel Proust's *A l'ombre des jeunes filles en fleur* was dedicated to Walter Berry; Winnaretta had refused to allow Proust to honor the memory of Prince Edmond de Polignac in the same manner.) Berry was fond of scapegrace Harry and was, from the distance of another generation, something of a foster father to him. Alone among members of the family, Walter Berry encouraged Harry to abandon his banking career to become a poet.

Walter van Rensselaer Berry lived in an eighteenth-century town house at 53 rue de Varenne where Edith Wharton had resided before she settled in her country house outside Paris. Berry had been a close friend and companion to Miss Wharton: it was believed that he had carried on a discreet liaison with her, or that they would surely marry – but actually Berry was a bon vivant in the tradition of the Belle Epoque, a gallant who preferred younger women and had a weakness for *les grandes horizontales*. Crosby and Berry shared a passion for sexual adventure, and books, which may have partly accounted for their mismatched friendship and unexpected rapport. Harry had access to Berry's exquisite collection of first editions, and through Berry's private library made his first acquaintance with Verlaine, Rimbaud and Baudelaire, the *poètes maudits* whose sexual and drug-taking excesses were as much an inspiration to Harry as was their poetry. Eventually Harry and Caresse moved into the same rarefied atmosphere of the faubourg St-Germain, to become neighbors at 19 rue de Lille.

In the autumn of 1927 Walter Berry was being treated by Dr Sergei Voronoff, the famous monkey-gland specialist, in a last effort to revive his failing body and sexual prowess. Berry died in October of that year, his death marked by *pompes funèbres* whose magnificence rivaled the procession for Marcel Proust five years before. As Janet Flanner, Paris correspondent for *The New Yorker*, remarked: 'The ceremonies of death are precisely graded in France.' Of these seven categories of pomp, even the highest has three sub-divisions: Berry's ceremony was in the very first rank. 'The plume-decked, broidered catafalque with its flowing curtains and silver insignia and its four plume-decked black horses with their somber caparisons and white reins, headed a procession in Mr Berry's last honor ... '

Harry and Caresse Crosby, Paris 1922.

Caresse *en plein air*, Paris 1928.

Obsessed as Harry was by death and all its trappings, he was not in accord with the French spirit of *pompes funèbres*; yet he undertook arrangements to have Walter Berry's body cremated. Although Berry's last wishes were that the ashes be scattered (and the idea particularly appealed to Harry), he acceded to Edith Wharton's request that the urn be buried in her garden. When Harry showed up with the urn he was accompanied by two gendarmes who had come along to make certain the ashes were buried according to French law. Miss Wharton was upset to have the police present during the burial, and blamed Harry for the crude intrusion of officialdom during a private memorial service to her dear friend Walter Berry. What Hemingway called Harry's 'wonderful gift of carelessness' was in some respects a kind of innocence, but Edith Wharton – author of *The Age of Innocence* – was unforgiving.

Berry's innocent bequest that his library of rare volumes be given to favorite-cousin Harry Crosby may have been another source of resentment. Harry was to take possession of the books only after Miss Wharton had made her choice from among them. She dallied over her choice of books from the Berry library, a way of annoying Harry for a time, but in the end she selected only a few sets as a token inheritance from her beloved friend, and washed her hands of the Crosbys forever after.

Word of the sybaritic pleasures of the Crosby ménage had got back to Miss Wharton long before the death of Walter Berry. 'Walter's young cousin,' she wrote, 'turns out to be a sort of half-crazy cad.' Edith Wharton would naturally bridle at Polly's change of name to Caresse, and disapprove of Caresse's whippet Narcisse, whose canine nails were painted gold and whose jeweled collars, like those of Josephine Baker's leopard, were changed daily. Further proof of Harry's 'half crazy' way of life was the vast sunken tub the young couple had installed in the 300-year-old house on the rue de Lille. The Crosbys, attired only in dressing gowns and slippers, would receive their guests in the bedroom and soon invite them to join their hosts in the tub, four or more persons at a time, with champagne and caviar sandwiches within casual reach. If the Crosbys came upon a group of art students who attracted them, the students were invited to an impromptu soirée and generously advised to 'bring friends'. By morning the beds and floors would be encumbered with intermingled bodies, Harry and Caresse somewhere part of the naked Laocoön tangle.

On his own, Harry picked up women as casually as he would pluck a flower for his buttonhole: women were drawn to the handsome, self-assured, free-spending individualist. He believed with Oscar Wilde (*The Picture of Dorian Gray* was his favorite novel) that 'the only way to get rid of a temptation is to yield to it'. If he saw a woman who attracted him at a café or in a restaurant, he was quite capable of abandoning his companion of the moment – including his wife – to introduce himself, then walk away with the beautiful stranger. No one remembered an occasion when Harry was rebuffed.

Caresse was in accord with this free-style sexual contract which allowed equal freedom to her, though she took less advantage of it, or had fewer opportunities, than Harry. She was certain Harry's temporary loves were nothing compared with his loyalty and devotion to her. His harem of women she considered merely 'décor'.

There was more than voluptuous pleasure-seeking to their lives: both Harry and Caresse began to produce poetry. Along with their literary ambitions, they had long wanted to be patrons of the arts in a practical way. In 1927 the Crosbys launched the Black Sun Press, not just a vanity-house outlet for their endeavors, but as a major showcase for the most important writers in Paris at that time. The Black Sun's list of authors included Ernest Hemingway, Archibald MacLeish, Kay Boyle, Ford Madox Ford, and of course Harry's particular idol, James Joyce.

The title of Harry Crosby's first volume of poems, *Red Skeletons*, suggests his characteristically morbid turn of mind. Skeletons fascinated Harry: he had purchased the skeleton of a young girl from a medical supply house, then hung it, draped in a yellow raincoat, from his bookshelves. After the revels of the Quatz'Arts students at the Crosby mansion on the rue de Lille, Harry wrote in his diary: 'a mad student drinking wine out of a skull which he had pilfered from my library as I had pilfered it a year ago from the Catacombs.' On the central staircase he had strung up another skeleton, with a contraceptive dangling from its jaws like a tongue.

Harry's verse showed only an occasional gift for expression or depth of feeling, and frequently the lines ran to doggerel. Yet he submitted to a grueling session of composition, from nine until noon, then again after lunch until often late at night – an extraordinary discipline inspired by the working habits of James Joyce. The discipline was considerably modified by Harry's addiction to drugs: at this time he was taking opium regularly, in the belief that the drug might help him write his way into the sacred precincts of art.

If Harry's own genius failed to emerge – through drugs, sun-worship, or a passion for death – he was more than willing to support the genius of others. Another sun-worshiper, D. H. Lawrence, was commissioned to write a work on Harry's obsessional sun-theme, to be called *Sun* and paid for in Harry's favorite form of currency, gold. (If Harry had not found the coins too cumbersome, he would have carried *pièces d'or* as pocket money: he was known to write checks on any convenient surface, a restaurant napkin, a page torn from a telephone directory, and once on a plate at Zelli's.) Since Lawrence was in Italy at the time, Harry went to the gare de Lyon with twenty gold coins of $20 each in a Diogenes search for a passenger on the Rome express with an honest face. Just before the train pulled out, Harry found his man, a complete stranger who asked simply, 'Is it a bomb?' 'No,' replied Harry, 'gold for a poet.' The gold pieces were delivered to Lawrence as planned; the messenger turned out to be the Duke of Argyll.

Harry needed constant stimulus, frequent opportunities for risk, and above all, variety. Every year he and Caresse attended the orgiastic Quatz'Arts Bal – once with Caresse riding bareback, and bare-breasted, on an elephant rented from 'Helen Scott Will Get It For You', an agency Americans turned to for such unlikely items. Harry carried a bag of live snakes and wore a neckpiece of dead pigeons: he distributed his snakes to the nude and gilded students, and one girl was seen to offer a bare nipple to the reptile Harry had given her. But even these outré episodes became routine. Harry hated predictability worse than death; rather, he loved death, the only pursuit worthy of his undivided attention.

On a trip to Egypt in 1928 Harry had himself tattooed on the soles of his feet, and Caresse tattooed on the shoulder, with the symbolic black sun. Egypt was a place of hard bright sun: Harry exposed himself to the burning orb by day, studied Egyptian funerary practices at night. The drugs that led through darkness into light were easily available in North Africa, and an open attitude toward homosexuality that led Harry to yield to that temptation as well, with a shepherd boy from Damascus. This affair no more disturbed Caresse than one of Harry's heterosexual escapades. He might occasionally wear his wife's lace underthings, not from any perverted inclination, but simply because he cared nothing about clothes and had run out of underwear of his own.

Egypt had provided Harry with another piece of wisdom to add to his crazy-quilt philosophy: a statement he picked up from a dervish and transferred to his diary, 'My wealth I can measure by the things I can do without'. Paris was hardly the place to practice the austerity this maxim implied, yet Harry did manage to divest himself of certain possessions, particularly the valuable editions from Walter Berry's collection he had once so coveted. He might surreptitiously place rare or first editions of Rimbaud and Baudelaire among the tattered second-hand volumes for sale on the bookstalls along the Seine. He could then imagine the delighted excitement of some buyer or bookseller coming across these unexpected treasures, gratis, among the dross. If Harry thought an item undervalued – he had his own system of values – he would insist on paying more than the asking price, to the confusion of shopgirls and salesmen.

A simpler life than Paris offered was often the shimmering ideal of the jaded rich. A young Dutch couple, Fran and Mai de Geetere, lived aboard a barge tied up beside the pont Neuf, and one day welcomed the Crosbys aboard. Kittens tumbled about on the rusted metal deck, Fran was playing the accordion and Mai offered the visitors a bowl of cherries – a scene so refreshing and in such contrast to the Crosby existence that the young de Geeteres became a new fascination for Harry and Caresse. The Crosbys began to visit the barge regularly: they brought friends to meet the extraordinary Dutch couple. Fran bartered Holland cheeses, traded sketch portraits for food, did sign-painting or any odd job for a living. Since there were no bathing facilities on the barge, the Crosbys offered their new friends the use of their sunken tub at the rue de Lille mansion: each Saturday Fran and Mai arrived with towels, soap and a change of clothes in a sailor's duffel bag.

Harry and Caresse helped the de Geeteres survive on their subsistence income, bought Fran's sketches, contributed food, delighted to participate even to this limited extent in the lives of the two attractive marginals. When the barge sprung a leak, Harry offered to pay the overhaul and towing charges. It was as if the wealthy couple had adopted their mirror-image counterpart.

Even as the barge was shipping water, the Crosbys sponsored a drydock party for the towing trip. The vessel was crowded with guests, including the Dolly Sisters then playing in Paris at the Moulin Rouge – they had come aboard carrying a case of champagne between them. There was Gouda cheese and wine and fruit, the kittens safely out of reach, Fran playing his accordion. The guests danced on, as the leaking water of the Seine reached their ankles.

*

Another celebrated barge party was the one given by Gerald and Sara Murphy after the opening of the 1923 Ballets Russes production of *Les Noces*. The Murphys had originally wanted to hold the party at the Cirque Médrano, but the director coolly informed them that all of Paris might seem to have become an American colony, but not yet Le Cirque Médrano. Instead, they discovered a *péniche* ordinarily used for official revels of the Chambre des Députés, but free on Sundays, a day of rest for the politicians. So the Murphys leased the barge for the first Sunday, 17 June, following the presentation of *Les Noces*.

The party was one of the first of those supreme *fêtes* the Murphys would become known for: an affair of careful planning that still allowed for spontaneity and fun. As a beginning act of spontaneity, Igor Stravinsky arrived before anyone else and promptly shifted the place cards so that he might sit next to the Princesse de Polignac. Outside, Cocteau lingered on the quai d'Orsay dressed as a ship's captain, but reluctant to board the tied-up vessel for fear of seasickness when passing river traffic rocked the barge. Cocteau watched his friends Chanel and Diaghilev cross the gangplank, then Picasso, Blaise Cendrars, Léger, Tristan Tzara – some forty guests in all, including the principal dancers from the ballet – before he decided the sightseeing boats had stopped running and he could safely join the party. Picasso was fascinated with the miniature toys the Murphys had provided instead of floral place settings (the les Halles flower market being closed on Sundays) and Boris Kochno managed to dislodge a wooden laurel wreath from the ceiling so that Stravinsky might leap through the vast horseshoe of carved leaves in an awkward balletic rite of spring. The party lasted until dawn, its evanescent spirit, as at any successful party, impossible to recall. Afterward guests agreed only that nobody got really drunk, everybody had an amazingly good time, and that the Murphys were an enchanted host and hostess. Gerald claimed that the gift of entertainment originated with Sara: 'I helped organize it.' Sara insisted: 'It wasn't parties that made it such a gay time. There was such affection between everybody. You loved your friends and wanted to see them every day, and usually you did see them every day. It was like a great fair and everybody was so young.'

Being young at a time when Paris was a great fair was one of the reasons Harry Crosby had been convinced life would be wasted at the Morgan bank: Gerald Murphy had come to the same conclusion about working in his father's exclusive leather-goods firm, Mark Cross. In 1921 Gerald took Sara and their three children to Paris, ostensibly to study landscape engineering in the city so lavishly endowed with formal gardens. Sara's share of her own family fortune brought in a comfortable $7,000 a year, and Gerald's money from Mark Cross made it possible for the Murphys to settle into a fashionable apartment on the rue Greuze in Passy. Gerald's father had once told a business partner, 'I don't *want* to make any more money', and Gerald shared his father's sentiment. Very soon after the Murphys arrived in Paris, Gerald was to discover an array of Cubist paintings at the Rosenberg gallery. He lost all interest in landscape engineering from that moment on: 'If that's painting, it's what I want to do.'

Unlike so many well-to-do dilettantes of the era, Gerald Murphy had more than an amateur's passing facility. Natalia Goncharova was his first teacher; his first painting project was to help restore the scenery for *Pulcinella*, along with Dos Passos and other volunteers, when the American colony learned that the Ballets Russes stage sets had been destroyed by fire. This unskilled workman's exercise, done with long-handled brushes from ladders and scaffolds, may have influenced Murphy's subsequent interest in painting on a vast scale. His 12-by-18-foot study of smokestacks and ventilator funnels, *Boatdeck Cunarder*, was accepted by the 1923 Salon des Indépendants over the protest that it was nothing but architectural drawing. Murphy had the support of Fernand Léger, who considered him the only American painter in Paris of any consequence. Like Léger, Murphy was fascinated with artifacts of the twentieth century, and painted in the hard flat colors of ad posters. Even Picasso murmured a rare comment of approval when he saw Murphy's curtain for the Cole Porter ballet, *Within the Quota* – beneath a Hearst-style headline UNKNOWN BANKER BUYS ATLANTIC an upended transatlantic liner was being measured against a skyscraper – 'C'est beau ça.'

Gerald Murphy had come late to painting, and if he had not come to Paris he would never have taken up a paintbrush at all. The Yale graduate born to a thriving family business feared that his interest in the arts would be considered neurotic or effeminate in America. But he was aware, even in France, of being a dilettante or part-time artist. The independent income, and a thriving social life, did not correspond to the classic image of a working artist. Léger once suggested to him that a painter could have a comfortable life with little likelihood that his work would be of great importance, but out of a difficult life came the only painting of any significance. Murphy might have pointed out their friend Picasso, at least the Picasso of the moment – rich, fashionable, gifted – as a rebuttal to this homily, but he knew his own work was not and never could be first-rate, 'and the world is too full of second-rate painting'. By the mid-Twenties Gerald Murphy decided he would never paint again, and he never did.

This was a time when the Riviera was being discovered, or re-discovered, as a carefree summer paradise. Formerly the resort cities of Nice and Cannes thrived in the winter months only, their wedding-cake hotels a hospice for the elderly rich, British tourists, and the infirm. The newcomers – Coco Chanel, Picasso, Cole Porter – were beginning to arrive in the unfashionable summer months, leading the way to undiscovered fishing villages and unpopulated stretches of virgin sand. On the crest of the latest wave, but in their own inimitable style, the Murphys staked out a seaside sanctuary they called Villa America, on the cap d'Antibes. Via *le train bleu* the Côte d'Azur had become a kind of overnight suburb of the Parisian social scene, now that the Murphys had transferred their hospitality to the Mediterranean shore.

*

In the spring of 1925 the Fitzgeralds made their second attempt to live in France, this time 'on practically nothing a year'. *The Great Gatsby* had just been published to excellent reviews but, in Fitzgerald's opinion, poor sales: the nothing-a-year amounted to the $7,000 he had so far earned from the novel. With their infant daughter Scottie, the Fitzgeralds sailed on the *Aquitania* to the Mediterranean, then made their way to Paris via Lyon in an automobile they had purchased on the Riviera. The closed car did not suit Zelda's penchant for riding with the wind in her hair, so at a garage in Lyon they had the metal top cut away like a sardine can. They continued driving north until the first spring rain soaked them thoroughly: the topless car had to be abandoned. It was a typical gesture of Scott and Zelda: a decision taken on a momentary impulse, an improvident fling to repent at leisure. The episode was the prelude to their 'summer of 1000 parties and no work'.

In Paris they settled into a flat at 14 rue de Tilsitt off one of the busy spokes of the Arc de Triomphe in what would appear to be the very center of things. Despite the impeccable address, the apartment was forbidding and none too clean, somberly furnished in a mixture of periods one guest called 'early Galeries Lafayette'. There was, at least, a telephone – or you could always get in touch with friends by *pneumatique*, the city-wide vacuum-tube message service. Otherwise you met by chance at the Dôme, American Express, or Zelli's.

The frantic pace of party life left little time for the expatriate parents to concern themselves with their daughter. The Fitzgeralds had high-minded theories of child-rearing, but turned Scottie over to a series of servants and nannies. On the one occasion anyone ever saw Zelda taking personal care of her daughter, she was bathing Scottie in the bidet.

The friendship between Ernest Hemingway and Scott Fitzgerald was based more on common literary interests than any natural affinity: they admired one another's work and enjoyed one another's company – the enjoyment more on Fitzgerald's side than on Hemingway's – but there was a strain to the relationship from the beginning. At their first meeting in the Dingo Bar, Fitzgerald praised his fellow author in embarrassingly extravagant terms, then very quickly lapsed into a kind of drunken paralysis after a single glass of champagne. Hemingway did not think much of a man who could not hold his liquor; then, there was something about Fitzgerald's mouth, a pretty-boy look to his face, that disturbed Hemingway. As for Zelda, Hemingway thought she was jealous of Scott's writing and would do anything to keep him from his typewriter.

There was some question as to which of the two, Scott or Zelda, led the other into the drunken pranks and party games – kidnaping waiters 'to saw in half with a musical saw', splashing through the fountain at l'Observatoire in evening clothes, returning home at dawn from les Halles in a camion loaded with carrots – the escapades that marked their time in Paris, a legendary hedonism, a doomed pursuit of sustained pleasure. A flaw in Fitzgerald's character, according to Hemingway, was Scott's awe of and attraction to the rich. In a hurt letter, Fitzgerald denied any such obsession, despite the evidence from his stories and novels very much concerned with the ethos of affluence. Certainly he was awed by the Old Guard, financial or literary; he was self-conscious about his own middle-American background and sensitive about being outclassed.

*

Fitzgerald's fascination with the rich led him into the irresistible orbit of Gerald and Sara Murphy and their Riviera coterie. Even the harder-

Zelda and F. Scott Fitzgerald with their daughter Scottie on board ship en route to Europe.

boiled Ernest Hemingway had succumbed to the Murphy charm, after having been introduced to them by Dos Passos. In a sense, Gerald and Sara Murphy were the chief witnesses to traumatic breakdowns in both the Hemingway and Fitzgerald marriages.

The Fitzgeralds survived, but barely, Zelda's casual and seemingly innocent flirtation with a dashing young French pilot, Edouard Jozan. While Scott was taking advantage of an exceptional period of productivity, writing most of the day at their rented villa in St-Raphael, Zelda was restless and bored, spending the sunlit hours on the beach, often surrounded by a group of officers from the nearby base at Fréjus. Zelda's particular favorite among this circle of bachelor admirers was Jozan, and the Murphys watched with some alarm Zelda's more than passing interest in her tanned and handsome beach companion. 'I must say,' reported Sara Murphy, 'everyone knew about it but Scott.' To Scott the situation seemed no more than Zelda's harmless beaux-collecting in Montgomery, Alabama, when he was one of the beaux proposing marriage to her. When it dawned on him that Jozan was more than a hopeless admirer of his wife, and that Zelda had become seriously attracted to him, there was a scene and an abrupt end to the affair. But neither Scott nor Zelda quite recovered from the episode, and both were sufficiently haunted by the memory of Edouard Jozan to use versions of him, if not the man entire, as fictional characters in novels: Tommy Barban in Scott's *Tender Is the Night*, and Jacques Chevre-Feuille in Zelda's *Save Me the Waltz*.

The Hemingway break was far more serious, leading to a trial separation between Ernest and Hadley, and finally to divorce. They had been staying with the Murphys at the Villa America when Bumby came down with whooping cough. In order to spare the Murphy children a dangerous contagion, Ernest and Hadley moved to a smaller villa in the neighborhood. Then Pauline Pfeiffer appeared on the scene: she had had whooping cough as a child, so she offered to join the Hemingways in their quarantine-isolation, an apparently benevolent gesture but one with motives beyond the call of friendship.

'Then, instead of the two of them and their child, there are three of them,' wrote Hemingway in *A Moveable Feast*. 'First it is stimulating and fun and it goes on that way for a while. All things truly wicked start from an innocence.'

A few months later, when the Hemingway marriage fell apart, Gerald Murphy offered Ernest his atelier on the rue Froidevaux in Paris, so

that he could set up a separate residence. In later years, Hemingway –
with his queer logic – blamed the Murphys for the breakdown of his
marriage with Hadley – 'Then you have the rich, and nothing is ever as
it was again' – and vilified Dos Passos as the 'pilot-fish' who had led
him to the rich.

*

In a reflective piece of fiction called *Babylon Revisited*, F. Scott
Fitzgerald makes a nostalgic tour of central Paris. The author's sense of
Parisian geography fails during the extended taxi journey – the two
banks of the Seine are somehow reversed – yet Fitzgerald's sense of the
city is right in more important ways. The protagonist, who might have
been Fitzgerald himself, directs the taxi past the ornate Opéra because
'he wanted to see the blue hour spread over the magnificent façade'.
The grill is being closed in front of Brentano's bookstore, and diners
are being served at the outdoor terrace of Duval's. 'He had never really
eaten at a cheap restaurant in Paris. Five course dinner for four francs
fifty, eighteen cents, wine included. For some odd reason he wished
that he had.'

Because of his bedazzlement by the rich, a large part of life in Paris
forever eluded Fitzgerald. Early success made it possible for Scott and
Zelda to imitate the lives of those whose insouciant style was sustained
by inherited wealth. This was a vain pursuit, as Fitzgerald was to admit
during the downturn of the Thirties, for a working writer dependent on
the sale of stories to *The Saturday Evening Post*.

When the taxi in *Babylon Revisited* does finally reach its destination,
the author-protagonist broods over his one large regret: 'I spoiled this
city for myself. I didn't realize it, but the days came along one after
another, and then two years were gone, and everything was gone, and I
was gone.'

CHAPTER EIGHTEEN

The Mood of '27

Harold Stearns had left America in disgust after compiling the volume *Civilization in the United States*, but he was just as disillusioned when American civilization pursued him to Paris. He saw the Dôme change from a dingy bistro with a billiard parlor in the back to the favorite tourist café in Montparnasse – the billiard parlor had been eliminated to make room for more Americans. To Ernest Hemingway's dismay his waiter-friend Jean at the Closerie de Lilas had been ordered to shave off his dragoon's mustache and wear a white jacket: the Lilas was being converted to a *bar Americain*. La Coupole had also become an American bar, and Jimmy's and Le Jockey introduced the New York speakeasy ambience to the Boulevard Montparnasse. When Richard Aldington returned to Paris in 1927, his favorite little café-restaurant on the rue de Rennes, where the prewar *menu fixe* had been 75 centimes, now served 'thirsty legions of contemporary genius' a forty-franc regional specialty.

The 1927 American Chamber of Commerce estimated that there were 15,000 Americans resident in Paris, but many Americans did not trouble to register with the police: the official estimate was closer to 40,000 – or perhaps it just seemed, to the French, there were that many. The American presence was everywhere evident as the transatlantic liners disgorged more and more tourists on the shores of France. These latecomers were not of the same species as those of the earlier migration, at the beginning of the decade. 'With each new shipment of Americans spewed up by the boom the quality fell off,' wrote Fitzgerald. 'Toward the end there was something sinister about the crazy boatloads.'

Fitzgerald himself did little to enhance the reputation of visiting Americans. Outside a night club the drunken author noticed a woman offering a tray of assorted trinkets for sale: he playfully kicked the tray from her hands, the pitiful collection of trivia went flying. Fitzgerald's companions were exasperated with his shameful behavior. 'But I gave her a hundred francs,' he said. 'Did you see me give her a hundred francs?' Lawrence Vail, 'King of Bohemia' (married to heiress Peggy Guggenheim), was arrested for publicly burning a 100 franc note during a café argument.

Americans would never realize how the French secretly felt about them. The childlike behavior and unconscious waste exhibited by visitors from the US was abhorrent to their old-world hosts. Yankee profligacy and frontier naiveté were qualities that aroused the French to indignation. British author Clive Bell explained the gap between the French and Americans this way: 'Some Americans had French mistresses, but very few had French friends.' (Man Ray was the exception – he had both.)

On the surface there seemed an equilibrium of interests. France was hard up in 1927. The economy was at the point of collapse, with the franc leading the way down. Americans were made welcome while the dollars flowed, for there were many Parisians who could profit from the bandwagon American boom. But the rest of France was left brooding and resentful. The Paris *Herald* ran a report on the increasing losses faced by hotels and restaurants in the vicinity of the north-eastern battlefields. Sentiment about the late Great War had so dissipated that families of the soldiers who had bled and died in France no longer took Cook's featured tour of Ypres, Verdun and the Marne. Overseas visitors bypassed the hallowed ground to make a beeline for Maxim's, the Café de la Paix and the Folies-Bergère.

An outrage that united the French as no other issue could was the recent demand by the US that France must pay its war debt. To the average Frenchman this situation was absurd: in the midst of its gravest financial crisis since the war, France was being dunned for funds borrowed from a rich wartime ally. President Doumergue was obliged to go to Washington to plead poverty to the US Senate – the French press referred to Uncle Sam as Uncle Shylock.

While most Americans did not at first recognize a growing anti-Yankee sentiment, certain shifts in attitude were becoming obvious. On one of his frequent return visits to Paris, E. E. Cummings – who now signed himself e. e. cummings – was arrested by the police for urinating on a darkened corner of rue Gît-le-Coeur. At the commissariat on rue de l'Abbaye, the arresting officer was asked the charge. 'Un américain qui pisse.' 'Quoi?' replied his superior, 'encore un pisseur américain?'

The surliness of service employees was a given of Parisian life – hadn't waiters and taxi drivers *always* been surly? But the indications were more ominous than that. An editorial in *Paris-Midi* deplored the habit of booing Americans on the street when they were heard to utter a phrase in English. An angry crowd forced the newspaper *Le Matin* to haul down an American flag displayed on the front of the building. A tourist bus was stoned by local residents when it passed through Montmartre.

Now that the Great War was seven years in the distant past, the memory of American doughboy heroes had faded. All the French needed was a single certified American hero to perform the most daring exploit of the century, and their anti-Americanism would reverse overnight.

*

Two French pilots, Nungesser and Coli, had earlier that year attempted the first flight across the Atlantic: their plane disappeared in the great void of the North Atlantic. The tragedy – four American pilots had already been killed in the same attempt – emphasized the danger of an inter-continental flying venture. In the summer of 1927 an air-link between Europe and America was still considered an impossible dream.

However, the Brevoort and Lafayette Hotel Group in New York was offering the $25,000 Orteig Prize for the first successful transatlantic flight, and a 25-year-old mail pilot, Charles A. Lindbergh, was determined to set off from New York bound for Paris, non-stop. His plane was a Ryan monoplane of metal superstructure and wooden wings: a consortium of Missouri businessmen had put up the money to build the flying machine, and named it *The Spirit of St Louis*.

On 20 May 1927, the Long Island weather reports were as favorable as Lindbergh could expect for the season: it was raining at Roosevelt Field, but clouds were lifting all across the Atlantic. Loaded with enough fuel for forty hours, the plane weighed 5,250 pounds – 1,000 pounds more than it had ever carried before – and there was some doubt that it could lift off from the muddy airfield. Lindbergh was up well before dawn with very little sleep behind him to sustain a forty-hour solo venture. Another problem was that the motor, during a warm-up session, could not rev up to full power. The mechanic considered the loss of power a temporary failure due to the weather: 'They never rev up on a day like this.'

The decision was made, Lindbergh was ready to fly. He had made up half-a-dozen ham sandwiches – 'If I get to Paris I won't need any more, and if I don't get to Paris I won't need any more either' – and a thermos of coffee. He tucked a wishbone in the pocket of his flying jacket, climbed into the cockpit, and adjusted his goggles. 'Well, boys, I'm off.' Mechanics and helpers had to push on the wing struts to get the plane moving. At take-off, *The Spirit of St Louis* skidded through a puddle of water and missed a stretch of telephone line by twenty feet, but Lindbergh was airborne and away. He took a bedraggled kitten along with him for company.

The French had been skeptical all along. In *Paris-Soir* an editorial expressed doubt that a lone flier could stay awake and alert enough 'to challenge successfully the dark forces waiting to do battle with him over the Atlantic'. Even the Americans, more optimistic by nature, called Lindbergh 'The Flying Fool'. The flight would have been hazardous under the best of conditions, but Lindbergh was sometimes obliged to fly as low as fifty feet from the surface of the water to avoid great banks of storm. After he had passed Newfoundland, cable reports began coming in from ships that had sighted the low-flying aircraft. Interested parties on both sides of the Atlantic began to take the exploit seriously: at le Bourget airport all planes were ordered grounded until further notice, vessels at sea were advised to keep a sharp lookout. Finally there was a sighting at Dingle Bay, Ireland, then another report from the coast of Cornwall. The news brought on the first wave of mass hysteria.

*

The romance and risk that informed Lindbergh's stunt so impressed Harry Crosby that he immediately identified with the Lone Eagle: he would have given his soul to change places with the solitary pilot then flying over the English Channel. His emulation was further encouraged by Caresse's declaration that Harry and Lindy looked alike enough to be brothers, except for Lindbergh's thatch of red hair. As soon as word reached Paris that *The Spirit of St Louis* had passed over the coast of France at Cherbourg, the Crosbys embarked in their chauffeur-driven limousine along the Route de Flandre leading northward out of Paris. The road was already as crowded with vehicles as when it served as the lifeline for a taxicab army en route to the Battle of the Marne.

Before the Cherbourg sighting, the afternoon crowd at le Bourget had been estimated at 45,000. By the time the Crosbys arrived, there were some 150,000 observers eagerly scanning the sky for the first sign

of the monoplane. US Ambassador Myron T. Herrick – considered by James Thurber to be publicity mad, forever elbowing his way into the front pages – was waiting for Lindbergh in the control tower with a delegation of French officials. Air space above le Bourget was closed to all traffic in order to keep the skies clear for the single-minded mail pilot from the west.

At twilight kleig lights were trained on the runways; police and airport personnel began to erect barriers to keep the growing crowd at bay. Meanwhile Lindbergh had twice passed over the Eiffel tower, but could not locate le Bourget.

'C'est lui!'

At a little past 10 p.m. Harry and Caresse Crosby, along with the thousands at the airfield, saw a sudden flash of silver against the moon. 'C'est Lindbergh!' Indeed, the frail monoplane was moving in and out of the banked clouds above le Bourget.

The Spirit of St Louis drifted lower and lower along a flare-lined runway, then made a smooth and precise landing. Lindbergh was prepared to taxi the plane in the direction of the hangars, but at that moment the impatient crowd broke through the police line and spilled over onto the field. There were cries of 'Lind-dee, Lin-dee!' as the first enthusiasts reached the aircraft. The Crosbys were unable to approach the center of all this excitement: the plane was completely cut off, surrounded by near riot. Harry and Caresse hovered on the periphery of the tumultuous crowd, quietly glorying in the triumph of their fellow American.

'Am I here?' asked the dazed pilot as he emerged from the cockpit. 'Is this really Paris?'

The wild display on all sides was answer enough. Exhausted by his thirty-three-hour ordeal, Lindbergh was more frightened of the surging, hysterical mob than by any possible danger he had imagined en route. He was then pulled as if by suction into the crowd, hoisted onto eager shoulders, paraded aloft. His headgear was pulled from his head and fell into the crowd: the cap and goggles were recovered by a mechanic, Harry Wheeler, who could no longer reach Lindbergh. A group of French pilots realized they might rescue Lindbergh if Wheeler donned the cap; he did, and was paraded around the field, thus diverting part of the mob who mistook him for Lindbergh. Meanwhile the real Lindbergh was freed by a cordon of gendarmes and several French pilots sent to his rescue. It was impossible to present Lindy to

The Spirit of St Louis flying over Paris.

his official welcoming committee in the besieged control tower, so the pilots escaped with Lindbergh by driving into Paris for a rendezvous at the Arc de Triomphe. Lindy spoke no French, but under the great arch his companions made known – in sign language and broken English – that here, beneath the eternal flame, lay the Unknown Soldier of World War I.

Meanwhile, furious newsmen at le Bourget learned that Lindbergh had been whisked away. A worse revelation was that some unscrupulous United Press correspondent had conspired to tie up all public telephones at le Bourget. In their frustration, a group of newsmen upturned the telephone kiosk occupied by the chief correspondent of the UP, trapping the hapless conniver inside, with the wires cut.

The shrewd and equally Machiavellian Hank Wales of the Paris *Herald*, knowing what the situation would be like at le Bourget, had not even ventured to the airport. He cabled a completely fictitious interview with Lindbergh made up of statements Lindy would have made under the circumstances: the scoop earned Wales a $500 bonus. (Wales arranged with connections at the US Embassy not to deny he had interviewed Lindbergh or release statements contradictory to those Lindbergh was supposed to have made in the exclusive interview.)

It took the Crosbys until long past midnight to get back to Paris through the tangle of traffic on the Route de Flandre. Montmartre was packed with celebrants: it was like New Year's Eve in mid-summer. Josephine Baker had stopped the show at the Folies to announce that Lindy had made it to Paris. The wildly exultant Crosbys spent the remainder of that historic night toasting the success of the Lone Eagle in champagne.

*

Lindbergh had been forty hours without sleep. He was driven to Ambassador Herrick's residence at 2 avenue d'Iéna for the luxury of a first bath, a meal of bouillon, poached egg and milk; then to bed by 3 a.m. wearing the ambassador's silk pyjamas.

While Lindy slept, Herrick assembled an appropriate wardrobe to the measure of the tall slim pilot – Lindbergh had brought along no change of clothes, no money; he had a passport, but no visa for France. The ambassador would arrange for the inevitable round of receptions: now that Paris was only thirty-three hours from New York, the man who made it possible was an instant celebrity. As long as Lindbergh remained in Paris, the American ambassador would be at his side: the

Embassy, and the United States at large, would benefit from the reflected glory of Lindbergh's extraordinary exploit.

The exhausted hero slept till noon. Next day – with his natural tact and a genuine concern – Lindbergh chose to visit Madame Nungesser at 33 faubourg du Temple, a call he put before any other official function. Nothing could have endeared him more to the French than to have paid homage to the mother whose son had been lost during a similar attempt to fly the Atlantic.

At a press conference in the Embassy residence, Lindy gracefully submitted to a hail of questions put by international newsmen. A persistent inquiry was how did the lone pilot urinate during the long flight; or, as Hank Wales – who was, this time, legitimately present at the interview – bluntly asked: 'Was there a crapper on the plane?'

'I had a sort of aluminum container. I dropped the thing when I was over France.'

To a woman reporter's question about his interest in the opposite sex, he replied, 'No, I am not married or engaged, nor have I any prospects of being married or engaged.' With all else, Lindy had instantly become the world's most eligible bachelor.

It would seem that nothing could have surpassed the glory of the flight itself, but an undreamed-of bonus was that the pilot should be a tall, handsome, unassuming young American. Lindbergh could do no wrong: at those first public appearances his modesty and boyish charm completely won the day. This clear-eyed, clean-living example of American manhood did much to obliterate the image of frivolity and debauch created by the café set.

President Gaston Doumergue presented Lindbergh with the highest decoration France could confer, the cross of the Legion of Honor – following which the flier uneasily submitted to the traditional kiss on each cheek. At a luncheon given by the Aero Club, Lindbergh was invited to step onto the balcony bedecked with French and American flags, to greet a cheering mob massed in the square below and spilling into the adjoining streets, a crowd of 50,000. A microphone was placed before him and Lindy spoke a few carefully chosen words in his first public address – then, at the elaborate French luncheon, drank his first glass of champagne. He went on to the Hôtel de Ville to be feted in the presence of the mayor of Paris, displayed like some glorious ornament against the backdrop of the medieval town hall: the 'Star-Spangled Banner' blared forth, followed by the 'Marseillaise'. The front page of every newspaper in Paris was filled with the details of Lindbergh's winged victory, column after column devoted to the most celebrated American-in-Paris of all time.

*

After the fanfare that greeted Lindbergh's great exploit, the French love affair with America was to last less than three months. Two anarchists, Nicola Sacco and Bartolomeo Vanzetti, had been convicted of murder and robbery in Dedham, Massachusetts. In what seemed to be a trial representing Boston's upper class versus two hapless Italian immigrants with unpopular political beliefs, the case aroused the French to a passion reminiscent of the Dreyfus Affair. There was evidence that the trial conducted by Judge Thayer had been unfair, and his statements outside the courtroom prejudicial. Demands for a new trial had been denied. To the French, and most Europeans, a conservative and repressive court system had condemned the men to death because they were poor, foreign, and proclaimed radical sentiments. National and international pressure for a stay of execution came to nothing. Sacco and Vanzetti were sent to the electric chair on 22 August 1927.

In Paris, news of the execution set off the most alarming riots of the decade. French mobs made the rounds of the cafés where Americans were known to congregate: many US citizens were badly beaten up or at the very least insulted in the street, publicly reviled for the Sacco-Vanzetti deaths. The expatriate colonies of Montmartre and Montparnasse were under siege. The gendarmes and mounted police who had only recently surrounded the American Embassy to hold back the crowds cheering for Lindbergh, now cordoned off the avenue Gabriel to protect Ambassador Herrick and his diplomatic staff from assault.

Feeling was still running so high by Armistice Day that William L. Shirer was pulled off an assignment to cover Isadora Duncan's funeral in Paris in order to cover the American Legion parade. His editor at the *Chicago Tribune* was certain there would be demonstrations against the 20,000 former doughboys marching down the Champs-Elysées.

In the late summer of 1927 Isadora Duncan had stepped into a motor car to go for a drive along the Promenade des Anglais in Nice. As she drove off she called out to friends, 'Adieu, mes amis, je vais à la gloire.' As the automobile picked up speed, Isadora's long trailing scarf – part of the loose-fitting, fluid dress style she had always favored – caught in one of the wheels. She died instantly from a broken neck.

Demonstration for Sacco and Vanzetti, Paris 1927.

The funeral cortege for Isadora Duncan was made up of only five carriages winding slowly to the Père Lachaise cemetery. The French government ignored the event, although Isadora had been a staunch friend to France: she had rented at her own expense the Metropolitan Opera House in New York, to plead the cause and raise funds for France at the outbreak of World War I; she had given up her château Bellevue, in Neuilly, to serve as a hospital for French wounded. None of Isadora's French friends walked behind the coffin.

Just after the Russian Revolution, Isadora Duncan had established a school of dance in Moscow, and she had married the Russian poet Sergei Esenin: the single imposing floral tribute at her funeral came from Russia: 'Le Coeur de Russie Pleure Isadora.' The heart of Russia wept for her, but the face of France was turned away.

*

Since Lindbergh's historic flight, Harry Crosby's death wish entered a new phase: he had himself taken to the air. Along with his friend, the Russian Prince Carageorgovich, Harry began taking twice-weekly flying lessons at Villacoublay. The air-crash death of a fellow student discouraged him not at all – rather, the tragedy could only add further glamor to Harry's newest obsession. Any adventure that attracted Harry Crosby must include the risk of sudden and dramatic oblivion.

At this time Harry came to know the French photographer Henri Cartier-Bresson, who spoke to him of what he called 'the decisive moment' in photography, the single instant of timing that renders a captured image into a work of art. For Harry, there must be a decisive moment concerning death; he had been reading Nietzsche, and was awed by the statement: 'Die at the right time'.

The decisive moment was not yet at hand, but flying exhilarated Harry in a bizarre new way: the airplane was surely the instrument for a perfect farewell to life. The Crosbys, like so many other wealthy expatriates, kept a second house outside Paris, the Moulin du Soleil – purchased from Armand de la Rochefoucauld, with a 'check' written on the cuff torn from Harry's shirtsleeve – a sanctuary from the frantic downward-spiraling city life. Harry convinced Caresse to join him in a death pact: when the time came, they would fly above the French woodlands surrounding their country property, then leap from the airplane together. To celebrate this macabre contract, Harry had gravestones prepared for himself and Caresse, and erected in the garden at the Moulin du Soleil.

Isadora Duncan and Sergei Esenin.

1

APRIL, 1927

transition

James Joyce, Kay Boyle, Carl Sternheim, Marcel Jouhandeau,
Hjalmar Söderberg, F. Boillot, Gertrude Stein, André Gide,
Robert M. Coates, Philippe Soupault, Archibald Mac Leish,
Paul Eldridge, R. Ellsworth Larsson, Else Lasker-Schüler,
Ludwig Lewisohn, Virgil Geddes, Marcel Noll, Bravig Imbs
Hart Crane, Evan Shipman, Georg Trakl, Robert Desnos,
Pavel Tselitsieff, Max Ernst, L. Tihanyi, Robert Sage.

Principal Agency : *SHAKESPEARE* and *CO*.
12, rue de l'Odéon, Paris, VIᵉ

Price { **10 francs**
        50 cents.

CHAPTER NINETEEN

The Time of *transition*

When tough-minded Daniel Darrah of the *Chicago Tribune* (Paris edition) needed somebody to take over Ford Madox Ford's literary column, he chose Eugene Jolas. Darrah wanted a newspaperman, not a 'writer', to write 'Rambles Through Literary Paris'. Jolas was both, and he would soon follow Ford Madox Ford in another area, that of editing one of the seminal little magazines of the 1920s.

Little magazines were dying off by 1927, but Eugene Jolas defiantly launched *transition* that troubled year. After *The Little Review* folded in 1926 – then came briefly to life in 1929, with a single issue to announce its demise – *transition* became the last important voice, a *cri de coeur* and occasionally a fanfare, of the fading decade.

Jolas brought a professionalism to *transition* in place of the haphazard approach or dilettante editing of so many of the literary journals of the era. Also, his French and German upbringing contributed to a European emphasis in *transition* beyond the familiar Anglo-American style and content. Surrealism was the dominant movement of the day, and *transition* was a reflection of this movement: Jolas was particularly influenced by the dream theories of Sigmund Freud, as were the Expressionists and Surrealists.

Under the twin dictatorship of André Breton and Louis Aragon, Surrealists commonly scorned or ignored publications of whatever intellectual pretension, except their own hard-line *La Révolution Surréaliste*. (When the movement became Communist-minded, the journal was renamed *Le Surréalisme au Service de la Révolution*.) Breton soon recognized the signal value and larger influence *transition* commanded among the Paris art and literary sets: his own work and that of fellow French Surrealists began to appear in the proscribed journal. In *transition 6* the Surrealists published one of their famous manifestos, 'Hands off Love', an impassioned defense of Charlie Chaplin, standing trial in the United States, and his inherent right to ask his wife to perform 'unnatural acts'.

A latecomer to the underground publishing scene, *transition* had less occasion to unveil new talent than previous journals of experimental work. The traditional standard-bearers of the avant-garde were once again the most remarkable of the contributors. Gertrude Stein was represented in the inaugural issue with 'An Elucidation' ('her first effort to explain herself'), and later with 'As a Wife Has a Cow: a Love Story'. And again, James Joyce's fragments from *Finnegans Wake* were included, for by now every small press and experimental magazine felt obliged to print a portion of his *Work in Progress* almost as an imprimatur of bona-fide modernism.

Of those writers not yet familiar to the expatriate reading public, Hart Crane, whose poetry was appearing in *transition*, was the most notable. At the Deux Magots, Eugene Jolas introduced Crane to Harry and Caresse Crosby, who were interested in publishing Hart Crane's long poem, *The Bridge*, in the Black Sun editions. The Crosbys were so impressed by the young poet – and Harry, by Crane's chaotic and self-destructive nature – that they invited him to the Moulin du Soleil where he was supplied with a tower room, paper, and his favorite scotch, Cutty Sark, in order to finish his masterwork. But the poet spent more time seducing the Crosby's chauffeur and the local chimneysweep (who left his sooty handprints over the white walls of Crane's ivory tower) than he did working on *The Bridge*. Crane exceeded even Harry's indulgent policy of laissez-faire with his savage drunken binges, and he was obliged to dispatch the poet to Paris with a final bottle of Cutty Sark and a return ticket by ship to New York.

Crane was one of *transition's* genuinely promising discoveries, but other contributors were truly second-rate. Jolas published Harry Crosby's 'Sun Death' even though he knew Crosby's poetry to be of questionable value: portions of Crosby's diary also appeared in *transition*, and if he had any gift at all it was in this expression of a bizarre attitude toward life. But Jolas was committed to an open-door policy at *transition*, hoping to foster a 'new language' in the style of the Surrealist automatic writing. If James Joyce and Gertrude Stein were to be permitted their experiments with language, why not Lincoln Gillespie? Gillespie was one of the café-terrasse writers Richard Aldington referred to when he wrote: 'In one place and in one moment of time were gathered together nearly as many specimens of the genus would-be-artist as all Europe had produced of the genuine article since the fall of Troy.' Gillespie's free-form prose was an unintentional parody of the works of James Joyce and Gertrude Stein rather than a new mode of literary expression, and might have had some value as satire if Gillespie had not taken himself so seriously. The notorious café dilettante became so inflated by his sudden celebrity that he broke with his wife, explaining: now that he was published in *transition* he could no longer live with a woman who was not his intellectual equal.

When Jolas worked on the *Chicago Tribune* he had been friendly with fellow correspondents Elliot Paul and Robert Sage. Jolas convinced Paul to join him as co-editor of *transition* and Sage as associate editor. The enterprise was financially shaky but courageously independent, which exactly suited Paul's temperament: he told Gertrude Stein, 'If ever there are more than two thousand subscribers, I quit.' There were never more than a thousand. Contributors were paid twenty francs per printed page; deficit expenditures came out of Jolas's pocket, or from supporters like Harry and Caresse Crosby.

Eugene Jolas's wife Maria also helped edit *transition*, and Kay Boyle, who had survived the dissolution of *This Quarter*, was recruited as an associate editor. The magazine was published in an office at 40 rue Fabert that had little to offer in the way of space or luxury – manuscripts were stacked on boards across the bidet and lavabo – except for the expansive view across the formal esplanade des Invalides to the mock-Byzantine domes of the Sacré-Coeur dominating the opposite side of the city.

Any journal that published both James Joyce and Gertrude Stein was certain to confront the ego-demands of both these *monstres sacrés*. Gertrude Stein could not understand why the Jolases would bother to be friends with Joyce and to publish him in *transition*, often in the same issue with her own work. 'Joyce is a third rate Irish politician', she told them. 'The greatest living writer of the age is Gertrude Stein.' The Jolases were not altogether convinced of this, and their attitude did not escape Gertrude's notice.

The reason Gertrude Stein received a large share of attention in *transition* was because of Elliot Paul's enthusiasm for her work. Miss Stein further alienated the Jolases by referring to Elliot Paul as the editor. 'Elliot Paul slowly disappeared,' she reported erroneously, 'and Eugene and Maria Jolas appeared.' It was Eugene Jolas who had founded the magazine, and then brought Elliot Paul in as co-editor – Paul lasted only a year, but that was the year Gertrude Stein's work was so ardently promoted.

The feud between Miss Stein and the Jolases may have been partly personal. Kay Boyle had once remarked about Maria Jolas: 'She had the large head of a Roman emperor and the wild gaze of a poet' – Gertrude Stein had also been described as having the head of a Roman emperor, and perhaps there was not room for two such imperial heads in one expatriate kingdom. Nothing by Gertrude Stein appeared in the final issues of *transition*, and for this reason, Miss Stein implied, '*transition* died'.

*

Alice Toklas continued to type the growing accumulation of unpublished manuscripts of Gertrude Stein, a huge inventory of unread work that was a constant source of unhappiness to the neglected author. It was Alice's idea to start a small press of their own, Plain Editions, which – unlike the other small presses in Paris – would print exclusively the works of a single author, Gertrude Stein.

Their first production was a short novel entitled *Lucy Church Amiably*. At Gertrude's request, the book was to look like a school book, and to be bound in the traditional blue of French textbook covers. Alice managed to get exactly the right shade of blue for the cover of *Lucy Church Amiably*, and to Gertrude's further delight the book was being displayed in the windows of the English-language bookshops. Gertrude, who loved to take long rambling walks in her favorite city, loved all the more to return from an outing and report to Alice she had seen *Lucy Church Amiably* in a bookshop window.

In addition to her long promenades through Paris, Gertrude Stein often strolled in her neighborhood park, the Luxembourg Gardens, a far more congenial and intimate exercise than walking through the Tuileries. In the Luxembourg Gardens the trees bore their familiar Latin name tags; there was a homely orchard, with apples in their little paper collars, there was even a miniature statue of liberty (all the statuary was on a far less heroic scale than in the Tuileries) which appealed to Miss Stein's undiminished patriotism. American she was and American she would remain, even if Paris, after all these years, was her 'home town'. She did not intend to go back to the United States until she was a lion, she declared: it would take the best-selling *The Autobiography of Alice B. Toklas* to make her lion enough for a brief return to America in the Thirties.

Meanwhile her entourage diminished as she became more and more content with her own, or Alice's, company. 'I like being alone with

Gertrude Stein and Alice B. Toklas in the late 1920s.

English and myself.' Now, instead of a young writer or neo-Romantic painter strolling beside her in the Luxembourg Gardens, she would more likely walk alone, or take her French poodle Basket for an airing. She still visited the art galleries, especially when she had an hour to kill while Basket was being trimmed and shampooed. Listening to Basket lap his water, Gertrude came to realize, as she told Alice, the difference between sentences and paragraphs, 'that paragraphs are emotional and that sentences are not'.

At the end of the Twenties, Gertrude had electric radiators put into the atelier, and a telephone was installed. The radiators overheated, and smelled. The telephone turned out to be a swift and efficient instrument for breaking off with no-longer-welcome friends. She was beginning to dismiss her young men of 26. She quarreled with Georges Hugnet, who was translating *The Making of Americans* into French, over her 'free translation' of his own *Enfances*. When Bravig Imbs had the impertinence to suggest that his wife Valeska might visit the region of Gertrude's summer house at Bilignin, Alice telephoned him to say, 'We want never to see you again'. Virgil Thomson received Gertrude Stein's calling card with the scribbled message: 'Miss Stein declines further acquaintance with Mr Thomson.' Plans went ahead, by letter, for Thomson to set *Four Saints in Three Acts* to music, even though the author and the composer were no longer speaking to one another.

Friends continued to call, but a cool reception meant that soon enough they too would receive a curt message of dismissal signed by Gertrude or a fatal *coup de téléphone* from Alice.

Pavlik Tchelitchev sidestepped the inevitable foreclosure of friendship with Gertrude Stein by removing himself from her sight. It was apparent that Gertrude had been unhappy with Tchelitchev's 'vulture-like' portrait of her and annoyed with him because of an open quarrel with Virgil Thomson that took place in her salon. (Frictions and rivalries among members of her entourage were permitted, even encouraged, but person-to-person wrangling in her presence was taboo.) Before Gertrude or Alice got around to breaking off the relationship, Tchelitchev met Edith Sitwell at 27 rue de Fleurus. The meeting was reported in *The Autobiography of Alice B. Toklas*: 'Then one day we asked Edith to lunch and Pavlik Tchelitchew [*sic*] came in and after lunch they left together and we never saw either of them again for a year – they had a very violent affair.' Said Gertrude: 'I liked to see people come and go but, just as much, liked to see them go.'

CHAPTER TWENTY

A Work of Art

'I never do portraits,' was Picasso's stock reply to any such request. The painter's reputation was secure, and growing; he was adamant about refusing commissioned work. But the affluent man-about-town might, on occasion, ignore his own rule and make the proposal himself.

'Mademoiselle, you have an interesting face. I am Pablo Picasso. Please, may I do your portrait?'

The name Picasso meant nothing to the blonde seventeen-year-old, but she was immediately charmed by the man. She had been window-shopping in front of the Galeries Lafayette department store when the stranger approached her with his blunt introduction. Although Picasso was approaching fifty – depressed at the thought, for he shared with Diaghilev an abhorrence of growing old and a dread of death – he was a dashing gallant in the presence of a lovely young girl like Marie-Thérèse Walter. The flair, finesse and superhuman vitality that went into his work were just as evident in his seductive personality.

Picasso's paintings of this period show the opposite side to his character: here was the violent misogynist, dismembering his women then reassembling their faces and forms in cruel distortions. The end to his marriage was in sight, he was restless in the confines of the bourgeois flat on rue La Boétie. His *Femme assise au bord de la mer* of 1929 might well have represented his repulsion to Olga, as theorists put forth; if so, he considered his wife a particularly monstrous form of praying mantis, a creature with sidelong teeth and jaws capable of devouring her mate. Whatever his feelings about Olga, or about women in general, Picasso fell in love with Marie-Thérèse and she with him.

Thus began the most discreet of Picasso's many love affairs. Marie-Thérèse was kept secret from even his closest friends, and certainly from Olga of the unpredictable Russian temperament. Picasso installed his new love in an apartment across the street from his own flat, near enough to the Galerie Simon on adjoining rue d'Astorg to offer an excuse to be with Marie-Thérèse without his wife suspecting the liaison. Although Picasso had already suggested a separation to Olga – a suggestion that triggered a tempestuous scene, though Picasso made no mention of another woman – Marie-Thérèse did not want him to divorce; she was perfectly content to remain in the shadows, an artist's anonymous mistress. In Marie-Thérèse's yielding nature and single-minded devotion to the older man, there was something of the young Jeanne Hébuterne who had loved Modigliani in the same self-effacing way exactly ten years before.

The year 1929 also marked the arrival in Paris of a young Catalan painter who immediately presented himself at Picasso's door. Salvador Dalí intended to visit the three great monuments of France: the palace at Versailles, the Grévin wax museum, and Pablo Picasso. Just as Picasso had helped Miró when that young painter first came to him in 1920, he now took the trouble to introduce Dalí to his own dealer, Paul Rosenberg, and to his sometime friend and still a force in art circles, Gertrude Stein.

Also, as if such echoes and impulses were cyclical at ten-year intervals, Picasso returned to a neo-classic style and theme once again. A wealthy young Swiss, Albert Skira, was casting about for some project to satisfy his mother's insistence that he take on some useful line of endeavor. At first Skira approached Picasso with the idea of illustrating a book – a book on Napoleon, for example – that Skira would publish. The Napoleon of modern art was not interested in the other Napoleon; besides, he did not accept commissioned work. That same summer, while Picasso was visiting Juan-les-Pins, he was waylaid by Skira's determined mother, who asked him to reconsider, or at least consider illustrations for some other book. By then Skira had thought of producing an illustrated edition of Ovid's *Metamorphoses*. Nothing could have appealed to the painter more than creating plates of Ovid's mythical creatures: the nymphs, satyrs and minotaurs that were to become a perpetually recurrent theme in the Picasso oeuvre. Delighted with his coup, Skira took rooms in the building next door to the Picasso flat. He hovered at the window awaiting the completion of each new engraving, signaled by Picasso himself, on a clown's antique trumpet blasting down the rue La Boétie.

From 1926 until 1928 Constantin Brancusi carried on a protracted litigation with the United States Customs over a piece of sculpture called *L'Oiseau d'Or*. The highly-polished feather-blade of bronze was priced at $600, but was being charged customs duty of $210 as 'a piece of detached metal' rather than as a work of art. The summary definition was more at issue than the excessive duty involved: the outcome of Brancusi's lawsuit would henceforth determine what line officials could take when confronted with a modern work like *L'Oiseau d'Or*.

At the hearings, Frank Crowninshield, publisher of *Vanity Fair*, testified that he had personally witnessed the crude metal formed and shaped by Brancusi; Edward Steichen, of the Museum of Modern Art, and the sculptor Jacob Epstein also testified to Brancusi's reputation and standing in the art world. In November 1928 the US government reluctantly conceded that *L'Oiseau d'Or* did possess qualities of 'an ornamental nature' and would no longer be classified as unworked metal. This trivial concession by United States Customs was nevertheless a significant victory in the realm of art. Also, for Brancusi, the triumph coming at the end of the decade partly vindicated a judgment at the beginning: in 1920 his *Princesse X* was condemned as 'obscene and phallic', then removed from the exhibit at the Salon des Indépendants in advance of an official visit by the French President.

At the age of eleven Brancusi left his home in Targu Jiu, Rumania, to see the world. By the early 1900s he was in Paris working by night at a restaurant in Pigalle, sculpting by day. To supplement his meager earnings he sang at the Rumanian Orthodox Church on rue Jean-de-Beauvais, but he was dismissed from the choir when the priest discovered he was eating the sacramental bread to appease his hunger, and worse – he was so excessively fond of any living creature he shared the bread with mice.

During World War I Brancusi became friends with the painters of La Ruche, and a close companion to Modigliani whom he taught the art of sculpture. He also came to know two other striking individualists like himself: Erik Satie and Marcel Duchamp. His work in wood, stone and metal became so simplified he referred to it as 'sculpture for the blind': figures and objects refined to their essences. He was first discovered by art patrons Walter Arensberg and John Quinn; by 1921 Ezra Pound was writing about Brancusi's art in *The Little Review*. Pound introduced the sculptor to James Joyce: the gentle Rumanian with his thick workman's hands and the half-blind Irishman of delicate build arrived at an instantaneous rapport. Perhaps the affinity between the two men led Caresse Crosby to ask Brancusi for a portrait sketch of Joyce to illustrate the Black Sun edition of *Tales Told of Shem and Shaun*. Brancusi was not the Crosbys' first choice: they had already been to Picasso asking for a sketch, but Picasso refused with his standard reply that he never did portraits.

The Crosbys, too, fell under Brancusi's spell. He must have seemed to them a kind of peasant-saint; they were attracted to him in the way they had taken up the Dutch couple Fran and Mai de Geetere, for that aura of unaffected charm, the example of a simpler way of life than they had ever known. Like his close friend Satie, Brancusi was sought after by a mixed social milieu, yet he remained a confirmed solitary. He lived alone at 8 impasse Ronsin with his white spitz, Polaris. Polaris went everywhere with his master, even to the cinema (Brancusi adored films), where Polaris sat beside him watching the flicker-antics of Charlot, the dog's seat reserved in advance.

When the Crosbys were invited to the two-room ground floor pavilion – workbenches strewn with chisels, saws hung from pegs, wood-shavings and stone dust underfoot – they were delighted to be served potatoes and chicken roasted in the sculptor's forge.

The portrait Brancusi submitted to the Crosbys was an impression only, but the sketch was used for the Black Sun edition of *Tales Told of Shem and Shaun*: an abstract spiral representing the author's inward-winding thought. When the portrait was shown to Joyce's father in Dublin, he remarked, 'The boy seems to have changed a good deal.'

*

'I never paint portraits,' was Picasso's final word, and the *frères* Abramowitz could not persuade him otherwise. The brothers were offering Picasso the opportunity to paint their client, the lovely German actress Maria Lani. As agents for the great star of the German stage and silent screen, they were having far more success in presenting Maria Lani to the Parisian art world than to the theater-going public. The Abramowitz brothers seemed indifferent to theatrical contracts: Maria Lani had yet to appear on the French stage – nevertheless, she was the toast of the 1929 season in Paris: gowned *gratuit* by the renowned couturiers of the day, perfumed by Worth and Chanel, courted, promoted, and above all, painted. Matisse had already done three portraits of the dark-haired beauty, Derain had painted two. It seemed that Maria Lani had attracted the eye and brush of every

Photo of Constantin Brancusi by Man Ray, and Brancusi's drawings of James Joyce for an edition of Joyce's *Tales of Shem and Shaun* published by The Black Sun Press. The realistic drawing (right) was turned down in favor of the abstraction (left).

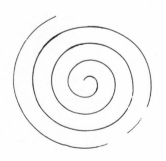

painter in l'Ecole de Paris, including Rouault, Foujita, Dufy, Vlaminck, Vuillard, Marquet, Marcoussis, Soutine and Bonnard. Picasso was unswerving in his refusal to execute a portrait of Lani even after his friend Cocteau – with his instinct for society's most fashionable figure of the moment – painted fourteen.

The last important group *vernissage* of the 1920s took place at the Georges Bernheim gallery: some fifty portraits of Maria Lani were to be presented. Before the scheduled opening, Maria Lani and the brothers Abramowitz (one of whom was really the husband of the actress, the other her brother) disappeared with the fifty treasured works of art. The only stage the actress had ever appeared upon was the party scene of the *haut monde* in Paris 1929. Actually, Maria Lani had been a stenographer in a business office in Prague. All trace of Maria Lani and her enterprising 'brothers' has been lost, but the portraits found their way through the clandestine American art market into several important collections, for the paintings were authentic if the subject was not.

Picasso illustration for Ovid's *Metamorphoses* – 'Four Women in Flight'.

CHAPTER TWENTY-ONE

Breakdown

The parties had become frenetic affairs, as if a last-of-the-wine fete could forever stave off hangover. During the final champagne years, Jean Cocteau had aggressive competition from social climber Elsa Maxwell in creating extravagant backdrops and original guest-lists for the frolics of the smart set. By the 1928–29 social season, Bébé Bérard – whose paintings Gertrude Stein was beginning to denigrate as 'almost something, and then they just are not' – left Miss Stein's circle to become set designer and costumer for parties of the hosts and hostesses stage-managed by Cocteau.

When white was in, the Picci-Blunt white ball was a snowy display of white furniture and white drapery against which drifted the ghostly dancers in white *tenue de soirée* – the only contrasting note was a bandstand of black jazz musicians, now *de rigueur* at any private party. Jean Patou's ball was arranged by Elsa Maxwell, the host's townhouse encased from rooftop to ground floor in silver foil. Scavenger hunts sent socialites scrambling over Paris in search of a Paraguayan flag or Mistinguett's slipper; Come-as-you-were parties requested guests to appear dressed as they were when the invitation was received, pyjamas and nightgowns predominating. The most original of invitations were sent by hairdresser Antoine to inaugurate his new *salon de beauté* and private living quarters on the rue Didier: the building was constructed entirely of Gobain sheet glass, with glass furniture and an interior staircase in pebbled glass – the invitations were engraved on thin sheets of glass, wrapped in parchment, delivered by hand.

The overcrowded *terrasses* on the place Vavin were less a sanctuary of the arts than a tourist stop for new hordes of poseurs. Harold Stearns described the Sélect as an example of the bistro scene of Montparnasse: 'a seething madhouse of drunks, semi-drunks, quarter-drunks and sober maniacs.' (Stearns had become temporarily blind, possibly from drink, and lost his job as 'Peter Pickem' at the *Chicago Tribune*: he was reduced to cadging drinks by telling a woeful tale of a decrepit racehorse.) The café circuit still served as a Bourse of the rise and fall of fluctuating reputations: Sinclair Lewis hoped to join with the younger generation of writers crowding the Dôme, but the fledgling littérateurs would have none of him; when Lewis stood at his table to make an impassioned point about Flaubert, somebody at an adjoining table shouted, 'Sit down, you're just a best-seller.'

Malcolm Cowley got into a fight with the patron of La Rotonde, and was hauled off to the commissariat: he managed to escape fine or imprisonment by a persuasive chorus of witnesses, French and American, who swore the patron was a troublemaker and had swung first. The café set of Montparnasse preferred Gaston, barman and part-owner of La Coupole, who was generous, good-natured and not easily provoked – yet they were drawn to La Rotonde and the Café Sélect where ugly scenes were more likely to occur, for what Robert McAlmon called the daily 'vaudeville'.

The commissaire was less tolerant of the vaudeville when Hart Crane got into a drunken argument with Madame Sélect in the summer of 1929. The formidable patronne of the Café Sélect, known to be sharp-tempered and vindictive, ordered the waiters to subdue Crane, then called the police. Crane was carried off by several *agents de police*, his head banging brutally against the paving stones on the way to the *panier à salade*, the police van. July was a bad time to be arrested in France: officialdom was in suspended animation during the vacation month, and Crane's friends were not immediately available. Word eventually filtered back to the Crosbys at Ermenonville, via McAlmon and Kay Boyle, but not before Crane had spent three weeks in La Santé prison. After Harry Crosby had arranged for Crane's release, a group of friends assembled at the bistro opposite the grim prison gates, A la Bonne Santé, to celebrate his return to freedom. Crane waved to them jauntily enough as he was led past the sentry box on the rue de la Santé, but during the festivities the pale and shaken poet admitted to Harry Crosby he was ready to make use of Crosby's gift ticket, second-class passage on the S. S. *Homeric* bound for New York.

That same summer Harold Stearns also decided to go home. 'It was a useless silly life,' he declared of his Paris sojourn, 'and I have missed it every day since.'

The great good place of every expatriate's dream was becoming a casualty ward. By 1929 the last wave of visitors to Paris seemed to want

Party time at La Coupole.

the cheap thrill of a ragged and disordered spectacle. The once lithe and glamorous Florence Martin of the Folies-Bergère, now a fading and foul-mouthed 'Flossie' of the café circuit, was said to have inspired the legend of the two middle-aged American women who drove up in a taxi to the Gypsy Bar, hesitant until Florence Martin entered, raucously drunk, screaming friendly obscenities at Jimmy the barman. One matron in the taxi opened the door to get out, saying to her companion, 'This must be the place.'

*

One of Gertrude Stein's young men of 26, surrealist poet René Crevel, wrote to Gertrude and Alice in his quaint English about the last of the non-stop partygoers, Scott and Zelda Fitzgerald: 'Curious and poor fellow. A boy. He has a wonderful wife, you know her, I think, but what this young charming and spirituel people has in the hed (tête)? I cannot say, but I want [to] speak about that with you and Miss Touclas.'

The rich, like Tom and Daisy Buchanan in *The Great Gatsby*, could retreat 'back into their money, or their vast carelessness', but the Fitzgeralds had to keep the party going at all costs. There were gnawing tensions behind the façade of gaiety and excess, not the least of which was that they were broke: Scott had earned $30,000 in 1927, and practically as much in 1928, but he had to borrow money from Scribner's to survive. He considered these loans an advance on his latest novel, *The World's Fair*, which had got off to a false start and would never be completed, though much of the Paris-Riviera background was used in *Tender Is the Night*, published in 1934.

What had been an idyllic interlude for Zelda, with a handsome French pilot on the sands of St-Raphael, would continue as a recurring nightmare for Scott, who was prey to fears of sexual inadequacy. Whether or not Scott confessed to Hemingway, 'Zelda said the way I was built I could never make any woman happy', and whether or not the two men went into the W.C. at Michaud's like little boys to compare penises, Zelda did once say to Scott she now realized he was homosexual, that he had come home the night before after a drinking spree with Hemingway and murmured in his sleep, 'No more, baby.'

But Zelda was making other wild assertions in 1929. After a visit to the les Halles flower market she revealed to Scott: 'The flowers are talking to me.' It could have been another one of her cryptic conversational ploys. She once remarked to Gerald and Sara Murphy, 'Don't you think Al Jolson is greater than Jesus?'

Au Bar – drawing by Cocteau.

Gerald Murphy introduced Zelda to Madame Lubov Egorova, former dancer with the Ballets Russes, one of the great ballet teachers in Paris at the time. Zelda had taken ballet lessons briefly as an adolescent; now, at an age when most ballerinas had completed the better part of their careers, she was determined to make herself into a professional dancer. According to Gerald Murphy: 'She wanted immediate success. Zelda wanted to dance for the world.' When the Murphys went to watch Zelda at practice for a recital, Gerald was embarrassed by her grotesque intensity. 'It was really terrible. One held one's breath until it was over. Thank God she couldn't see what she looked like.' Zelda recorded her own impression of that time as: 'I worked constantly and was terribly superstitious and moody...full of presentiments. Scott drank.'

*

Morley Callaghan had worked on the *Toronto Star* with Ernest Hemingway, and was a devotee of the Hemingway mystique: he wrote on the same subjects as his idol, and in the same style. When he brought his wife Loretto to Paris in 1929, he was in a sense attempting to relive the Hemingway legend. Callaghan's first impressions of Paris echo Hemingway's original enthusiasm for the city, but at a distance of eight years, seen through the opposite end of a telescope. Callaghan's Paris was the last act of a disintegrating pageant, the tag-end instead of the bright beginning of a decade.

The young couple stayed first at the Paris-New York Hotel until the depressing view from their window of a flower-laden hearse parked in the cul-de-sac made them decide to move to the rue de la Santé – with an only slightly less depressing panorama of La Santé's cinder-colored prison walls. Their Paris sojourn was something of a second honeymoon, a late-sleeping leisurely time that began with waking to a summer's day in Paris, then the delight of coffee and steamed milk with croissants. They took a ritual lunch at La Coupole, then went for their mail at the American Express. If they remained on the Right Bank for the afternoon it was to window-shop in the place Vendôme and shop at the Galeries Lafayette. By late afternoon they might stroll along the Champs-Elysées or explore the hard bright streets around the Opéra, searching for the perfect café where they might savor that evening's exceptional experience, the apéritif hour, amidst businessmen rattling the pages of *Figaro* and French shopgirls in their black stockings trying to pronounce the words to the popular song 'Constantinople'.

Zelda Fitzgerald in ballet attire.

At night they went to Zelli's and Bricktop's to dance, and passed the Jockey on the way home, the jazz and cigarette smoke blowing into the street. The Callaghans were doing the things one did in Gay Paree; in truth, they were searching for Hemingway, but the famous writer was not to be found in the famous cabarets. Naturally Callaghan asked Sylvia Beach at Shakespeare and Company to help him get in touch with his former colleague on the *Toronto Star*, but Miss Beach had become chary of giving out the addresses of her better-known clients. 'You could leave a message,' she said, to Callaghan's annoyance. The dilemma solved itself when Hemingway one day came knocking on the Callaghans' door and invited the young couple to his apartment on the rue Ferou.

At the end of 1928 Ernest Hemingway's father had committed suicide. Hemingway's mother, at her son's macabre request, sent him the pistol Dr Hemingway had shot himself with – a grim trophy the writer would brood over in his thirtieth year, 1929. Married to Pauline Pfeiffer now, with money from her generous Uncle Gus and his own expanding income, Hemingway enjoyed a style of life that was a large remove from the place Contrescarpe. The Callaghans were properly impressed with the spacious apartment Ernest and Pauline had taken just off the Luxembourg Gardens, in the shadow of St-Sulpice.

Hemingway's now traditional trip to Pamplona was a far more luxurious excursion than that famous trip in 1925 described in *The Sun Also Rises*: the Hemingways motored down to Spain in their new Ford roadster. Spain, to Hemingway's disgust, had been invaded by American chewing-gum and Coca-cola. He indulged so richly and copiously in the food and wine of the country that he returned to Paris with all the symptoms of gout – he was obliged to go on a diet, and drink mineral water only.

The Hemingway acquaintanceship was propitious for the Callaghans: suddenly the young couple were no longer tourists, but had penetrated the inner circle of celebrated expatriates. And Hemingway could indulge the ego satisfaction of having a young writer – new to Paris, and open to instruction – dogging his footsteps. Loretto did not get on as well with Pauline Hemingway, who seemed patronizing, especially concerning *la mode* and a milliner she knew but whose name she was reluctant to divulge to Loretto. The two men had more in common. Morley Callaghan had been a collegiate boxer, and Hemingway was anxious to work off the slackness and paunch of the good life.

Hemingway and his second wife, Pauline.

For Callaghan, some of the glittering allure of his hero dimmed under the stress of a competitive sport. Instead of being instructor to the younger man as he was in the literary arena, Hemingway immediately found himself being outboxed by the swifter, better-trained Callaghan. Once, when Hemingway's lip was cut by Callaghan's barrage of lefts, Hemingway spat blood directly into the young man's face. They made it up over beers at the Falstaff Bar where the banter with the English bartender, who had been a professional lightweight fighter, put both men in a better mood.

Loretto cut her hair in the new style, like a boy's, and Morley approved. The flat on the rue de la Santé had to be given up when the Callaghans discovered they were being bitten by bedbugs; they left the prison district with regret, they rather liked their Russian concierge whose lover, a Russian cabbie, took them on Sunday excursions outside Paris in his workday taxicab. But Edward Titus, husband of Helena Rubinstein, offered them the free use of his own apartment. Titus was the new editor of *This Quarter*, an outlet for Callaghan's fiction. With the move to Titus's flat on the rue Delambre, the Callaghans became all the more intimate with the overlapping café and salon life. They met Gertrude Stein, and Scott and Zelda Fitzgerald.

At their first meeting with the Fitzgeralds, Scott stood on his head. When Hemingway heard this, he simply shrugged and said, 'That's Scott.' But he asked the Callaghans not to pass on his address to the Fitzgeralds.

In *That Summer in Paris* Morley Callaghan evokes the small, quiet Miró dressed in his old-fashioned dark suit, striped shirt and bowler hat, acting as timekeeper with great Spanish dignity for one of the Hemingway-Callaghan bouts at the American Club. On another occasion, Fitzgerald was the ill-chosen timekeeper, and allowed one dramatic round to exceed the two-minute limit. The thickset Hemingway was dumped by his sparring partner during the overtime, and Fitzgerald announced with chagrin that he had carelessly allowed the round to run beyond the limit. Hemingway was furious with Fitzgerald, and went to wash the blood from his face. He had accused Fitzgerald of maliciously allowing the round to run overtime. Fitzgerald was aghast: 'He thinks I did it on purpose,' he said to Callaghan. It was significant that Hemingway had come to the bout after eating a heavy lunch of lobster thermidor with white burgundy at Prunier's – formerly he would have done his boxing on little more than *poireaux en salade*.

The incident, trivial as it was, would have gone no farther than the gossip-grapevine of Montparnasse had not Isabel Paterson picked up the story for her book column in the New York *Herald Tribune*. Hemingway's growing literary reputation made him Stateside news: unfortunately, Paterson reported that Ernest Hemingway had been knocked out by Morley Callaghan, not just knocked down. With Hemingway's hair-trigger temper and tender ego, the ridiculous episode grew into a cause célèbre. Morley Callaghan soon realized his friendship with Hemingway was shattered because he had once, briefly, inadvertently, toppled the giant.

Meanwhile Fitzgerald foolishly allowed another lapse to be scored against him when he drunkenly related to Hemingway a story going the rounds of New York, spread by Robert McAlmon, that Ernest was a homosexual and Pauline a lesbian. Hemingway's bull rage over the slander was scattershot and all-inclusive: Fitzgerald was somehow associated with McAlmon, who was 'too pitiful to be beaten up' (though Hemingway had every intention of doing so), and Fitzgerald suffered the fate of those messengers who bear ill-tidings to the king. After 1929 the blood-brotherhood of 1925 could never be the same.

*

'There were Americans at night, and day Americans,' wrote Zelda Fitzgerald, 'and we all had Americans in the bank to buy things with.' This was in the autumn of 1929 when Zelda was fifteen pounds underweight, pushing herself to exhaustion at ballet practice. Hemingway had described Zelda's eyes as those of a hawk, and watching her face 'you could see her mind leave the table and go to the night's party and return with her eyes blank as a cat's . . . ' The alternating avidity and blankness in Zelda's face became all the more pronounced as she lived on the illusion that agents from Diaghilev had come to watch her dance. She awaited an offer from the Ballets Russes when, as it turned out, the agents were actually from the Folies-Bergère looking for a potential shimmy-dancer. Madame Egorova reported a visit with Zelda alone, for tea, when her student's voice and facial expressions shifted bizarrely, and Zelda finally dropped to her knees and embraced Madame Egorova's feet. Zelda was beginning to hold onto the sides of the table to get through a meal.

The Fitzgeralds invited Morley and Loretto Callaghan to James Joyce's favorite restaurant, Les Trianons. It was a somber occasion. Joyce did not appear that night, as he frequently did; Scott seemed withdrawn, perhaps brooding over his failure to get back to work on *The*

World's Fair. (The sterile summer was ending, and Hemingway admonished him to get on with his novel, with the fall coming on and the feeling of death in the air, the time when 'the boys' did their work.) Zelda was agitated throughout the meal: 'What will we do next?' she kept asking. When she insisted they all go roller-skating, Scott became stern and paternal – strangely, Zelda reverted to a complaisant child.

'You're tired,' he informed her, then went for a cab. Like a little girl, Zelda meekly wished the Callaghans goodnight, then allowed herself to be put into a cab by her husband and sent home, presumably to bed. Morley asked Scott what the trouble was, and Scott replied that Zelda worked far too hard at dance practice.

'Why is she working so hard at it?'

'She wants to have something of her own, be something herself.'

Not many months later, just as the decade ended, Zelda's anxiety and depression required her admission to Malmaison, the mental institution just outside Paris where former President Deschanel had been confined exactly ten years earlier. Zelda arrived at Malmaison slightly intoxicated; a week later she abruptly checked herself out of the clinic, against the advice of her physician. When she returned to their apartment in Paris, Scott had been giving a series of parties: Zelda found herself in the midst of a sustained and familiar alcoholic nightmare. Within three weeks her condition was compounded by an inexplicable eczema and recurrent delirium: 'There was music that beat behind my forehead and other music that fell into my stomach from a high parabola...' She agreed to submit to treatment at Les Rives de Prangins, near Nyon on Lake Geneva, where her condition was diagnosed as acute schizophrenia, a term only recently invented by Dr Paul Bleuler, her consulting psychiatrist. Unlike Nicole Diver in *Tender Is the Night*, Fitzgerald's composite character based on his wife and Sara Murphy, Zelda would never recover from her breakdown.

*

James Joyce was the most superstitious of men. When Robert McAlmon reported having seen a rat at the Closerie de Lilas, Joyce cried out, 'That's bad luck, that's bad luck!' and had to be taken home. Dates and numbers took on extraordinary importance. He would put Sylvia Beach to any amount of trouble to obtain the first bound copy of *Ulysses* by 2 February 1922, the exact date of his fortieth birthday – or he could turn pale at the realization that he had just asked a guest to dinner who would make thirteen at table.

A Dublin friend, Thomas McGreevy, had called to wangle an introduction to Joyce for a young admirer of the writer, Samuel Beckett. Only after McGreevy hung up did Joyce make a mental count of the prospective diners: thirteen! Immediately he got in touch with another guest who could be persuaded to accept an alternate invitation, thus Samuel Beckett's first meeting with James Joyce was as a member of a more comforting quorum of twelve.

At dinner Joyce sat with his slim legs twisted to one side; he was dressed in a waistcoat of embroidered flowers, wearing a large ring that caught the light as he gestured with one thin hand. Living in self-imposed exile, Joyce closely questioned Beckett concerning the news and gossip of Dublin. Like Diaghilev meeting a fellow Russian émigré, Joyce relentlessly pumped newly-arrived Irishmen for scraps of information about the home to which he would never return. (In Trieste, Italo Svevo said to him: 'It is dangerous to leave one's country, but even more dangerous to go back to it.')

Samuel Beckett had just been appointed *lecteur* in English at the prestigious Ecole Normale Supérieure for the 1928–9 academic year. Just out of Trinity College Dublin, Beckett was uncertain about teaching as a career or of following a creative literary bent of his own. He had of course wanted to meet the celebrated author of *Ulysses*, and McGreevy, his predecessor at l'Ecole Normale, was delighted to bring the two Dubliners together. Joyce and Beckett were twenty-four years apart in age, but Joyce felt an immediate affinity with the hawk-faced young lecturer. In a very short time Beckett found himself with the unexpected role and questionable honor of serving James Joyce as man of all work.

Before Beckett had arrived upon the scene, a series of young (but not always young) men and women of willing disposition fulfilled the appointment as spare-time secretary to Joyce. Both Sylvia Beach and Robert McAlmon felt obliged to do considerable legwork for Joyce, as well as being his publishers. Or any casual acquaintance might be inveigled into rendering service to the master: Philippe Soupault, Surrealist author, remembered being asked by Joyce, 'Which way are you going home?' – then discovered he was involved in a complicated time-consuming errand for Joyce on the opposite side of the city. Because of Joyce's near-blindness, and in respect for his genius, any favor or assistance offered to the author was considered an act of homage. But McAlmon, who had assumed the role of spare-time secretary to Joyce prior to Beckett, was disenchanted with the man and his oeuvre. Joyce could be high-handed and infinitely demanding in his attitude toward underlings and patrons alike. If the money McAlmon regularly advanced to Joyce did not arrive when promised, Joyce sent his benefactor blunt little reminders: 'I shall be greatly obliged if your monthly cheque arrived punctually.' For Joyce's part, McAlmon was far too flippant in his manner: the young man was sadly lacking the respect and subservience Joyce demanded of an acolyte.

When the unpaid assistantship fell to Beckett, he was flattered and eager to be of service. Though never in any official sense Joyce's secretary, Beckett made himself available to the author's every need or whim: research at the Bibliothèque Nationale, transcriptions at all hours of the day or night, reading aloud to Joyce as the author swabbed his pained eyes following an attack of iritis.

Since Beckett never rose before noon, he arranged to hold seminars with his sole student in the late afternoon, when the two would read Shakespeare together at the Dôme. The art patron Peggy Guggenheim remembered Samuel Beckett as the apathetic Irish counterpart of Oblomov, the protagonist of Goncharov's novel. Descriptions of Beckett at this period vary from 'a small redhaired Irishman' (Adolph Hoffmeister) to 'a blond beanpole with glasses' (Nino Frank), his eyes alternately colored blue, then green. The most consistent of remembered impressions is the intensity of Beckett's gaze, and his profound seriousness. McGreevy called his young friend The Melancholy Irishman, which was close to Joyce's own reference to himself as Melancholy Jesus. Beckett frequented the small Dublin circle of Irish expatriates: Arthur Power, Francis Stuart (married to Maud Gonne's natural daughter, Iseult), Thomas McGreevy, and occasionally mingled with the French Surrealist poets, but he chiefly preferred the company of James Joyce, or his own solitude. He haunted the residence halls on the rue d'Ulm, playing dirges on a flute in the late hours. His favorite subject of conversation was the philosophic implications of suicide.

Adrienne Monnier spoke of Beckett – as perhaps Beckett thought of himself – as the new Stephen Dedalus, following the Joycean path of 'silence, exile, and cunning'. Beckett then began to assume the traits of his idol: he pretended to be more nearsighted than he was, holding reading matter very close to his eyes as Joyce would do; his cigarette dangled carelessly from his fingers, and he crossed his legs in the same fashion. Actually the two men were very alike in character and interests:

introverts both, traditionally Irish in their awe of the supernatural. Both men were proficient linguists; they were fascinated scavengers of obscure facts, odd turns of speech, esoteric knowledge.

From the first, Beckett looked up to Joyce as would an adoring son. The two men became as close as Joyce's guarded nature would allow – throughout the friendship they called one another 'Mr Beckett' and 'Mr Joyce'. Beckett may have wanted to be the spiritual son to James Joyce, but Joyce had a son, Giorgio, and the only love he had had to spare was rationed out to Nora Barnacle, Giorgio and his daughter Lucia.

Beckett became so involved with the Joyce family that he decided to forgo his Christmas holiday with family in Dublin in order to be of assistance to Joyce during Nora's hospitalization following a hysterectomy. Joyce was lost without his wife; Beckett felt he could not leave him at that critical time.

A disturbing aspect of Beckett's relationship to the Joyce family was the growing attachment Joyce's daughter felt toward her father's handsome young companion-assistant. Lucia was a graceful, tentative and shy creature – attractive except for the strabismus which brought her gaze into a slightly cross-eyed squint. This defect was a greatly enlarged deformity in the sensitive girl's mind: she dwelt on the matter of her appearance with all the morbidity of post-adolescence. Furthermore, her lonely life in Paris – she was not fluent in French, kept changing schools and languages, was uneasy with every shift of background in her father's nomadic exile – increased an already unstable nature. Lucia was a bundle of complexes and turmoil.

Mildly attracted to Lucia, Beckett treated her with a young man's attention to the young lady of the house – but it was her father he truly cared about, and whose attention he sought. With a delicacy and polite reserve Beckett had learnt from Joyce himself, the young man seemed to be paying court to the daughter. Nora and James Joyce observed the one-sided romance develop without realizing how hopeless the affair was to be. Beckett never revealed to the Joyces that he was in love with a girl in Germany, a girl he was determined to marry if she would have him.

The parents considered a match between their daughter and the quiet, intelligent Irishman an ideal alliance. For the first time, the affections of the withdrawn Lucia were aroused: she made no secret of *her* intentions, though the object of her desire might himself show every reluctance. Beckett now tried to avoid seeing Lucia, timing his visits when she would most likely be away – but he did not always succeed. In order to see and be with the admired father, he was continually at risk of a compromising entanglement with the determined daughter.

By now Beckett had become all too aware of Lucia's disturbed and disturbing behavior. Formerly too shy to join in conversation, she now chattered obsessively in company, was nervously animated, childishly hyperactive. Lucia's mind wandered from one subject to the next in no orderly or reasonable pattern: her disconnected monologues reminded Beckett of 'the father's mind running rampant in the daughter'. Beckett was not alone in his belief that Lucia might be insane, although his feeling that she might be on the verge of suicide was perhaps due to his own obsession with self-annihilation. Joyce's translator, Valery Larbaud, had always been convinced that Lucia's bizarre mannerisms indicated neurosis; Eugene and Maria Jolas were alerted to Lucia's condition by a doctor who remarked that her abstracted manner was cause for real concern.

Only Joyce seemed entirely unaware of Lucia's alarming symptoms. The father was consumed by the task of putting together *Finnegans Wake*, distracted by financial worries (*Ulysses* was being pirated in the United States by renegade publisher Samuel Roth), exhausted by overwork and attacks of iritis that left him 'literally doubled in two from fatigue and cramp'. He was losing the confidence of friends and defenders like Ezra Pound and Wyndham Lewis who declared *Finnegans Wake* a hopeless puzzle and literary dead end. (Nora's reaction to the work in progress was, 'Why don't you write sensible books that people can understand?') Hovering over him was the necessity of another dread eye operation, his ninth.

Lucia's single psychic outlet was the dance. In turn she had attempted drawing lessons, piano, singing, and had given them all up, but from 1926 until 1929 she worked and practiced her dance for as many as six hours daily. A series of teachers that included Raymond Duncan, Jaques Dalcroze, and Egorova of the Ballets Russes, encouraged her and expressed some acknowledgment of her gifts. In April 1929 Lucia entered an international dance competition at a *bal musette* in Montparnasse, the Bal Bullier. Her costume was that of a graceful glittering undersea water sprite, as if she danced as the legendary Ondine who could become mortal by marrying a human being. She was much applauded – the audience called for an encore by *l'Irlandaise* – although

Lucia Joyce, photographed by Berenice Abbott, Paris, 1926.

she did not receive a prize. This was to be Lucia's only moment of glory after three years of intensive study, for she never danced again.

*

Ezra Pound was briefly back in Paris to look up old friends and revisit the scene of his halcyon days. Settled in Rapallo now, he was no longer the open, free-spirited iconoclast who became every artist's publicist and friend. Pound's occasional irascibility and incipient paranoia had been fueled by the demagoguery of Benito Mussolini's Fascist regime in Italy. Pound, the longstanding spiritual exile, had at last found sanctuary in a nation that satisfied his most outrageous prejudices.

Ezra Pound joined the Joyce family, along with Samuel Beckett, for dinner at Les Trianons. Here Joyce reigned in unquestionable majesty – even Pound must have been impressed by the esteem and respect he commanded. The proprietor kept Joyce's customary table on permanent reservation, the head waiter took the trouble to read the entire menu aloud to Joyce so that the near-blind author did not have to carry eyeglasses or resort to a magnifying glass.

For all his pleasure in dining out, Joyce came from a nation without traditional cuisine and was admittedly no gourmet. He chiefly delighted in the role of host, and savored the pleasure of entertaining a few close friends whenever he was in funds. He pressed his guests to choose the most expensive items on the menu, while he as host ate sparingly and would have been just as content on a steady diet of tinned salmon and boiled lentils. Joyce preferred to drink white wine, especially Swiss, but the cheapest would do, as long as there was plenty of it.

At dinner Beckett was his usual quiet and modest self, all the more so in the overwhelming presence of Joyce and Pound: to Joyce he showed a characteristic deference, noticeably solicitous toward the older man. Pound interpreted Beckett's manner as that of a sycophant, and was to say so later on. He was impatient and rude to Beckett, offering not the slightest interest or customary generosity to a new young literary hopeful. Nor did Pound and Joyce find one another's company agreeable: their views were too divergent now to allow for the easy relationship begun in 1920; they were, despite the polite pretense, no longer friends.

Meanwhile Beckett was, in a slow and irregular fashion, moving away from his total commitment to James Joyce. He had begun to write prose and poetry of his own: his first short-story, 'Assumption', was published in the same issue of *transition* as his scholarly essay on the Italian influence on James Joyce's work. McGreevy encouraged him to write a poem for the contest sponsored by Nancy Cunard; Beckett completed his entry only minutes before the midnight deadline, then slipped the poem 'Whoroscope' under the door of the Hours Press. Nancy Cunard was so impressed with this initial work by an unknown poet that she awarded Beckett the first prize of £10. Later she arranged to meet the prize-winner himself, and was further impressed with his 'profile of an Aztec eagle'. With Nancy Cunard as a patron, Beckett was launched. Three hundred copies of *Whoroscope* were printed as a separate pamphlet by the Hours Press, Beckett's first independently published work.

By now Beckett had wandered out of the exclusive orbit of James Joyce and his family, but Lucia was as much in love with him as ever – and ever more mentally unstable. Finally she attempted to confront her reluctant lover alone, out of range of her all-absorbing father and from under the weight and pressure of family. She invited Samuel to lunch at a Montparnasse restaurant, an invitation Beckett could in no diplomatic way refuse. Instead, he took the precaution of bringing along his student and drinking companion, Georges Pelorson: he may have thought to divert Lucia's interest to the other young man; at any rate, it was a deliberate ploy to provide a third-person buffer between himself and Lucia.

When two men, instead of Beckett alone, appeared at the restaurant, Lucia's dismay was immediately evident. Disappointed and melancholy at first, she eventually slipped into a manic stage, became bizarrely agitated, her hands brushing her face in futile gestures that smeared her make-up and disarranged her hair. Neither man dared interrupt her disconnected monologue. The luncheon was a Mad Hatter's party, an embarrassment for Beckett and his unwelcome friend, a crushing disaster for Lucia.

The girl's condition could no longer be ignored, and Beckett had no intention of allowing her delusions about him to continue. When next Lucia met him at the door, Beckett blurted out the unhappy truth: the purpose of his call was to see and be with her father. He went on to explain that he did think of her as a friend, with almost brotherly devotion, but that she was not the object of his visits to the Joyce apartment. Lucia was shocked and hurt. When James and Nora Joyce learned of Samuel Beckett's blunt declaration to their daughter, they considered his behavior a low deception all along. The friendship was over, their door was closed to him. The young Dubliner could never be the foster son to James Joyce he had so wanted to be, and never the son-in-law Joyce intended.

The relationship was not repaired until the Thirties, after Lucia had been diagnosed as schizophrenic and became a patient at Les Rives de Prangins where Zelda Fitzgerald had been under treatment a few years before.

Sketch by F. Scott Fitzgerald.

Paris, July 1928

18 Rue D'Odeon
Festival of St. James

CHAPTER TWENTY-TWO

The Snow of '29

'The snow of '29 wasn't real snow. If you didn't want it to be snow
you just paid some money.'

F. SCOTT FITZGERALD

The mood was upbeat. By October of 1929 the Paris *Herald* had
become so prosperous the publishers announced the building of
modern and spacious quarters on the rue de Berri, just off the
Champs-Elysées. The franc was selling at 25.5 to the dollar, and
American dollars were still turning into eminently spendable francs. At
the Gaumont Palace Maurice Chevalier was appearing in his first
talking picture *La Chanson de Paris*, while the optimistic Emile Coué
had carried his own happy song to America: 'Every day in every way I
am becoming better and better.'

Coué's auto-suggestion appeared to be having its effect. Following
the nasty scandals of the Harding era, Coolidge had served a term of
tranquil prosperity, and Hoover had eased into office on the same ticket
of rising affluence. Since 1925, with stocks such as Radio, ATT, US
Steel, and Montgomery Ward moving ever upward, Paris branches of
American brokerage houses were doing unprecedented business. At
high tide it was time to get into the swim. Hairdressers and bootblacks
listened for market tips from their customers, cabbies spread the latest
word on the hottest issues; everybody borrowed on next month's salary
to get in on today's sure thing.

There were noticeable cracks in the Wall Street façade: US business
activity was sluggish, unemployment at an unhealthy level; yet speculation grew all the more frantic. In February there had been a brief
collapse of stock values, possibly a warning tremor of deeper soundings
to come, but eager investors quickly reacted to the downturn by
pushing popular issues to new highs. Bargain hunters were ever poised
to swoop in and take up the slack at the first symptoms of slump.

The Federal Reserve cautiously pressured member banks to restrict credit to brokers and to discourage loans that were purely speculative. The warning was ignored. Credit was a staple of the marketplace, as real as currency itself. Since the end of World War I, economic policy had been updated to accommodate Maynard Keynes's theory that potential wealth was a useful correlative to apparent wealth.

The stock market came to represent the great democratic meeting place where J. P. Morgan and his chauffeur both had a piece of Anaconda Copper. The wonder is not so much that his chauffeur was converted to the gospel of unlimited growth, but that J. P. Morgan became a true believer: the affluent plunged as recklessly as the financial amateurs. Speculation had become a national pastime. Smaller investors flocked to the mostly unregulated investment trusts being built as pyramids of dubious paper. In the summer of 1929 more than a million shareholders were building the pyramids.

On 3 September, six months after Hoover was inaugurated as President, the stock market reached its all-time high. Prices slipped later in September, but this only brought out the bargain hunters in force.

On Tuesday, 22 October, a day that became known as Black Tuesday, the frenzy of activity on Wall Street was inexplicable and unprecedented. A dramatic shift of trading patterns took place as six million shares of stock changed hands. For every sell order there was a buyer, but the drop in prices was disastrous. By the next day a torrent of sell orders flooded the trading floor, and by the end of the day the tape was still two hours late with price quotations. Long dormant fears of ruin had replaced the buoyant optimism of the bulls. After a heady five-year climb, the market plunged backwards into the abyss.

By noon on Wednesday, brokers could not keep up with calls to 'sell at the market' for they were too busy sending out distress calls for margin coverage to their customers. Prices became impossible to quote: the stock-trading system collapsed into chaos. A messenger boy idly bid a single dollar for White Sewing Machine, quoted at 48 when the market opened, and acquired a block of 100 shares in the absence of any other bid. The trauma was so great that brokers wandered the littered floor like zombies: several whispered to themselves; one man giggled hysterically, another wept. A consortium of bankers led by J. P. Morgan injected a modicum of hope by ostentatiously buying up large blocks of stock: the market steadied temporarily. But 12,894,650 shares had been sold off in a single session, and the nightmare drop in prices could not be camouflaged. In the sickening slide, the paper gains built up since 1925 had all but vanished by the closing gong at 3 p.m. The bankers' consortium discreetly retired from the field. By 29 October investors were fighting to sell. There were still shares of pie in the sky on the market, but not even the bargain hunters were buying. The market hit bottom on 13 November: the Coué formula echoed like a bad joke on the floor of the New York Stock Exchange.

*

A six-hour difference in time isolated the Paris brokerage houses from the Wall Street drama. Telephone lines were jammed: the absence of confirming information from New York only increased the panic and terror of investors living in Paris. The sluggish Paris Bourse had never achieved the scale of US investment activity: French issues were affected only psychologically and superficially, but many Frenchmen of means had succumbed to the American fever and invested in Wall Street as well. They now gathered in large numbers outside the Paris Bourse.

Inside, prices were still recorded on a chalkboard behind the old-fashioned railings – 'the gold-skinned men,' as Joyce described them, 'quoting prices on their gemmed fingers' – but the Paris Bourse was no help in keeping American investors informed. Hundreds of calls went through to the Paris *Herald* switchboard where extra staff tried to assuage the fears of Americans in Paris during the financial crisis at home. Other groups of Americans joined pockets of French businessmen gathered outside the Banque de Saint-Phalle and the Guaranty Trust awaiting some mysterious signal of reassurance. The word from home, when it filtered through, was a confirmation of disaster.

Many of the expatriate colony living the life of *rentiers* in France were no longer solvent. Americans who had been dependent on remittances from home joined the queue at the embassy for emergency funds to return to the US. The cafés and hotels of Montparnasse emptied out: letters addressed to those who had already left for home piled up in the patrons' mail rack at the Dôme, unread.

The smaller-scale French economy had not shared in the American boom, except obliquely through the hordes of tourists in Paris. France was still a nation of shopkeepers and small farms, gold was the traditional investment of most Frenchmen. Those who did climb on the

American bandwagon were also affected by what became known as Le Krach. Maurice Sachs wrote in his diary for 24 October: 'Nous n'avons plus rien' – 'We have nothing left.' His mother had suffered a heart attack at the news of the crash; his uncle, Richard Wallanson, had committed suicide.

Americans had been the foremost purchasers of French art throughout the Twenties, pushing prices to the same incredible levels as prices on the stock exchange. There were few buyers left in Paris to maintain the unrealistic art prices: galleries on the rue de Seine and rue La Boétie closed down; affluent painters began to move back into the cheap ateliers of another, simpler age. 'We don't sell our paintings anymore!' cried André Lhote. 'Painting is saved!'

*

After the years of dissipation, Harry Crosby returned to the United States in December 1929 looking remarkably youthful, apparently in excellent health. His tanned and handsome visage showed little trace of the sexual excess or the drugged and drunken escapades in Paris. It was as if his favorite author Oscar Wilde had modeled *The Picture of Dorian Gray* on Harry Crosby's life, and the real portrait was in Harry's steamer trunk.

In New York he began to look up acquaintances from the Paris years: Hart Crane, Archibald MacLeish, E. E. Cummings; and he had taken up with an old flame, the now married Josephine Rotch Bigelow. On 7 December Hart Crane gave a party for Harry and Caresse Crosby in his Brooklyn apartment with its view of the famous bridge, the subject of Crane's long poem. Present were Cummings, William Carlos Williams, the Malcolm Cowleys, Walker Evans the photographer, and a group of homosexual sailors. In the course of the evening someone was shuffling a deck of playing cards; he extended a hand of cards to Harry and told him to pick a card. Calmly Harry crossed himself, predicted he would choose the ace of hearts, then did exactly that. To the others, the random selection of an ace of hearts was a party trick or a coincidence, but the card was of great significance to Harry. He knew something no one else at the party knew.

Before they left that night, the Crosbys invited Hart Crane to join them for dinner three days hence, at the Caviar Restaurant. Also on that date, the 10th of December, Harry had an earlier appointment with his uncle J. P. Morgan, possibly to discuss the matter of the Crosbys having drawn heavily on capital during the binge years in Paris. The discussion was never held, for Harry did not show up. Nor did he appear at the Caviar Restaurant where Hart Crane sat waiting with Caresse and her mother-in-law.

When the dinner hour passed, and still no sign of Harry, Caresse thought of calling Harry's friend Stanley Mortimer who sometimes lent Harry his studio at 1 West 67th Street. Mortimer admitted he had given Harry the key to his studio, and agreed to stop by the studio to see if Harry might be there. He did not want to tell Caresse that he was certain Harry had gone to the studio, and with Josephine Bigelow.

The door to the studio was locked from inside, and there was no answer to Mortimer's persistent knocking: by 10 p.m. he was obliged to ask the building superintendent to help him break into the studio on the ninth floor.

Two inert bodies, fully clothed, lay across the bed, a .25 caliber Belgian pistol – a sun symbol engraved on its side – dangled from Harry's lifeless hand. A single bullet had passed through Josephine's left temple; in Harry's right temple was an identical gaping bullet hole. Their shoes were off, and on Harry's bare feet were the tattoos he had acquired in North Africa: a Christian cross on the bottom of his right foot, a pagan sun symbol on the left. Josephine was wearing a gay corsage of orchids and Harry carried with him at the end a whiskey flask, the gift of his fellow corpsmen in the Norton-Harjes Ambulance Service. There was no note.

Hart Crane wrote an elegy for Harry Crosby called 'The Cloud Juggler', the last published work before his own suicide in 1932, but E. E. Cummings wrote the epitaph:

> 2 boston
> Dolls; found
> with
> Holes in each other
> 's lullaby

*

Everyone left Paris in August, but Diaghilev fled the city as if it were the source of his personal plague. His body had erupted in running sores: Kochno and Lifar bathed his feverish body with alcohol, changed the soiled dressings on his sores. Dr Dalimier diagnosed diabetes, and placed Diaghilev on a spartan diet: he could take no alcohol whatsoever, and was to replace sugar with saccharine. The continental bon vivant

Coco Chanel, Paris 1929.

could not accept the doctor's regime and would not admit to debility. He gaily cheated on the diet: 'But today is *Sunday*,' he would say to his watchguard Kochno as he poured himself a forbidden flute of champagne. Dalimier advised Diaghilev to go to Switzerland where a treatment for diabetes by insulin injection had proved successful. Instead, the impresario hastily embarked on the last of his classic Grand Tours, when he introduced the latest of his protégés – in 1929 Igor Markevitch – to the cultural treasures of Europe. Switzerland meant clinics, regime and hypodermic needles. With his horror of growing old or ill, Diaghilev had always surrounded himself with youth and beauty, hoping to dwell forever removed from all that was associated with sickness, decline and death.

More than once Diaghilev had presented a copy of Thomas Mann's novella *Death in Venice* to a favored young man on the eve of a trip to the city of canals. Ironically, Igor Markevitch interrupted their tour in Germany to visit family in Switzerland, while Diaghilev, as if he had an urgent appointment in Samarra, went on alone to Venice.

Meanwhile, Diaghilev's two closest women friends, Coco Chanel and Misia Sert, were cruising the Dalmatian coast with Bend'or, Chanel's latest lover. Both women had reason to hope for distraction from their own unhappy circumstances: Bend'or was being blatantly unfaithful to Coco; Misia's marriage to José-Maria Sert was breaking up.

In Misia's case, a peculiar triangle had resulted when the Serts 'adopted' young Roussadana Mdvani, an art student who appeared at their door seeking painting instruction from Sert. At twenty, Roussy was an extraordinary beauty in the eyes of her fifty-year-old art teacher. She soon became Sert's mistress – with Misia's knowledge if not wholehearted approval, for Misia had fallen in love with the girl as well. Roussy became an established member of the household: student, daughter, mistress – something of a love kitten to the older childless couple. The affair had reached the point where Sert wanted to marry his young mistress. Misia had miserably agreed to an arrangement whereby she would become the set-aside member of the ménage-à-trois, hovering at the edge of the triangle yet not altogether divorced from the lives of the other two.

For once it was Chanel who could offer consolation to Misia, even though she was having problems of her own. On the cruise with Bend'or they managed to put aside their personal dilemmas and giggle together like schoolgirls over the Duke's vulgar taste in canopied beds and the ornate antique furnishings of a yacht so lightly named *The Flying Cloud*.

Then came the telegram from Serge Lifar, dictated by Diaghilev: 'Am sick, come quickly, Serge.'

The Flying Cloud changed course, bound for Venice. As soon as the yacht tied up, Diaghilev's two friends rushed to the Grand Hôtel des Bains where the sick and fading impresario lay in pain. It was shocking to come upon Diaghilev, wasted and colorless, his condition obviously grave. His eyes were animated for the first time as Misia and Coco materialized at his bedside. He was shivering under the blankets, wearing his dinner jacket in bed to keep warm, although the room was suffocatingly hot.

'Oh, how happy I am to see you.' He spoke in a hoarse whisper, for his voice had begun to fail. 'I love you in white. Promise me you will always wear white.'

These were the last reasonably coherent thoughts he would express. Later in the day he lapsed into delirium and fever, spoke of himself in the past tense while muttering in a disconnected way about the romantic music of Tchaikovsky. 'The *Pathétique*, that's what I loved most in my life . . . quick, go hear it and think of me.' When asked how he felt, he replied, 'I feel drunk.'

Misia slipped out quietly to purchase a sweater to replace the unseemly dinner jacket he wore in bed. She found a doctor, a German (the Italian doctors Vittoli and Bidali were baffled by his illness, insisting that the patient suffered from rheumatism), and she engaged an English nurse to stand watch in place of the faithful duo, Kochno and Lifar. Suddenly Diaghilev seemed to improve. His temperature was down, he insisted on wearing his plate, he rambled – but hopefully – about a trip to Palermo. Chanel left to rejoin her lover on *The Flying Cloud*; Misia stayed behind to keep company with Lifar and Kochno at Diaghilev's bedside.

On the evening of 18 August, Misia returned exhausted to her hotel across the lagoon, the Danieli, while Kochno and Lifar remained with Diaghilev. 'They were so white,' Diaghilev whispered over and over. 'All in white. They were so white.' The airy chimera of youth and whiteness hovered about the overheated room. The sick man lapsed into a coma. As soon as the nurse recognized the terminal symptoms she began packing her valise. Kochno called Misia at the Danieli.

When Misia arrived she was accompanied by Father Irineus of the Greek Orthodox Church, who had come to administer the last rites for the dying. At dawn Diaghilev's heart ceased to beat. A ray of sunlight struck Diaghilev's forehead, then the hotel room gradually filled with the light of day. Misia was awed by the theatrical spectacle of the lagoon suddenly and gloriously come to life just at the moment of death's visitation, as if the magnificent charlatan, now silent, had himself arranged the lighting for his adieu.

The nurse bent over the still form to wipe away a tear running down his cheek, and to close the staring eyes.

The private funeral took place among a few close friends assembled in Diaghilev's hotel room. All the currency Diaghilev had carried with him, 6,000 francs, Misia turned over to Lifar and Kochno: she had intended to pay for the funeral and burial by selling her diamond necklace in Venice, but she met Coco Chanel rushing toward her in the piazza San Marco. Chanel had been overcome with a premonition of Diaghilev's death. At her very first meeting with him, Chanel had offered a generous check to the bankrupt impresario: now, at the end, the gesture was the same. Chanel assumed the last worldly expenses of the man who had forever banked on charm instead of money.

A solemn mass was held for Diaghilev at the Greek Orthodox cathedral in Venice, then the coffin was placed aboard a slim black funeral gondola, its prow carved with gilded angels, the coffin flanked by black-robed priests. The body was borne to the island cemetery of San Michele: Misia Sert and Coco Chanel followed in the first gondola of the floating procession. At the island Kochno and Lifar were preparing to crawl behind the coffin on their knees to the graveside, but a sharp rebuke from Misia brought them to their feet – she was not quick enough, however, to prevent Lifar's theatrical leap into Diaghilev's open grave. Attendants drew him out of the grave, and while the priests restrained Lifar, mourners filed by dropping flower petals onto the coffin, offering a last homage to the vanished conjurer of the arts, bidding an era farewell.

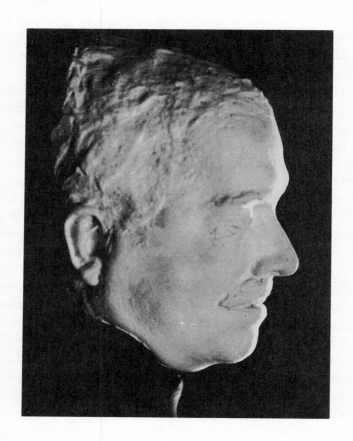

Diaghilev's death mask.

Epilogue

The hotel across from mine is now a youth hostel, the animated accents from Germany, Spain, and North Africa spilling into the rue Pélican from its windows, but in the 1920s and before, it was a house of prostitution called A la Patte de Chat where this narrow *allée* turns into the wider thoroughfare of rue Croix-des-Petits-Champs – as the bordel's business card informed prospective clients.

In this same quarter of the 1st arrondissement, Palais Royal, Vita Sackville-West lived with her lover Violet Trefusis just after World War I, Vita swaggering down these streets disguised as a sailor, a bandage across her forehead. Neither Violet nor Vita may have been aware that another bordel, the Chabanais, was located nearby, just behind the Palais Royal beside the Bibliothèque Nationale. Here Violet's putative father (the Prince of Wales, her mother's lover) disported himself in sumptuous private chambers furnished with a copper *baignoire* filled with champagne, and a throne of his own design that permitted semi-reclining dalliance with more than one favorite at a time. That famous address on the rue Chabanais, number 12, is now a bureau of hostess-secretaries 'au service de l'homme d'affaires' known as La Gentilhommière.

At breakfast I take coffee with steamed milk and croissant at a café on rue St-Honoré, admiring the fluid style of the barman who operates the levers of an espresso machine, then juggles cup and saucer, spoon and sugar cubes, with the circus grace of a Fratellini. A *garçon de café*, as Jean-Paul Sartre remarked, plays at being *garçon de café*. Beside me at the crowded *comptoir* a trio of apprentices in blood-stained white coveralls (from the wholesale *boucherie* on rue du Louvre) take turns ordering rounds of thin red breakfast wine from the barman's liter bottle.

I fix the familiar café and its particular moment in my mind's eye: this could as well be a Parisian bistro of sixty years before, despite the strip of neon that illuminates a row of apéritives ranged along a mirrored shelf and an unfortunate pinball machine crouching in one corner, mercifully silent at this early hour. The café tables have round marble tops rimmed in brass, set upon a base ending in three metal claws, though in many cafés the base is modified *style-moderne*, perhaps the filtered-down influence of Brancusi and Léger. The apéritives are the same; the waiter still wears a white apron down to his ankles, the chairs are wicker. My change arrives in a classic saucer – the saucer, alas, is plastic.

'The memory of each person who has lived in Paris differs from that of any other,' wrote Hemingway. My experience relates in no way to Morley Callaghan's summer of 1929 or to Henry Miller's Paris of the 1930s, or even to that of the GIs who lingered in the city after World War II in the hope of becoming a new generation of expatriate poets, painters and musicians. I first came to Paris in 1960, and my recollections date from January of that year – forty years after President Deschanel's breakdown and Modigliani's funeral cortege. A connecting thread does run through everyman's Paris; there are prototypes, touchstones: the eternal café, the central bridges (except for the sadly missing pont des Arts), a gray changeable coloring like no other, smells and sounds, a mood due as much to the city as one's self, an alternating low fever and sometimes depression broken by sudden and unexpected delight.

On the street where I lived, rue Tiquetonne, the *filles de joie* would whisper 'Tu viens?' – as they did to Thurber, Cummings and Dos Passos – until they saw me often with my *petite amie*, recognized me as a denizen of this turbulent quarter, knew me as a neighbor. We all ate together at a cheap restaurant in the passageway of Le Grand Cerf off rue St-Denis; the restaurant is still there, and still cheap, left high and dry after the floods of change, its mixed and close-packed clientele served three generous courses on squares of paper tablecloth, wine and service *compris*, twenty-five francs.

Again, in the Seventies when the market sheds were obliterated, I daily passed the great gaping hole in the Belly of Paris where only a colony of rats crept stealthily through the ruins. An underground shopping center known as Le Forum des Halles erupted from the crater; now, from ground level, an Art Déco structure in chrome and glass rises from the excavated site like some temporary Paris Exposition 1982, or a penny arcade, an unlikely and inadequate replacement for the classic Baltard ironwork of the market sheds.

Across the boulevard Sébastopol the Centre Pompidou offers its shock effect: a colorful boilerworks turned inside-out, not necessarily an aesthetic triumph but surely a joyful, lively, imaginative playground-monument. Set beside the main building like an afterthought is Brancusi's reconstructed studio, its forge and proportions a duplicate of the original atelier on the impasse Ronsin, even to the racks of lyre-shaped saws and stone chisels. The center is familiarly known as Beaubourg, after the neighborhood that was razed to make way for it, rather than after the politician whose idea it was. I wander through a Braque retrospective, then examine the Surrealist production of Yves Tanguy in the next gallery. From the upper level of the zigzag glass-enclosed escalator one looks down on the open plaza alive with specta-tors circled around performing hypnotists, fire-eaters, troubadours. At the St Merri end of the complex, adjoining an incongruous public baths with institutional façade of terrazzo and yellow brick, is a small *place* named for Igor Stravinsky. One side of the *place* is lined with ventilator funnels like a brass ensemble of tubas protruding from Beaubourg's cave: schoolboys scramble after a soccer ball, a solitary flautist leans against the side of St Merri cathedral playing a dirge to himself.

On the other side of rue du Temple, where the rue Rambuteau becomes rue des Francs-Bourgeois, a community center is showing the later works of Picasso lent by his wife Jacqueline, mostly portraits of herself. (For some obscure reason all the attendants, guards – even the cashier – are Chinese.) There is a heavily respectful and passionless mood to all of this. We reflect on Jacqueline's several profiles, *en passant*, moving from gallery to gallery on a wooden catwalk, filing past the Picasso oeuvre as if attending *pompes funèbres*.

Before leaving the ancient quarter of Le Marais I make a stop at rue Dupetit-Thouars, in the northerly direction of République. The five-storey building, number 8, forms a corner with the rue de la Corderie: here the poet E. E. Cummings slept in pristine innocence with the prostitute Marie-Louise. The double row of stark windows faces l'Ecole des Arts Appliqués à l'Industrie and looks out upon the ironwork rooftop of the Marché du Temple – a souvenir of the vanished market sheds of Les Halles – where crowds of mostly North African shoppers hover over bins and plywood tables stacked with American blue jeans, made in France.

Back through the maze of streets in the Temple and Hôtel-de-Ville arrondissements, then across the pont Marie to the Ile St-Louis side of the bridge: at a café that is not called Le Rendezvous des Mariniers I order a *demi* of French beer. But the café could as well be Madame LeCompte's hotel-restaurant where Dos Passos was sheltered after World War I during the composition of *Three Soldiers*. As a *site classé* the island is untouched and untouchable by change. The façade at 29 quai d'Anjou has been renovated, but only superficially and in harmony with the medieval façades on each side. The cellar where *Transatlantic Review* was edited, the home of Three Mountains Press, is now a private *cave*, perhaps reverted to a *cave aux vins* of centuries before – but I am unable to confirm this, or run the blockade of workmen in the inner court. Apartments on the Ile have become museum pieces, almost priceless real estate: a fitting testimony to a time when the wealthiest expatriates chose to live here – Nancy Cunard in her Afro-Surrealist apartment on the rue Le Regrattier; the Crosbys, with their commuter-canoe tied up at the quai d'Orléans.

Via pont St-Louis and the pont au Double, I take a diagonal course across the Seine to the Left Bank, past the graceful gothic buttresses of Notre Dame that seem to sustain the great thrust and spirit of the city itself.

Tucked into a niche of the quai de Montebello is a reincarnation of Shakespeare and Company, for some thirty years under the management of a goateed expatriate from America, George Whitman. I first crossed the threshold of Shakespeare and Company my first winter in Paris, frozen out of hotel solitude to seek the comfort and warmth of George's fire and bookshelves. In design and intent the second Shakespeare and Company is not unlike Sylvia Beach's famous establishment, though possibly attracting a less celebrated roster of authors, in a less celebrated literary age. A young, footloose, international band of scriveners and book-lovers inhabits the complex of upstairs rooms, making tea and poetry, browsing through George's private library and important collection of 1920s lore, issues of *transition, This Quarter, Transatlantic Review* and the magnificent original editions of Joyce's *Ulysses* and *Finnegans Wake*. If the ghosts of Hemingway and Joyce do not wander the midnight quai de Montebello, there is surely a benevolent and literate spirit permeating the premises George calls the Tumbleweed Hotel.

For a time James Joyce and Ernest Hemingway lived within a few steps of one another, but this was before they met. At 74 rue du Cardinal Lemoine, the erstwhile *bal musette* at street level – where Hemingway took Hadley for an evening out – is now a pocket theater, the 400 Coups. Across the street at number 71 is a passageway leading to an inner court and private garden, an assortment of dwellings hidden from the street. In one of these Joyce lived (in Valery Larbaud's borrowed flat) and here completed his masterwork, *Ulysses*. There is no plaque to mark his temporary sojourn in this secret corner of Paris.

The *terrasse* tables around the place de la Contrescarpe are crowded with tourists; somehow this has become a 'quaint' neighborhood, a quarter of inexpensive restaurants feeding troops of sightseers. *Clochards* still gather around the square: two of them, with a common liter bottle, lean against one of the ruined trees like Vladimir and Estragon in *Waiting for Godot*. Samuel Beckett lived and taught at the nearby Ecole Normale Supérieure on the rue d'Ulm; between the school and the place de la Contrescarpe is an obscure residential street, rue Amyot, where Jeanne Hébuterne threw herself from a window after the death of Modigliani.

At 39 rue Descartes, Ernest Hemingway wrote short-stories about his boyhood Michigan, in an unheated attic room. On the ground floor is a restaurant, Chez Alexandre, every table taken; another restaurant – on the other side of the entryway, beneath a plaque commemorating the death of Paul Verlaine – remains empty, with a sign in the window: 'Restaurant de charactère à vendre.'

In the 14th arrondissement, Observatoire, an aged lady sporting wisps of beard directs me to La Santé prison. She appears far more interested in pointing out the hospital on the other side of boulevard Arago, Sainte-Anne, where – and the bearded lady puts a finger to her temple – another kind of incarceration takes place.

The Callaghans, Morley and Loretto, lived on the rue de la Santé, in one of the buildings facing these grim cinder-colored walls. I take a cognac at the famous bistro, A la Bonne Santé, where Harry and Caresse Crosby, Kay Boyle, Robert McAlmon and a group of the poet's friends waited for Hart Crane's release in the summer of 1929. Two guards chat together in the sentry box, behind them a queue of wives and sweethearts (they are all women, young, several with children) waiting for visiting hours to begin. The gates swing open only for a moment to admit a delivery van: there is a brief view of vines like nooses dangling from a roof in the courtyard. No one emerges, and the great gates close again.

The Dingo Bar on the rue Delambre has become a restaurant, l'Auberge au Centre; the Jockey is still at 127 boulevard Montparnasse,

Jimmy's is called the New Jimmy's. Where boulevard Raspail crosses boulevard Montparnasse, the café du Dôme and La Rotonde stand fast: the Dôme, dominating the place Vavin, now a restaurant as well as a *café-terrasse*. Diners study menus under orange Belle Epoque lamps, photographs of their celebrated predecessors ranged along the wall of the *salle*.

I take my lunch at La Coupole: *paupiette de veau* with a half bottle of wine; at least three waiters attend to my simple repast. At the next table a white-bearded diner sucks at his oyster shells, then delicately dabs a napkin at his chin where the taste of the sea runs into his beard. Students hurry past Le Sélect carrying under their arms large portfolios that match the green awning of the café. They are headed no doubt for the rue de la Grande-Chaumière, that street of painters still, home of the Académie de la Grande Chaumière. Here at La Coupole the Russian ambience is gone, but I notice a rack of newspapers on spindles, a memento from the time when Lenin and Trotsky awaited news of insurgency at home.

From outside, the Closerie de Lilas retains something of its former garden ambience, but the cocktail lounge interior would not be conducive to a young Hemingway lingering over his notebooks and a single café-crème. A well-weathered Maréchal Ney forever contemplates the mythical maidens of l'Observatoire holding the universe aloft. Around the corner, a piece of real estate has absorbed the sawmill at 113 rue Notre-Dame-des-Champs, no clue to its existence at the time Hemingway lived at that address with Hadley and their infant son Bumby.

A plaque does mark Gertrude Stein's place of residence at 27 rue de Fleurus: 'Gertrude Stein 1874–1946 – Ecrivain américain vécut ici avec son frère Léo puis avec Alice B. Toklas. Elle y récut de nombreux artistes et écrivains de 1903 à 1938.' With the homage generally reserved for eminent Frenchmen, Gertrude Stein, among all the expatriates of the 1920s, has had the last word. Through the grillwork of the entryway a green and pleasant patch of garden is visible beside the glassed-in atelier. Gertrude would have been happy with the garden, but as a dog lover might have objected to the vile yellow powder a concierge has sprinkled at the door to keep dogs from urinating against the cornerstones.

For some reason the large *bassin* in Gertrude Stein's favorite park, the Luxembourg Gardens, has been drained, its shallow depth a swamp of mud. The palais du Luxembourg no longer harbors the Impression-ist collection: the paintings are now housed in the Jeu de Paume at the Concorde end of the Tuileries. Across from the palais, on rue de Vaugirard, the Hôtel Foyot where Raymond Radiguet lived (and was said to have died) is no more. Around the corner on the tiny rue Ferou is a modish town house where Hemingway lived with his second wife, Pauline, at number 6, the most lavish of Hemingway's Paris addresses.

The rue de l'Odéon is still a street of booksellers, more so than ever, long after the time of Adrienne Monnier's Les Amis des Livres and Sylvia Beach's Shakespeare and Company. Across the boulevard St-Germain, and deeper into the heart of the Latin Quarter, I find Natalie Barney's ancient dwelling at number 24. The door to the passageway is open; inside, a friendly tenant who has just come in from the rue de Buci market informs me that the Greek temple is behind a high wall, the garden patrolled by dogs. He adds, by way of postscript: 'The garden once extended to the rue de Seine where Colette lived. Colette made rendezvous with Mademoiselle Barney by way of the garden.'

I would try to see the temple from the back street running parallel to rue Jacob, the rue Visconti. Another tenant, equally helpful, at the house just the other side of Natalie Barney's walled garden allows me to pass through his apartment to a children's play area, with swings and sandbox and a miniature slide. Not even from the top of the slide could I see over the wall, but the tenant assures me the Greek temple is still there, *un monument historique*, where Valéry read his verses and naiads played out their pageants.

*

On another tour I travel even deeper into Montparnasse: first to the commercial-residential rue Blomet, a noticeable gap at 45 (there were already complaints in the 1920s that the building was about to collapse), where Miró lived beside Masson and where the Rue Blomet Group was born. Instead of the single lilac tree around which the poets and painters disputed the tenets of art, there is a verdant park, including a club house and a boules court hemmed in by modern apartment buildings. An old man sits in this garden spot reading *Le Matin*, his cane hooked to the back of a park bench. We two are alone in this removed place at so early an hour. Directly in front of the old man's bench is a sculpture by Miró – he is altogether unaware of the object, or is accustomed to its presence – a strange artifact in so plebeian a garden, its rhinoceros-like protuberances apparently out of place here:

but what place more fitting? There is a remarkable absence of graffiti. It would seem that children are not disturbed by the creature in bronze: the upturned horns are worn smooth by hands that have clung to them, climbing; the base of the sculpture is ringed around with the imprint of bicycle tires in the dust.

On the far side of rue de Vaugirard, at the outer limits of the 15th arrondissement, the rue Dantzig runs to the edge of the seacoast of Bohemia. On a fork called passage Dantzig stands La Ruche, comfortable and with appropriate dignity, like the old man on the park bench, settled into its *troisième age*. I find no trace of a slaughterhouse in the vicinity despite the notation on a recent map of an *Abbatoir, Rive Gauche*. There is still a Café Dantzig, where the butchers drank with painters and sculptors. The outbuildings of La Ruche, as well as the stockyards, have been removed to make room for the HLM (high-rise apartment buildings) walling in Paris. Yet the queer five-sided structure of La Ruche still serves a new generation of 'bees' or provides studio space for ancient residents.

I encounter two elderly tenants (in their eighties, surely) who lived at La Ruche before World War I. Monsieur D ('Do not mention my name, it means nothing, to anybody') is a sculptor, still working in the atelier where he and Madame once lived. They invite me to their new flat, eager to talk about the great days of La Ruche; they live in comfort now, isolated comfort, in one of the HLM of the quarter. While the white-haired grandmotherly Madame D prepares tea (she is of Russian origin, her French still accented), Monsieur complains of the neglect so many tenants of La Ruche suffered (himself, I fear, among them) because their work was never à la mode. He lists their names – genius unrecognized, reputations never achieved – on his fingers. Madame disputes his memory from the kitchen. Monsieur D, and so many others, were never taken up by a Gertrude Stein or a Dr Barnes.

From the porte de Vanves there is only one Métro change to the Right Bank stop at Trocadéro. This end of avenue Henri-Martin has become avenue Georges-Mandel (a latter-day politician shares the homage paid to an earlier one), and the concierge of number 43 is troubled by shifts in nomenclature, especially now that the street at the juncture of the Polignac estate, rue Cortambert, is being renamed to honor a local Protestant pastor. I would assume she calculates still in old francs and centimes, though the system of *francs nouveaux* was established in 1960, my first year in Paris. She wears black, I nod in sympathy to her complaint. Together we mourn the changes that disrupt our shared philosophy, knowing that the changes are what keep Paris alive.

The great mansion serves today as the administration offices of the Singer Foundation established by the Princesse de Polignac in 1928. With a slender loaf of bread as a pointer, the concierge indicates the large bow windows of an upper storey, the vast music salon of Winnaretta's day. 'They have taken the organ out,' she says, as if I were listening for music – and for a moment I do listen. I nod again as she informs me that all the musical instruments have been removed.

At l'Etoile I reflect on the name change to place Charles de Gaulle: it will take the French another generation, or more, to think of this central arch surrounded by spirals of perpetual motion as anything but l'Etoile. On the nearby rue Daru there is no traffic at all. The Russian Cathedral, Saint Alexandre-Nevsky, is the same kind of anachronism as Miró's sculpture on the opposite bank: one of those unexpected treasures Paris tucks away almost as a secret from itself.

Picasso married a czarist colonel's daughter under these upturned turnip domes of gilt; Stravinsky and Diaghilev inhaled the heavy incense of its jewel-box interior, the remembered scent of Mother Russia. Part of the roof is terraced with scaffolding, a dome to be restored: a plea for funds, in Russian and French, appears on the church bulletin board.

Across the street is the restaurant A la Ville de Petrograd, where Stravinsky wolfed down Nicolas Nabokov's *cotelette Pojarsky*. One has the choice of several imported vodkas with dinner, and *caviar gris* at 400 francs the 125 grams. The restaurant accepts Soviet travelers checks.

Rue La Boétie is now much less a street of art galleries – La Licorne has become a post office, but there is a Bernheim Gallery at 35 – than a long thoroughfare of commercial societies, Persian carpets and *la mode*. Picasso lived with his wife Olga at number 23; a rug merchant occupies one of the ground-floor premises, the other is a clothier featuring T-shirts inscribed with mottoes appropriate to city jogging.

Behind l'Opéra, just off the place Diaghilev today, Picasso met young Marie-Thérèse Walter and offered to paint the girl's portrait. Beside their meeting place, Galeries Lafayette, rue de Provence comes to an end, with its celebrated address One-Two-Two. This bordel closed down in 1946 when the 'Marthe Richard' law effectively banished houses of prostitution from metropolitan France. (The massage parlor replaced the *maison close*, and prostitutes simply took to the streets in greater numbers.) In place of the One-Two-Two is a Club des Tanneurs, situated between two banks.

The neighborhood of the Madeleine exudes an atmosphere of money: shoppers are headed for Fauchon's fancy goods, and more than one black limousine with diplomatic license plates drives by. Jean Cocteau's mother, according to Maurice Sachs, was a fixture of the salon at 10 rue d'Anjou, perpetually at her needlework, graciously receiving her son's strange assortment of friends. In this same building Marcel Proust climbed to visit Madame de Chevigny, obliged to rest on the window seat of each landing in order to catch his breath and still his heart. For many years Cocteau, too, hoped to be received by his distinguished neighbor one flight below, whom he knew only as her fictional counterpart, Madame de Guermantes in *Remembrance of Things Past*.

To reach Coco Chanel's town house, Cocteau needed to walk only half a block to the rue du faubourg St-Honoré where number 29 faces rue d'Anjou. The fashion house of Chanel still dominates rue Cambon, but here ironically the streetside address is given over, ostentatiously, to Pierre Cardin. Directly behind the commercial premises lies a graveled courtyard with parking space for several automobiles, then the façade of Chanel's former *hôtel particulier* with its impressive fan of canopied glass. The great houses of another age have been subdivided into luxury apartments, the entryways guarded by security cameras instead of concierges. I stroll past the electronic eye unchallenged.

The corner of rue Boissy d'Anglas and the rue du faubourg St-Honoré reflects the style and ethos of this quarter of Paris, with Lanvin on two sides, Hermès and Limoges on the other two. Again, convenient to the Cocteau residence, was Le Boeuf sur le Toit, around the corner on the rue Boissy d'Anglas. Farther along the rue St-Honoré, the place Vendôme carries the motif of wealth and chic to its ultimate extreme: Charvet, Schiaparelli, Cartier, the Rothschild bank. The Morgan Guaranty Trust is solidly fixed at number 14 where Harry Crosby served his apprenticeship as playboy banker opposite the Ritz Hotel.

Diaghilev's favorite hotel, the Continental on rue Castiglione, is now part of the Intercontinental chain, and so named. The accents in the lobby and bar are a reminder of the continued American presence in Paris: there are 50,000 Americans resident, approximately the same number as in the 1920s, until the figure was halved in 1929. At rue

Royale I observe a shipment of vintage Chambertin being delivered to the service entrance of Maxim's, along with an equal consignment of crates of Coca-cola.

*

The cemetery of Arceuil is a bleak and uninspiring walk from the RER train stop; in a distant corner of the cemetery is the grave of Erik Satie. I had accepted in good faith the information that Satie's tomb had been designed by Brancusi, but apparently it is not: the slab stone covering of Satie's resting place is a duplicate of the many unadorned grave markers in the Montparnasse and Montmartre cemeteries, as well as the Père Lachaise. Satie's hermit-abode is in another part of Arceuil, in the shadow of the Arceuil-Cachan aqueduct. The building at the junction of rue Cauchy and the avenue François Vincent Raspail bears a plaque: 'Erik Satie 1866–1925 a habité cette maison 1898 à sa mort.' There is a couscous restaurant on the ground floor; I ask the Algerian waiter about the room where Satie once lived.

'Did you see the plaque? All private flats now. A writer, n'est-ce pas?'

'A composer,' I reply.

*

The public *pissoir* was once as familiar a sight as the kiosk plastered with concert and music hall posters. It would seem that the last of the outdoor urinals are to be found at the entrances to city cemeteries: the one at Père Lachaise has taken on the moss-green patina of metal sculpture, its yellow-stained grating choked with wet leaves, a joke the Dadaists have placed among the monuments and memorials of this vast burial ground.

I approach the guardian's lodge under a lowering sky: all the blended grays of paved courtyards, the sides of tilted buildings, stone bridges and the Seine itself gather in a flat cloudbank stretched over the city of the dead in Menilmontant. A guard in the *képi* of an *agent de police* proffers a map of the place; he indicates with a ballpoint Bic several celebrated burial plots, and a crematorium, for my benefit. My gratuity finds its way into a pocket of the uniform; I receive a salute.

Along the avenue Laterale N. I pass a row of upright family mausoleums like sentry boxes stuffed with dead flowers, broken crockery, artificial fern. A rose-colored slab of marble in Section I informs me: 'Ici Repose Colette.' A light rain falls through the tall trees arched above the avenue Feuillant. Never mind – I will briefly visit the Stein-Toklas plot, and the adjoining Division 96 where Modigliani and

Jeanne Hébuterne lie side by side, then be on my way. At Division 89 is a huge sculpture by Jacob Epstein, in memory of Oscar Wilde: a winged figure, the stone penis broken off by a vandal. The monument is a gift from an anonymous admirer of the poet-playwright who died in Paris beyond his means.

The ballpoint dots on my map have blurred in the rain. But I manage to locate the slab that covers Amedeo Modigliani and Jeanne Hébuterne, the inscription in Italian, the dates of their deaths only a day apart: 24 Gennaio 1920 – 25 Gennaio 1920. Jeanne is described as the painter's devoted companion who for love of him 'fino all'estremo sacrifizio'.

Others on this funereal pilgrimage are better prepared than I: they carry umbrellas, wear plastic hoods – a band of tourists or a family group.

'Apollinaire is in Division 86,' one of them calls out.

'Did you find Edith Piaf?' asks another.

I dart haphazardly through Division 94 in the rain, unable to find the names Gertrude Stein and Alice Toklas commemorated anywhere here. A thunderclap seems to signal an increase in the downpour. I am obliged to take shelter in a doorless mausoleum: opposite me, in its own marble sanctuary, a stray cat eyes me suspiciously across the wet void. The wait is long, there is something gloriously contemplative about my situation. I ask myself one or two tart questions.

Someone shouts something about Molière, and receives a reply about La Fontaine. The umbrellas pass on. The cat has the crazy-quilt markings of its inbred cemetery tribe. I am certain I can hear Gertrude's rich laughter and see Alice's shrewd smile as I wait out the thunderstorm in my tomb. At last I am driven to make a run for it. With a graveyard cat watching my getaway I dash down the avenue des Acacias, around the carrefour du Grand Rond, and out of Père Lachaise at the rue de Repos. I can make out the watery neon of a café ahead as I flee these ghosts and find my way back into the living city.

Author's Acknowledgments

I am grateful to the following institutions for assistance with the research and writing of this book: Bibliothèque Nationale, Paris; British Museum, London; Centre Culturel Americain, Paris; Centre Pompidou, Paris; Humanities Research Center, Austin, Texas; Linen Hall Library, Belfast; The Queen's University Library, Belfast; Shakespeare and Company, Paris.

I would like to express my thanks to Leo Bukzin, Diane and Daniel Harlé, Ted Hickey, Siobhan Kilfeather, the late Igor Markevitch, Elizabeth McCrum, Arthur Power, Cecile Richard, David Sturdy, and George Whitman for information, texts, reminiscences they were good enough to share with me – and to several anonymous individuals willing to talk about Paris, then and now.

Photographic
Acknowledgments

BBC Hulton Picture Library: 81, 91b, 193, 232; The Bettmann Archive Inc.: 186; Bibliothèque Nationale: 107a; Boyer-Viollet: 249; Branger-Viollet: 14; Collection Viollet: 17, 87b, 128b, 136, 145, 190/1; Harlingue-Viollet: 43b, 54/ 5, 97, 115a, 115b; John F. Kennedy Library: 27a (Photo no. EH 6897P), 69 (Photo no. EH 4308P), 215 (Photo no. EH 6940P); The Landowska Center: 107b; Lipnitzki-Viollet: 72, 102b, 156; May Ray: 149a, 149b, 205; Courtesy Igor Markevitch: 102a; Popperfoto: 6; The Sylvia Beach Collection, Princeton University Library: 35, 47, 53 (Photo Man Ray), 63b, 128a, 129, 162; The F. Scott Fitzgerald Collection, Princeton University Library: 179; Private Collection: 8a (Photo Sotheby Parke Bernet Inc.), 8b (Photo Giraudon); Roger-Viollet: 98, 209, 236; Musées de Rouen: 132 (Photo Lauros-Giraudon, painting by Jacques-Emile Blanche); Sotheby Parke Bernet & Co.: 211; Reproduced with permission of The Poetry/Rare Books Collection of the University Libraries, State University of New York at Buffalo: 58b; Special Collections, Morris Library, Southern Illinois University at Carbondale: 170a, 170b; Beinecke Rare Book and Manuscript Library, Yale University: 33 (Photo ascribed to Carlo Linati), 119 (Photo Man Ray), 125 (Photo Thérèse Bonney), 199, 223 (Photo Berenice Abbott).

Bibliography

The following books were consulted by the author.

Ackroyd, Peter *Ezra Pound*, 1980

Aldington, Richard *Life for Life's Sake*, 1941

Alexander, Sidney *Chagall*, 1978

Allan, Tony *Americans in Paris*, 1977

Allen, F. L. *Only Yesterday*, 1931

Alpers, Antony *The Life of Katherine Mansfield*, 1977

Anderson, Sherwood, *Letters*, 1953

Baker, Carlos *Ernest Hemingway*, 1969

Baker, Josephine *Josephine*, 1978

Battersby, Martin *Art Deco Fashion*, 1974

Battersby, Martin *The Decorative Twenties*, 1969

Beach, Sylvia *Shakespeare and Company*, 1959

Belle, Jean-Michel *Les Folles années de Maurice Sachs*, 1979

Berger, John *Success and Failure of Picasso*, 1965

Bernstein, Burton *Thurber*, 1975

Blair, Deirdre *Samuel Beckett*, 1978

Borgal, Clément *Radiguet*, 1969

Boyle, Kay (with Robert McAlmon) *Being Geniuses Together*, 1938

Brassai *Le Paris secret des années 30*, 1976

Bruccoli, Matthew *Some Sort of Epic Grandeur: The Life of F. Scott Fitzgerald*, 1981

Buckle, Richard *Diaghilev*, 1979

Buckle, Richard *Nijinsky*, 1971

Cabanne, Pierre *Pablo Picasso*, 1977

Callaghan, Morley *That Summer in Paris*, 1963

Chagall, Marc *Ma vie*, 1957

Charles-Roux, Edmonde *Le Temps Chanel*, 1974

Chisholm, Anne *Nancy Cunard*, 1979

Conte, Arthur *Le Premier Janvier 1920*, 1976

Cowley, Malcolm *Exile's Return*, 1951 (1934)

Cowley, Malcolm *Second Flowering*, 1937

Crespelle, Jean-Paul *La Folle époque*, 1968

Crespelle, Jean-Paul *La Vie quotidienne à Montparnasse*, 1968

Crosby, Caresse *The Passionate Years*, 1953

De Cossart, Michael *The Food of Love*, 1978

Dos Passos, John *The Best Times*, 1966

Dupin, Jacques *Miró*, 1962

Earnest, Ernest *Expatriates and Patriots*, 1968

Ehrlich, Blake *Paris on the Seine*, 1962

Ellmann, Richard *James Joyce*, 1959

Fifield, William *Modigliani*, 1976

Fitzgerald, F. Scott *The Crackup, with other Pieces and Stories*, 1965

Fitzgerald, F. Scott *The Great Gatsby*, 1925

Fitzgerald, F. Scott *The Letters of F. Scott Fitzgerald* (ed. Andrew Turnbull), 1963

Fitzgerald, F. Scott *Tender is the Night*, 1934

Flanner, Janet *Paris was Yesterday, 1925–1939*, 1972

Ford, Hugh *Published in Paris*, 1975

Gajdusek, Robert *Hemingway's Paris*, 1978

Giedion-Welcker, Carola *Constantin Brancusi*, 1958

Gold, Arthur and Fizdale, Robert *Misia*, 1980

Goldbarth, Albert *Different Fleshes*, 1979

Gorman, Herbert *James Joyce*, 1974

Green, Christopher *Léger and the Avant-garde*, 1976

Guggenheim, Peggy *Out of this Century: Confessions of an Art Addict*, 1979

Guilleminault, Gilbert *Le Roman vrai des années folles 1918–1930*, 1975

Gurdjieff, G. *Meetings with Remarkable Men*, 1963

Harding, James *Erik Satie*, 1975

Harding, James *The Ox on the Roof*, 1972

Hemingway, Ernest *In Our Time*, 1925

Hemingway, Ernest *A Moveable Feast*, 1964

Hemingway, Ernest *Selected Letters* (ed. Carlos Baker), 1981

Hemingway, Ernest *The Sun Also Rises*, 1926

Heymann, C. David *Ezra Pound: The Last Rower*, 1976

Hobhouse, Janet *Everybody who was Anybody*, 1975

Huddleston, Sisley *Paris Salons, Cafés, Studios*, 1928

Josephson, Matthew *Life Among the Surrealists*, 1962

Kennedy, Richard S. *Dreams in a Mirror*, 1980

Kenner, Hugh *The Pound Era*, 1972

Kiki *Memoirs of Kiki*, 1929

Kochno, Boris *Diaghilev*, 1970

Lania, Leo *Hemingway*, 1960

Lifar, Serge *Serge Diaghilev*, 1977

Loeb, Harold *The Way It Was*, 1959

Longstreet, Stephen *We All Went to Paris*, 1972

MacMillan, Douglas *Transition 1927–38*, 1976

Mann, Carol *Modigliani*, 1980

Mansfield, Katherine *Letters and Journals of Katherine Mansfield* (ed. C. K. Stead), 1977

Markevitch, Igor *Etre et d'avoir été*, 1980

Mellow, James R. *Charmed Circle*, 1974

Meyers, Jeffrey *Katherine Mansfield*, 1978

Milford, Nancy *Zelda*, 1970

Mizener, Arthur *The Far Side of Paradise*, 1951

Mosley, Leonard *Lindbergh*, 1976

Neagoe, Peter *Americans Abroad*, 1932

Nicolson, Nigel *Portrait of a Marriage*, 1973

Norman, Charles *The Magic-Maker: E.E. Cummings*, 1958

O'Brian, Patrick *Picasso*, 1976

Paul, Elliot *The Last Time I Saw Paris*, 1942

Potts, Willard (ed.) *Portraits of the Artist in Exile*, 1979

Power, Arthur *Conversations with James Joyce*, 1974

Power, Arthur *Paris and Dublin in the 1920s*, unpublished ms.

Putnam, Samuel *Paris Was Our Mistress*, 1947

Rey, Anne *Erik Satie*, 1974

Rhys, Jean *Smile Please*, 1979

Ross, Ishbell *The Expatriates*, 1970

Sachs, Maurice *La Décade de l'illusion*, 1950

Samuel, Claude *Prokofiev*, 1978

Secrest, Meryle *Between Me and Life*, 1976

Shattuck, Roger *The Banquet Years*, 1955

Shirer, William *Twentieth Century Journey*, 1976

Stein, Gertrude *The Autobiography of Alice B. Toklas*, 1933

Stein, Gertrude *Selected Writings of Gertrude Stein*, 1972

Stravinsky, Vera (with Robert Craft) *Stravinsky*, 1979

Thomson, Virgil *Virgil Thomson*, 1967

Toklas, Alice B. *What is Remembered*, 1963

Tompkins, Calvin *Living Well is the Best Revenge*, 1972

Vorobëv, Marevna *Life with the Painters of La Ruche*, 1972

Werner, Alfred *Soutine*, 1978

White, Ray Lewis *Sherwood Anderson's Memoirs*, 1969

Wickes, George *The Amazon of Letters*, 1977

Wickes, George *Americans in Paris*, 1969

Wilson, Edmund *The Twenties*, 1975

Wolff, Geoffrey *Black Sun*, 1976

Index